Locating Queer Histories

T0398149

Locating Queer Histories

Places and Traces across the UK

Edited by
Justin Bengry, Matt Cook and Alison Oram

BLOOMSBURY ACADEMIC
LONDON · NEW YORK · OXFORD · NEW DELHI · SYDNEY

BLOOMSBURY ACADEMIC
Bloomsbury Publishing Plc
50 Bedford Square, London, WC1B 3DP, UK
1385 Broadway, New York, NY 10018, USA
29 Earlsfort Terrace, Dublin 2, Ireland

BLOOMSBURY, BLOOMSBURY ACADEMIC and the Diana logo
are trademarks of Bloomsbury Publishing Plc

First published in Great Britain 2023
This paperback edition published 2024

Copyright © Justin Bengry, Matt Cook and Alison Oram, 2023

Justin Bengry, Matt Cook and Alison Oram have asserted their
right under the Copyright, Designs and Patents Act, 1988,
to be identified as Editors of this work.

For legal purposes the Acknowledgements on p. x constitute
an extension of this copyright page.

Cover image © Nigel Swallow/Anni Agnise

All rights reserved. No part of this publication may be reproduced or transmitted
in any form or by any means, electronic or mechanical, including photocopying,
recording, or any information storage or retrieval system, without prior
permission in writing from the publishers.

Bloomsbury Publishing Plc does not have any control over, or responsibility for,
any third-party websites referred to or in this book. All internet addresses given
in this book were correct at the time of going to press. The author and publisher
regret any inconvenience caused if addresses have changed or sites have
ceased to exist, but can accept no responsibility for any such changes.

A catalogue record for this book is available from the British Library.

A catalog record for this book is available from the Library of Congress.

ISBN: HB: 978-1-3501-4372-2
         PB: 978-1-3502-5253-0
         ePDF: 978-1-3501-4373-9
         eBook: 978-1-3501-4374-6

Typeset by Integra Software Services Pvt. Ltd.

To find out more about our authors and books visit www.bloomsbury.com
and sign up for our newsletters.

Contents

Figures

Every effort has been made to trace copyright holders and to obtain their permission for the use of copyright material. The publisher apologizes for any errors or omissions in the above list and would be grateful if notified of any corrections that should be incorporated in future reprints or editions of this book.

Contributors

Justin Bengry is Lecturer in Queer History and Director of the Centre for Queer History at Goldsmiths, University of London, where he convenes the first MA in Queer History. He worked with Matt Cook and Alison Oram on the AHRC research project 'Queer beyond London' and with Alison Oram undertook Historic England's project 'Pride of Place: England's LGBTQ Heritage'. Justin's other research explores histories of homosexuality and consumer capitalism, Britain's 'gay pardons' for past homosexual offences and queer microhistories. He is completing a book entitled *The Pink Pound: Capitalism and Homosexuality in Twentieth-Century Britain*.

Sean Brady is Lecturer in Modern British and Irish History at Birkbeck College, University of London. His research interests encompass questions of gender and sexuality in relation to religion and politics since 1800. His recent publications include *From Sodomy Laws to Same-Sex Marriage: International Perspectives since 1789* (2019), co-edited with Mark Seymour.

Caroline Bressey and **Gemma Romain** explored the Barbara Ker-Seymer albums in the Tate Archive while undertaking research for their UCL-based, AHRC-funded project 'Drawing over the Colour Line: Geographies of Art and Cosmopolitan Politics in London 1919–1939' (AH/I027371/1) between 2012 and 2014. Caroline Bressey's work focuses upon the Black presence in nineteenth- and early-twentieth-century England, anti-racist reading communities and archival access. She is Reader in Cultural and Historical Geography in the Department of Geography, UCL, and the author of *Empire, Race and the Politics of Anti-Caste* (2013). Gemma Romain is now an independent historian of Caribbean and Black British history, with a focus on archives, art and queer histories. She is the author of *Race, Sexuality and Identity in Britain and Jamaica: The Biography of Patrick Nelson, 1916–1963* (2017).

Alan Butler is a lecturer at Plymouth Marjons University, a trustee of the Oral History Society and current chair of the Community Archives and Heritage Group, who are a special interest group of the Archives and Records Association. In 2016 he completed an AHRC-funded collaborative PhD called *Performing LGBT Pride in Plymouth 1950–2012* with the University of Plymouth, which involved the formation of a specific LGBT+ history accession for the Plymouth and West Devon Record Office (now The Box). All this work supports and extends his role as co-director of Pride in Plymouth CIC, which is a social enterprise dedicated to raising visibility of the LGBT+ communities in Plymouth.

Rachel Hope Cleves is Professor of History at the University of Victoria in British Columbia and Member of the College of the Royal Society of Canada. Her book about Norman Douglas, *Unspeakable: A Life beyond Sexual Morality* (2020), is the winner of the 2021 Wallace K. Ferguson Prize from the Canadian Historical Association. She is also the author of *Charity and Sylvia: A Same-Sex Marriage in America* (2014) and *The Reign of Terror in America* (2009). Cleves is currently at work on two book projects: a biography of a once notorious nineteenth-century American courtesan, and a study of the intersections of food and sex in the transatlantic imagination from the eighteenth century to the present day.

Matt Cook worked on the AHRC-funded research project 'Queer beyond London' with Alison Oram and Justin Bengry. He is Professor of Modern History and a specialist in queer history at Birkbeck College, University of London. He has edited three other collections on LGBTQ histories and is the author of *London and the Culture of Homosexuality, 1885–1914* (2003) and *Queer Domesticities: Homosexuality and Home Life in Twentieth-Century London* (2014). *Queer beyond London*, co-authored with Alison Oram, was published in 2022 and his *Writing Queer History* is due out with Bloomsbury in 2023.

Margaret Greenfields is Professor of Social Policy at Anglia Ruskin University and Visiting Professor in Social Policy and Community Engagement at Buckinghamshire New University. She has a particular focus on participatory action research programmes leading to effective policy interventions to enhance inclusion and cohesion. Margaret frequently works closely with LGBT+ members of faith communities: Gypsies, Travellers and Roma, vulnerable migrants and refugee/asylum-seeking women.

Dominic Janes is Professor of Modern History at Keele University. He is a cultural historian who studies texts and visual images relating to Britain in its local and international contexts since the eighteenth century. Within this sphere he focuses on the histories of gender, sexuality and religion. His latest book is *Freak to Chic: 'Gay' Men in and out of Fashion after Oscar Wilde* (2021).

Searle Kochberg is a maker, writer and teacher in film, and has a practice-based PhD in co-creative documentary practice. Recent research work includes the two research projects: *Rainbow Jews* (2012–14, funded by National Lottery Heritage Fund) and *Ritual Reconstructed* (2014–16, funded by AHRC, as part of the Connected Communities strand). Searle is a Visiting Research Fellow at the University of Portsmouth. He has edited and co-written the textbook, *Introduction to Documentary Production* (2002) and contributed to *Introduction to Film Studies* (2012) and *Promotion in the Age of Convergence* (2013).

Gareth Longstaff is Senior Lecturer in Media and Cultural Studies at Newcastle University. He works on queer theory, history and archiving, with a particular focus on the relationship between gay male sexuality, celebrity and pornography. In his forthcoming book *Celebrity and Pornography: The Psychoanalysis of Self Representation*

(2022), he explores self-representational media, pornography/sexual representation, and digital/networked archives of desire.

Alison Oram is Senior Research Fellow at the Institute of Historical Research, University of London, and Professor Emerita at Leeds Beckett University. She has published widely on twentieth-century queer British history and on the representation of LGBTQ histories in heritage, especially historic houses. She led 'Pride of Place: England's LGBTQ Heritage' for Historic England in 2015–16, and her books include *'Her Husband Was a Woman!' Women's Gender-Crossing and Modern British Popular Culture* (2007); *The Lesbian History Sourcebook* (2001, with Annmarie Turnbull); and, with Matt Cook, *Queer beyond London* 2022.

Louise Pawley is interested in lesbian stories in twentieth-century archive collections and has completed an MA on this subject at the University of Sussex. She went on to work at the nearby Keep Archive Centre, focusing in part on the cataloguing of the Brighton Ourstory Archive, Brighton's largest lesbian, gay and bisexual collection.

George Townsend is a PhD candidate in English at Birkbeck College, University of London, where he is studying the cultural history of public bathing places, focusing specifically on the history of Parson's Pleasure, Oxford.

Alva Träbert is a gender historian and feminist sociologist based in Bochum, Germany. Her work focuses on queer identities, gender-based violence and the challenges refugees face in accessing legal protection and healthcare. She leads a state-wide training programme that aims at implementing violence protection measures for queer and trans refugees and provides advocacy for refugees claiming asylum based on their sexual orientation and/or gender identity.

Acknowledgements

This collection emerged from the 'Queer Localities' conference we organized at Birkbeck College, University of London, to mark the end of our 'Queer beyond London' project in December 2017. It was a remarkable event – bringing together academics and community historians, archivists and activists from across the UK and well beyond. Many shared with us the sense of connection and comradeship they felt participating in the day's rich and creative discussions. It was one of those events that – even as you are experiencing it – you know you will remember as having been unique. We want to thank all the participants for showing us so vividly how locality could matter to understandings and experiences of sex, desire and sexuality, and in particular our keynote speaker, Valerie Korinek, for unfurling the queer Canadian prairies. Chris Waters gave a bridging keynote between our event and another queer gathering the day before. We owe a debt to Craig Griffiths for thinking so flexibly about the 'Queer Lives Past and Present' event he organized and to Chris for joining us together so deftly. We are grateful to Birkbeck for providing us with the space; to the AHRC for their generous funding of both the conference and project; to Carlie Pendleton for assistance in preparing the manuscript; and to Katy Petit, our wonderful administrator and overall fixer, whose centrality to the project was confirmed when she coined the moniker 'Queer beyond London' as a deft alternative to our more dour 'Sexualities and Localities'.

Since that conference the Covid crisis has made such in-person gatherings impossible and has posed enormous professional and personal challenges to many of those involved in this book. We are hugely grateful to all our contributors and all at Bloomsbury – especially our editors Abigail Lane and Emily Drewe – for working with us in such adversity. We also want to thank project manager Dharanivel Baskar and the copyediting and production teams at Integra for all their help.

Matt missed the conference because of a new arrival to his family; the period since saw the death of a close friend. For him this book is a welcome to Harrison Cook and a farewell to Andy Saich, an avid explorer of queer localities the world over. It is dedicated to them both.

Introduction

Matt Cook and Alison Oram

George Montague, Brighton's self-described 'oldest gay in the village', was a fixture of the famously gay-friendly English seaside resort until his death in March 2022 at the age of 98. For more than a decade he participated in Brighton's Pride parade, zipping along in his mobility scooter unmistakeably festooned with rainbow flags and activist messages for the crowds lining the streets. Montague's placards celebrated his pride, love and marriage. They also demanded change: a care home for 'grey gays' and an apology from the British government, which criminalized and convicted men including himself for historic homosexual offences. Montague's largest placard, declaring himself the oldest gay in the village, neatly encapsulates issues of isolation, belonging, community and locality that thread across this collection.

A playful reinterpretation of the expression 'only gay in the village' made famous by Matt Lucas's *Little Britain* character Daffyd from the seemingly isolated village of Llanddewi Brefi in Wales, Montague's reworked version signalled not loneliness but community. Of course, Daffyd was never actually alone in his Welsh village, and this is mirrored in many of the locations and histories across this collection that extend well beyond London and other urban centres. Nor was George Montague alone in Brighton. His activism was roundly supported, and his absence from Brighton Pride in 2016, in the midst of his campaign for a state apology, was noted in the gay press. For Montague, the word 'village' did not signal the loneliness of small and isolated locations, but instead the rich and vibrant locale in which he claimed a superlative place.

Queering locality

Let's start with our title, which highlights the idea of locality, and the queer histories connected to place. In recent years, this relationship (between queer place and queer history) has come to the fore for both historians and geographers, and in this collection we extend their conversation. We have gathered together chapters which are extraordinarily varied in terms of time periods, places and disciplinary approaches as they traverse the UK and beyond. They present a kaleidoscope of located histories of queer Britain and Northern Ireland: gleams and sparkles of colour and life that suggest further rich seams to be uncovered, and point to future understandings of queer history and place elsewhere. These histories are evocative of so many different queer kinds of place and the variety of experiences, meanings and perceptions that constitute a sense of place.[1] People form multiple identifications in relation to the places they live, visit and imagine. Their expression and experience of identity shift as they move between them, and in this way queer people and queer behaviour create distinct cultures of place – complicating the meanings and associations of particular localities.

People create 'places' but this is not a one-way process. Cultural geographers argue that space and place are active in the production of social norms, counterculture, a sense of self, fleeting or even more sustained community, and a range of associated feelings and desires. That this conception of locality has become axiomatic owes much to the arguments forged by postmodern and cultural geographers like Edward Soja, Henri Lefebvre and Doreen Massey in the 1980s and 1990s. Their work (among others) prompted the so-called spatial turn in the humanities. Space, place and locality are now woven more fully into social and cultural analysis across the disciplines, though how these terms are understood varies.[2] Space and place are seen as distinct by geographers, for example, while historians can tend to use them interchangeably, rather, as people have tended to do in the sources they draw upon (in oral histories, for example). Across the chapters to come we see spatial vocabulary used in various ways, signalling different dimensions and conceptions of locality and place. We invite our readers to be alert to these uses and open to the different understandings they signal. If a place is a specific location, for example, then the queer places visited across this collection are very different in terms of scale and definition. They include the capital cities of Edinburgh, Belfast and London, the province of Northern Ireland, the Jewish suburbs of London, the leisure spaces of Brighton beach, a swimming site in Oxford and a plant hunter's garden in Yorkshire. Each of these places configures queer desires and behaviours, but in very different ways – and sometimes fleetingly, sometimes for more persistent periods of time.

Locating queer

The chapters map some of the UK's differently scaled localities and their associated temporalities – from a single ritualistic moment to an entire century. Sexual identity is shown to matter deeply in some places, and to be more diffuse or displaced in others. Our contributors use the term 'queer' variously to specify identity in the manner of LGBTQ and to trouble such apparently coherent ideas of selfhood. We use queer in the title and in this introduction because it is capacious enough to embrace the sense of shifting ground and shifting desires that emerges in the collection. It usefully troubles ideas of permanence or totality – including in ideas of space, place and locality. What the contributors show between them, for example, is that we can't speak with any ease or conviction about a singular or homogeneous queer Britain. Instead, they demonstrate that locality matters profoundly in texturing and differentiating queer lives, experiences and self-understandings.

Our contributors include an archivist, a community historian, a film-maker and early career and more senior academics from history, media studies, literature, geography, art history and social policy. Together, they explore the queer dimensions of places across Britain and beyond, with several also looking at the significance of movement and what that does to the experience of the places of origin and destination – in the transplanted Englishness of an ex-pat community in Florence, for example, or in a televisual and personal shuttling between Newcastle and London.

The chapters identify the dynamics and cross-cutting identifications relating to class, race, religion and gender. Gemma Romain and Caroline Bressey suggest the ways in which Black interwar bohemians might have felt a different sense of being in and out of place to others in their circle. Sean Brady demonstrates the potency of religiously defined localities to queer experience in Northern Ireland. And while Parson's Pleasure, the Oxford bathing spot explored by George Townsend, functioned homosocially and to the exclusion of women, Rachel Hope Cleves shows how the Florentine English 'colony' was marked by a convivial mixing of men and women in a heterosociality often overlooked in queer scholarship.

As well as coming from different disciplinary directions, the chapters mobilize different approaches; histories from below and thick descriptions sit alongside social, cultural and media analyses. The 'traces' of our title refer in part to the sometimes indistinct and ephemeral evidence of queer lives and communities which nevertheless allow our contributors equivocally to locate queerness and queer locality in Britain. This material is wide-ranging, including interwar photography and 1980s activist ephemera; oral history; sacred texts and rituals; literature, TV and autobiographies; and horticulture (in Dominic Janes's exploration of transplanted Alpine plants). It is through such sources that different localities come to be experienced, traced and understood. The collection is thus in part about competing and jostling meanings and associations, and about what different materials and disciplinary approaches bring to understandings of locality.

What the chapters have in common, beyond their seductive invitation to value the local and the regional more powerfully in queer history, is the work they do to challenge, raise questions about and push forward many of the themes around place and time that are currently preoccupying queer historians and geographers in particular. We touch on these in the remainder of this Introduction, fanning out from the cities which have tended to dominate in analysis of queer lives to take in the suburbs, smaller towns and rural areas which have come into queer focus over the last decade. We suggest that the regions and constituent nations of the UK can be seen as larger but no less distinctive queer localities, and consider the significance of movement between them in the UK and beyond. Finally we mark the significance of Empire and race to understandings of queer place and dynamics of time. These are the broad frameworks within and against which our contributors are working.

Queering and queer in the city

Early historical work in the 1990s on the emergence of gay identities and cultures focused on large metropolitan cities, initially in the United States, with work on New York, San Francisco and Philadelphia.[3] These studies showed how the texture of queer life differed from place to place and how areas and sites within these cities affected the way desires were felt, understood and acted upon. In their oral history of the butch-femme lesbian bar scene in Buffalo (New York state), for example, Madeline Davis and Elizabeth Lapovsky Kennedy showed how the bars sustained certain patterns of desire and identification. The particular dynamics of the city, certain areas within it and the bars themselves mattered to the way women understood themselves and felt community there.[4]

The so-called new queer British historians of the early 2000s shifted the focus to Britain – though primarily to London. Between them they showed how the inner west suburb of Notting Hill (for example) fostered particular forms of queer community that were distinct from those associated with Soho or Bethnal Green. They suggested that such areas and specific places within them (from boarding houses and university settlements to theatres and cosmopolitan bars) mattered not only as backdrop and context but as an active constituent in the play of desire, identity and community.[5] This work demonstrated that the capital was perhaps better understood as a series of differently scaled localities than as an iconic whole – though mythologies about London were also important, not least in informing people's decisions to move there to live out a queerer life or else to steer well clear. David Higgs' edited collection, *Queer Sites: Gay Urban Histories since 1600* (1999) and then *Queer Cities, Queer Cultures: Europe since 1945,* edited by Matt Cook and Jennifer Evans, drew together accounts of a range of European cities, from the queerly iconic to those with little or no such notoriety. These collections show that iconic or not, these cities were all places where queerly identified people lived out their lives and where the particularities of urban planning, history and culture shaped the understanding and experiences of sexual desire.[6] This body of work entrenched the idea of the city and metropolis as axiomatic to queer life and culture, but it also suggested the need to understand it as a contested and variable terrain – tacitly inviting a turn to the queer significance of localities within these bounds and beyond.

What geographers, social scientists and historians have noted is that intersecting urban processes have led to businesses and communities clustering in particular spots in cities. This includes, especially in the post–Second World War period, the emergence of loosely or more specifically queer bars, streets and areas, and the formation of 'gay ghettos' or 'gaybourhoods'. These have been analysed as essential mechanisms through which gay sub-cultures have formed, been sustained, or indeed lost and compromised.[7] In these areas, queer people could find relative tolerance and a degree of safety in community. Historically often on the edge of city centres, and allied with spaces open to other outsider or marginalized groups (shift workers, sex workers, racial 'others'), increasing knowledge about their existence was built and disseminated among queer people via gossip, observation and the gay and lesbian press. In the Plymouth of the 1950s to the 1990s described by Alan Butler in Chapter 9, cross-over pubs, bars and cafes on the city's Union Street became notorious for hard drinking sailors and queer sexual opportunities; the specifically gay places were meanwhile often half-hidden, as they also were in other towns and cities at least until the 1970s.

In recent years gaybourhoods and gay villages, and the scholarly preoccupation with them, have been criticized for their exclusion of lesbians, bisexual and trans people, as well as those who cannot afford to socialize in commercial bars or the rents and house prices of gentrifying gay districts. There is also a contemporary concern about these queer social places disappearing, as well as debate about whether gay ghettos and villages are as necessary and relevant now that legal equality has equivocally come to pass in the UK.[8]

Beyond the city

If the city centre and the inner suburbs (often run-down in the late twentieth century) have compelled the gaze of those investigating queer lives, places beyond – suburbs, small towns, villages, the countryside – have been associated with oppressive norms from which queer people have or should want to flee.[9] This is partly because the much touted division between the city and its surrounds has real-life effects – and not least in the decisions people make to leave or stay. Yet in recent years places beyond the city have not only become newly desirable to some queer people in changed times but have also been re-evaluated as highly significant to the ways queer lives have been lived and understood. Suburbia has been reclaimed,[10] for example, in a move encapsulated in this collection by Searle Kochberg and Margaret Greenfield's Chapter 7. They show how the capital's suburbs have particular resonance for queer Jewish Londoners because of the ways religious ritual and queer memory and mobility intertwine.

Other work in Britain and other national contexts has resuscitated the queer dimensions of regional cities, small towns and rural areas.[11] While London tended to dominate and the queer historical patchwork as it extended beyond the capital was relatively threadbare until the mid-2000s, there has been a flowering of LGBTQ community history over the past 15–20 years – underpinned in large part by grants from the Heritage Lottery Fund (*c.*130 of them for LGBTQ groups between 2003 and 2018). Brighton Ourstory, which mobilized in the aftermath of the passing of Section 28 of the Local Government Act forbidding local authorities from 'promoting' homosexuality, was the first UK community history project to suggest the significance of locality. It highlighted the town's queer exceptionalism, already apparent in the 1950s and 1960s.[12] The later upsurge from the early 2000s opened out LGBTQ histories ranging from that of Plymouth in England's southwest (on which Alan Butler reflects in his chapter) to those garnered by Ourstory Scotland in the north (and on which Alva Träbert draws). Anchored often in oral histories, this work has drawn attention to the local fabric of lives lived in part against the grain and beyond the country's iconic queer sites.[13]

Many local libraries and museums collaborated with these projects and exhibited the materials they gathered. They did this often as part of LGBT history month (from 2005) or of the Pride events which have proliferated over the last decade beyond London (Francesca Ammaturo counted 109 nationwide in 2018 including one on a caravan park in North Wales).[14] The repeal of Section 28 in 2003 (in Scotland, 2000) freed the hands of local authorities (and so many of those local museums and libraries) to engage with LGBTQ community work. They were further prompted by their new obligations under the 2010 Equalities Act. St Fagans National Museum of History in Wales, for example, developed a policy of actively collecting objects, documents, photographs and oral histories to represent and include the lives of LGBTQ people across the country. The uneven cultural shift towards greater toleration and acceptance mobilized many to engage with histories which had previously felt challenging, marginal or taboo.

This renewed queer historical consciousness began to nuance London-centric presumptions and carried with it distant echoes of the pioneering and more overtly political community history work in the 1970s and 1980s. It is probably no coincidence that this consciousness has re-emerged during a wave of closures of lesbian and gay venues across the UK: there has been a sense of urgency for some to record and remember such places in recent community oral history projects, and often with a mix of nostalgia and pride. In these accounts of the ebb and flow of social spaces and of gay politics, the historic power of alternative and gay bookshops as community centres frequently surfaces (as it does in this volume for Edinburgh and Plymouth). So too does the importance of 'finding' pride and building a historical archive of people's particular queer everyday lives. More than this, they speak, collectively, of the local queer cultures of place and how these have changed.[15]

This local and regional turn has demonstrated considerable differentiation among towns and cities beyond London. In *Gay West* (2011) Robert Howes looked at the particular complexion of lesbian and gay politics in Bristol and Bath since gay liberation, showing how it related to other local countercultural and political networks.[16] Focusing on northern England, Helen Smith found distinctive patterns of casual sex between working-class and often married men in the first half of the twentieth century. Through her analysis of court cases in the mid-1950s she also discovered striking differences between male sexual networks and associated self-conceptions in Yorkshire, the West Midlands and London.[17] Paul Flynn's *GAY* (2017) meanwhile showed how Manchester's cutting-edge dance, music and bar scenes affected and reflected wider national change.[18] Matt Cook and Alison Oram's *Queer Beyond London* (MUP, 2022) demonstrates the particular queer dynamics and cultures of four provincial cities – Brighton, Leeds, Manchester and Plymouth – underscoring the need to take these places on their own terms as well as in conversation with wider national and international social, cultural and economic shifts.

Pioneering studies of the southern states of the United States, New Zealand and Canada have shown how the specificities of rural life modulated queer identification and desires in these nations with vast tracts of countryside. These studies took the focus even further from iconic queer cities and showed how there was no queer wasteland beyond them.[19] But even in the densely populated UK, rurality has meaning. There have long been alternative narratives of rural retreats for queer expression – the goings-on at country house parties, and the potential for outlawry in the 'greenwood' E. M. Forster imagined at the end of his novel *Maurice* (1913). Socialist and homosexual rights advocate Edward Carpenter (1844–1929) also valued closeness to nature in his writing, living on the smallholding he shared with his lover George Merrill (1867–1928) in Millthorpe, Derbyshire. Hebden Bridge and Todmorden, small country towns in northern West Yorkshire, have become known for their high density of lesbians (and gay men).[20] But Caroline Bressey and Gemma Romain put a new spin on this in Chapter 6, exploring the place of interwar queer people of colour outside the city (and specifically outside central London), queering the assumed whiteness of rurality between the wars as well as the urban-centredness of Black British queer histories. George Townsend, too, describes how the bathing spot Parson's Pleasure in Oxford occupied a liminal place between town and country, between heteronormative bathing rules and decidedly queer pleasures.

Further layers of association and identification relate distinctly to the regions and nations of Wales, Scotland and Northern Ireland – as recent place-based queer histories by Daryl Leeworthy (2019), Norena Shopland (2017), Jeff Meek (2015) and Marian Duggan (2016) suggest. The four UK nations have somewhat different legal regimes and varied cultures, economies, geographies, religious and national identities and histories.[21] These have spawned distinctive queer lives and communities in these places and also between different urban and rural localities within them. In Chapter 3, Sean Brady shows how politico-religious divisions and the depth of religious fervour and affiliation constructed (and inhibited) ways of being queer in Northern Ireland, marking it out from other regions and nations of the UK. Alva Träbert's Edinburgh migrants (in Chapter 1) describe personal processes of becoming identified with distinctive aspects of Scottishness, even though they had mostly moved from other countries entirely. In England, Gareth Longstaff (in Chapter 2) shows how the putative north-south divide plays out for this northerner moving south to London in what seems a classic gay migration story. Yet once in the capital he found himself captivated by an episode of Channel 4's pioneering lesbian and gay magazine programme *Out on Tuesday* (1989–94). The show depicted gay bar patrons in the 1980s in the north-eastern city of Newcastle deploying and redefining heteronormative stereotypes of northern working-class and hard masculinities. It suggested to Longstaff how gender as well as sexuality is refracted through place and region, casting his migration in new light.

The ways in which urban and rural places are haunted with personal and collective histories, connections and associations allow for everyday difference and also resistance.[22] These spectres are especially evoked in the movement between places in two recent works. In his memoir *Between Worlds* (2021) pioneering gay historian and sociologist Jeffrey Weeks suggests how the particular working-class culture of the Rhondda valley in south Wales shaped his sense of – and response to – his emergent desires in the 1960s. If Weeks's earlier work signalled the centrality of the capital to the lesbian and gay movement, here he draws the place of his upbringing into an account of living 'between worlds' that have, for him, been unevenly present to each other: the Rhondda affecting his life and perspective in London; London infusing his visits to the Rhondda.[23] Jeremy Atherton Lin's tour through the gay bars of London, San Francisco and Los Angeles (in *Gay Bar*, 2021) meanwhile culminates in Blackpool, in England's north-west. On a weekend trip from London, Atherton Lin found queer experience and a particular brand of seaside drag modulated by nationalism, racism, economic hardship and a distinctive sense of class identity. This felt to him very different to the queer localities he'd got to know well in the capital.[24]

Seaside resorts like those visited by Atherton Lin have long been associated with liminal sexualities of all kinds; they seem to offer pleasurable freedoms and an escape from the everyday. In this respect, Brighton on the south coast has many commonalities with Blackpool, also a gay playground, even though their hinterlands are very distinct – the latter drawing its visitors from across the industrial and post-industrial northern cities and north Wales; the former a refuge from London and for gay people from the wider UK. Louise Pawley (in Chapter 8) discusses how the beach in this 'gay mecca' became a venue for lesbian and gay activism and remembrance in the late 1980s, and how resistance there sometimes came through the evocation of a camp, carefree seaside spirit. The coastal context is very different in Plymouth further along the south coast to the west. Butler shows that in this patriotic military city there was a concern to remain 'below the radar': gay people took pride in passing as straight or ambiguous, in contrast to the seeming imperative in Brighton to be out and proud. A key influence was the military ban on lesbians and gay men which endured until 2000, reminding us again of the varying cycles and time frames influencing queer visibility and confidence in different parts of the city. Yet the blurring of boundaries between land and sea produced an intensely queer culture in Plymouth; its sailors straddling the watery world of their ships and onshore carousing, many of them shuttling between queer and straight sexual pleasures during their shore leave. Butler's account of homophobic abuse and violence amidst the city's homoerotic pleasures touches a theme running across the book: the intermingling of safety and danger in queer and other places. Known queer-friendly districts or certain cities like Brighton have been particularly attractive but are still tinged with risk.[25] Where is it safe to be evidently queer or trans? Where is it wise to exercise caution? These constant adjustments and anxieties are further nuanced by gender and racial belonging. Safety in particular places is an everyday concern for queer people, though one that has changed in its valence and nature over time.

Queer movements

Such feelings of safety and danger often underpin long and short-term movements and migrations of queer people between localities, another cross-cutting theme of the collection. Classically this movement is imagined as going away from family and place of origin (often pictured as a small town or suburban or rural locality). A typical example is the character of Ritchie in Russell T. Davies's TV drama *It's a Sin* (2021), who flees the Isle of Wight at the first opportunity for a wild gay life in 1980s London. This trajectory has increasingly come under fire for being inaccurate and overly simplistic, though it remains relevant to many young people. The idea of moving to find and make LGBTQ community in a new place continues to have resonance and is often linked to the idea that a fulfilled gay life can only be lived out in the city, ideally a larger metropolis. Alva Träbert's chapter tracks a set of very different migrants to Edinburgh between the 1970s and the 2000s. While this was queer migration to a big(gish) city, it was not a migration south to London or Manchester – indeed one man moved north in a period when sex between men was still illegal in Scotland though no longer entirely so in England. The political culture of Edinburgh and Scotland attracted these people, whose identities often developed and changed in ways they did not foresee.

An even more adventurous or necessary route, for those with the opportunity or means to afford it, has been the escape to another country entirely. In Chapter 10

Rachel Hope Cleves documents the flight to Florence of generations of British and American queers, drawn by its long-standing history of equivocal tolerance as well as its reputation for the arts and culture. Especially from the late Victorian period, queer men and women escaped punitive UK and US laws and social attitudes to settle in this city, while retaining their identification as English (or American) and drawing a sense of Englishness and of English place into this provincial Italian city – a fusion which Henry James described as 'queer, promiscuous and polyglot'. For plant-hunter Reginald Farrer, queer desires were projected onto 'the perverse little people of the hills', the alpine plants he tracked down and onto the male travelling companions with whom he had various degrees of romantic attachment. Moving in the other direction to the queer men and women exiling themselves in Florence, Farrer brought the Alpine plants he loved back home to Britain. They were, Dominic Janes suggests, repositories of his queer desires, transplanted from the Himalayas to northern England.

Queer identifications and desires might form and change in such movements, through the act of movement and in settling 'somewhere else'. Movements may not be linear, from A to B, but roundabout or there-and-back, with queer meanings and associations snowballing in the process.[26] Chosen and enforced travel, as well as imagined and desired movement, is a keynote in queer testimony and history. By looking across and between localities, between countryside and city, and across regions we gain a sense of that dynamism and the significance of an intra and international queer diaspora which can be missed or lost in a focus on single places. This attention to movement and to the places left behind sharpens our understandings of being in or out of place (or of feeling both at once). Cleves thus describes a sense of alien belonging in Florence for the queer English colony as places and times cluster and create layers – in a conjunction of outsider status and white elite privilege. Queer desires, ideas and understandings are again shown to be in dynamic relationship to time and locality.

Themes of Empire and colonialism are writ large in Cleves's piece, but all of the chapters in some way have Britain's imperial and post-imperial character as their backdrop, from the discussion of a world-travelling collector to the queer configurations of Northern Ireland. Bressey and Romain's chapter tracks some interwar queer Black people and their travels remind us that some of those people were in the UK because of colonial links to the Caribbean. Others among them were American and part of the wider Black Atlantic diaspora. Their chapter alerts us to a particular form of white sensibility among (moneyed) London bohemians who were keen to engage with certain Black cultural forms which fascinated them. White identities based on imperial assumptions were fostered at British public schools and universities, training white men of the higher social classes to serve and regulate the colonies. The homosociality of these places of education, which would be reproduced in the administration and military activities of empire, can be traced through to the seemingly innocuous pleasures of men's river bathing at Oxford and through plant-hunter Reginald Farrer's sense of an automatic right to collect plants abroad and bring them back to Britain.

Time and place

Material and spatial contexts, cultural geographers have argued, can evoke other places and temporalities which curtail and open out different possibilities. It is these layers of space and time and their effects in particular localities which compel the contributors to this book.[27] While these chapters each refer to queer places and place-making during certain time spans, they only tangentially fit a conventional trajectory of queer history with its oft-evoked landmarks (including, for example, Oscar Wilde and Radclyffe Hall's encounters with the law in 1895 and 1928, and the Sexual Offences Act of 1967). Those dealing with the late nineteenth and early twentieth centuries have the context of contemporary persecution of sex between men in the UK, meaning that queer desires often had to be veiled in various ingenious ways – expressed through codes and allusions, articulated through the natural world or through objects, or pursued through travel to other places. Other chapters pick up themes that cluster around the 1980s, years of more intense political activism than earlier or since. But beyond the ostensible time periods they deal with, most chapters discuss places and spaces that evoke and draw in other earlier periods and ways of experiencing and understanding time at odds with the notion of steady linear progression.

Parson's Pleasure often acted as an escape from time for the men swimming there – evoking an older temporality, a stepping into other times. The building up of traditions about the spot, Townsend shows, is an accretion of times past, some actual, some mythical. At particular moments, such as the Victorian fin de siècle, men might actively call into play the Greek classical past to frame their enjoyment of friendship and romance there. The political flyers produced in 1980s Brighton to promote anti-Section 28 activism on the beach evoked cheeky seaside graphics of an earlier era. One of the more sobering trajectories of time is the premillennialism espoused by some Ulster protestant sects, which they used to justify their rabid homophobia and anti-feminism, the context for the Save Ulster from Sodomy campaign described in Brady's chapter.

The collection is of course not comprehensive in its coverage; there are gaps and silences, voices unheard, localities ignored. Though gender is at issue across the chapters, for example, there is no detailed consideration of trans identification and its relation to different localities in Britain. What we hope, though, is that individually and collectively the chapters that follow open out questions, trouble trenchant presumptions and provide fresh insights into the queerness of locality. Because each of the chapters is multifaceted we decided against sectionalizing them – a structural approach which would box them in. Instead, we chose to arrange them in an unruly geographical sweep from north to south, tracing and gathering up different configurations of queer life across Britain (and Britain abroad) as they go. The more arbitrary structure we settled on gestures to our interest in space and place, movement and migration, but more importantly allows very differently conceived and argued chapters to come side by side, generating unexpected resonances and dissonances between queer localities.

Notes

1   T. Cresswell, *Place: A Short Introduction* (Oxford: Blackwell, 2004); Doreen Massey, 'Places and their pasts', *History Workshop Journal* 39 (1995): 182–92; Michael Rustin, 'Spatial relations and human relations', in *Spatial Politics: Essays for Doreen Massey*, ed. David Featherstone and Joe Painter (Malden, MA: Wiley-Blackwell, 2013).

2   Richard Rodger and Susanna Rau, 'Thinking spatially: New horizons for urban history', *Urban History* 47 (2020): 372–83.

3   Elizabeth Lapovsky Kennedy and Madeline D. Davies, *Boots of Leather, Slippers of Gold: The History of a Lesbian Community* (New York: Routledge, 1993); George Chauncey, *Gay New York: Gender, Urban Culture, and the Making of the Gay Male World, 1890–1940* (New York: Basic Books, 1994); Nan Alamilla Boyd, *Wide-Open Town: A History of Queer San Francisco to 1965* (Berkeley: University of California Press, 2003); Marc Stein, *City of Sisterly and Brotherly Loves: Lesbian and Gay Philadelphia, 1945–1972* (Philadelphia: Temple University Press, 2003).

4   Kennedy and Davies, *Boots of Leather, Slippers of Gold*.

5   See, for example, Matt Cook, *London and the Culture of Homosexuality, 1885–1914* (Cambridge: Cambridge University Press, 2003); Matt Houlbrook, *Queer London: Perils and Pleasures in the Sexual Metropolis, 1918–1957* (Chicago: University of Chicago Press, 2005); Morris B. Kaplan, *Sodom on the Thames: Sex, Love, and Scandal in Wilde Times* (Ithaca: Cornell University Press, 2005); Frank Mort, *Capital Affairs: London and the Making of the Permissive Society* (New Haven: Yale University Press, 2010); and Simon Avery and Katherine M. Graham (eds), *Sex, Time and Place: Queer Histories of London, c.1850 to the Present* (London: Bloomsbury, 2016).

6   David Higgs (ed.), *Queer Sites: Gay Urban Histories since 1600* (London: Routledge, 1999), Matt Cook and Jennifer Evans (eds), *Queer Cities, Queer Cultures: Europe since 1945* (London: Bloomsbury, 2014).

7   Catherine J. Nash and Andrew Gorman-Murray, 'LGBT neighbourhoods and "new mobilities": Towards understanding transformations in sexual and gendered urban landscapes', *International Journal of Urban and Regional Research* 38, no. 3 (May 2014): 756–72.

8   See Kath Browne and Gavin Brown, 'An introduction to the geographies of sex and sexualities', in *The Routledge Research Companion to Geographies of Sex and Sexualities*, ed. G. Brown and K. Browne (London: Routledge, 2016); Ben Campkin, *Queer Premises: London's LGBT Night Spaces* (London: Bloomsbury, 2022); Amin Ghaziani, *There Goes the Gayborhood* (Princeton, NJ: Princeton University Press, 2014).

9   Kath Weston, 'Get thee to a big city: Sexual imaginary and the great gay migration', *GLQ: A Journal of Lesbian and Gay Studies* 2, no. 3 (1995): 253–77.

10 Gavin Brown, 'Urban (Homo)sexualities: Ordinary cities and ordinary sexualities', *Geography Compass* 2, no. 4 (2008): 1215–31. Gordon Waitt and Andrew Gorman Murray, 'Homemaking and mature age gay men "down under": Paradox, intimacy, subjectivities, spacialities, and scale', *Gender, Place and Culture* 14, no. 5 (2007): 569–84; Martin Dines, *Gay Suburban Narratives in American and British Culture: Homecoming Queens* (London: Palgrave, 2009).

11 See Matt Cook and Alison Oram, *Queer beyond London* (Manchester: Manchester University Press, 2022); Daisy Payling, 'City limits: Sexual politics and the new urban

left in 1980s Sheffield', *Contemporary British History* 3, no. 2 (2017): 256–73; Japonica Brown-Saracino, 'How places shape identity: The origins of distinctive LBQ identities in four small U.S. cities', *American Journal of Sociology* 121, no. 1 (2015): 1–63; Tiffany Myrdahl, 'Ordinary (small) cities and LGBQ lives', *ACME: An International E-Journal for Critical Geographies* 12, no. 2 (2013): 279–304; Nick McGlynn, 'Slippery geographies of the urban and the rural: Public sector LGBT equalities work in the shadow of the "gay capital"', *Journal of Rural Studies* 57 (2018): 65–77.

12 Brighton Ourstory Project, *Daring Hearts: Lesbian and Gay Lives of 50s and 60s Brighton* (Brighton: QueenSpark, 1992).

13 For more discussion of local LGBT history projects in Britain see Alison Oram, 'Making place and community: Contrasting lesbian and gay, feminist and queer oral history projects in Brighton and Leeds', *Oral History Review* (forthcoming, 2022).

14 Francesca Ammaturo, unpublished paper delivered at the 'Stonewall 50 Years On' conference held at Manchester Metropolitan University, 2019.

15 Oram 'Making place and community' (2022).

16 Robert Howes, *Gay West: Civil Society, Community and LGBT History in Bristol and Bath 1970 to 2010* (Bristol: SilverWood, 2011).

17 Helen Smith, 'Working class ideas and experiences of sexuality in twentieth century Britain: Regionalism as a category of analysis', *Twentieth Century British History* 29, no. 1 (2018): 58–78; see also Helen Smith, *Masculinity, Class and Same-Sex Desire in Industrial England, 1895–1957* (London: Palgrave Macmillan, 2015).

18 Paul Flynn, *Good as You* (London: Ebury Press, 2017). Also see Mike Homfray, *Provincial Queens: The Gay and Lesbian Community in the North-West of England* (Oxford: Peter Lang, 2007). Kath Browne and Leela Bakshi, *Ordinary in Brighton?: LGBT, Activisms and the City* (London: Routledge, 2016).

19 John Howard, *Men Like That: A Southern Queer History* (Chicago: University of Chicago Press, 1999); E. Patrick Johnson, *Sweet Tea: Black Gay Men of the South* (Chapel Hill, NC: University of North Carolina Press, 2007); Scott Herring, *Another Country: Queer Anti-Urbanism* (New York: New York University Press, 2010); Chris Brickell, *Mates and Lovers: A History of Gay New Zealand* (Auckland: Godwit, 2008). Valerie Korinek, *Prairie Fairies: A History of Queer Communities and People in Western Canada, 1930–1985* (Toronto: University of Toronto Press, 2018).

20 Darren P. Smith and Louise Holt, 'Lesbian migrants in the gentrified valley and "other" geographies of rural gentrification', *Journal of Rural Studies* 21, no. 3 (2005): 313–22.

21 Jeffrey Meek, *Queer Voices in Post-War Scotland: Male Homosexuality, Religion and Society* (Basingstoke: Palgrave Macmillan, 2015); Daryl Leeworthy, *A Little Gay History of Wales* (Cardiff: University of Wales Press, 2019); Marian Duggan, *Queering Conflict: Examining Lesbian and Gay Experiences of Homophobia in Northern Ireland* (London: Routledge, 2016); Norena Shopland, *Forbidden Lives: LGBT Stories from Wales* (Bridgend: Seren, 2017).

22 On this idea of haunted places see Michel de Certeau, 'Walking the city', in *The Practice of Everyday Life* (Berkeley: University of California Press, 1984).

23 Jeffrey Weeks, *Between Worlds: A Queer Boy from the Valleys* (Cardiff: University of Wales Press, 2021).

24 Jeremy Atherton Lin, *Gay Bar: Why We Went Out* (London: Granta, 2021).

25 Andrew Gorman-Murray 'Intimate mobilities: Emotional embodiment and queer migration', *Social & Cultural Geography* 10, no. 4 (2009): 441–60; see also Browne and Brown (2016).

26 Rebecca Jennings, "'It was a hot climate and it was a hot time'": Lesbian migration and transnational networks in the mid-twentieth century', *Australian Feminist Studies* 25, no. 63 (2010): 31; Weston, 'Get thee to a big city' (1995); Gorman-Murray, 'Intimate mobilities' (2009); Alison Oram, 'Circling around: Migration and the queer city', in Cook and Oram, *Queer beyond London* (2022).

27 And in ways which resonant with Michel Foucault's use of heterotopia – rehearsed in Michel Foucault, 'Of other spaces', in *The Visual Culture Reader*, ed. Nicholas Mirzoeff (1986; London: Routledge, 1998), 22–7.

1

Great expectations: Migrating to Edinburgh

Alva Träbert

Introduction

The idea of queer[1] people moving to the metropolis to find their place in the world is a familiar one. While UK localities beyond London are gradually receiving their due attention as historic and current draws for queer life, the cities commonly associated with vibrant queer communities in the UK are still conventionally found south of the Scottish border. This chapter examines Scotland (and specifically Edinburgh) through the eyes of four individuals who chose to make it their home, and who migrated there at different points in time from rural Scotland, England, the United States and Jamaica.

As a destination for queer migrants, Edinburgh's position is unique in several ways. With a population of less than 500,000 it is comparatively small for a capital city, offering somewhat less anonymity than other national capitals. Decriminalization of consensual sexual activity between male adults arrived in 1980, thirteen years later than in neighbouring England and Wales, and the strong influence of the Church of Scotland has done little to facilitate public visibility for queer and trans people. However, in 2000 Scotland was also the first nation within the UK to repeal Section 2A, which prohibited local authorities from 'promoting' homosexuality and furthered the isolation of and discrimination against queer people.[2]

Many queer and trans migrants take an active part in shaping the political and social landscape of Scotland as well as Scottish attitudes towards migration. Alongside the narrative of young queer people leaving Scotland for a southern metropolis such as London or Manchester, there have always also been those who were drawn to Scotland. This includes some who left England to seek their fortune north of the border, even at a time when this meant moving back into criminality. Interviews undertaken with Ellen, Matt, Oonagh and Jaime explore some of the hopes and fears that brought them to their current home, the (queer) infrastructure and attitudes they found upon arrival, and the places and spaces they helped carve out, celebrate and preserve for themselves, their families and their communities. I am particularly interested in teasing out the tensions between expectations and the lived experience of this specific locality.

It is useful to situate these stories within the developments and trends of queer migration research in recent years. Migration studies have largely conceived of migrants as male workers seeking to improve their labour conditions. Subsequently, migration historians '"found" female migrants' and added a gender dimension to their analyses.[3] Social historian Nancy Green argues that this was partly due to an increased study of community formation, different forms of oppression, but also agency from the 1970s onwards.[4] Still, until fairly recently, this growing body of work largely assumed migrants to be heterosexual.[5] Gradually, this position is being challenged by scholars centring the migration experiences of gay, lesbian, queer and trans people, arguing that 'sexuality and sexual identities, practices and desires may be pivotal factors for migration'.[6] This focus on sexuality and sexual orientation in migration emerged in the late 1980s and early 1990s, catalysed by a number of political and social factors, such as the development of queer as well as race/ethnic studies, the rise of HIV/AIDS and the growing contributions of feminist academics.[7] Arguably, the latter have played a central role in shifting the focus beyond merely tracking the movement of individuals and groups, and instead 'exploring processes of subject and identity formation through migration' processes.[8]

What do we mean by queer migration? Social and cultural geographer Andrew Gorman-Murray offers the following definition: 'Queer migration occurs when the needs or desires of non-heterosexual identities, practices and performances are implicated in the process of displacement, influencing the decision to leave a certain place or choose a particular destination.'[9] In terms of what this may look like, researchers have offered a variety of – sometimes competing, sometimes complementary – narratives. For some, queer migration is fundamentally an act of emancipation.[10] There is the now common trope of queer people leaving their childhood homes to begin a completely new life in the metropolis – the very real foundations of which have been documented by the anthropologist of kinship, class, gender and sexuality Kath Weston, among others.[11]

For many, however, the roots and goals of migration choices are less straightforward. Not every queer migrant cuts ties to their childhood family or to social networks who disapprove of their sexuality. Scottish journalist and oral historian Bob Cant suggests 'two-mindedness' as a way to conceptualize the everyday 'work of translation'.[12] Queer people perform, he argues, concealing parts of their lives from others while simultaneously refusing to completely disavow either sexuality or (family) origins, paving the way for 'the possibility of new forms of belonging that are not predicated on single, unitary identities'.[13] The idea of a queer diaspora has also been invoked to explore the ways in which sexuality and sexual identity can change when queer individuals cross literal and figurative borders, taking their social, cultural and political ideologies with them.[14] Offering an alternative approach to the diaspora model, English theorist and queer studies pioneer Alan Sinfield emphasizes not the act of leaving home but that of assembling in a new home, which is 'not an origin, but rather a destination; there is no return, only arrival'.[15] Contrary to the idea of queer individuals leaving a familiar place that feels like home, 'narratives of queer migration-as-homecoming thus locate estrangement in the original home. The movement, here, is a movement away from being estranged'.[16]

The spatial and social complexities of more traditional models of migration are hardly captured by the quantitative data available, such as census statistics. This is even more true for queer people and motives – which is why qualitative, narrative research (and oral history in particular) lends itself to filling some of the many remaining gaps in research. Sociologist Anne-Marie Fortier beautifully describes the ways in which 'memory becomes a primary ground of identity formation in the context of migration… tied to the creation of the identity of places'.[17] In queer peoples' tellings of migration, of uprooting, searching, relocating and homecoming, we can learn about their beliefs and politics, as well as the social and material processes by which they have shaped themselves as well as their chosen homes.

The stories of Ellen, Matt, Oonagh and Jaime stood out because of the role that changing location played in their lives and in the ways they related to their current home in Edinburgh. They add to the rich tapestry of queer oral histories and work on queer identities in Scotland undertaken over the past decades. This includes seminal collections of Scottish queer life stories by Bob Cant,[18] oral and public historian Amy Tooth Murphy's work on post-war lesbian domesticity,[19] legal scholar Brian Dempsey's publications on lesbian and gay activism,[20] and social historian Roger Davidson's work on Scottish gay men's experiences with medicine and psychiatry as well as law reform.[21] Human geographer Grant Anderson's recent PhD thesis examines gender queerness in Scotland.[22] Building on his work on same-sex desire in Scotland and specifically on gay and bisexual men, social and cultural historian Jeff Meek has more recently focused on Scotland's path to decriminalization as well as issues around reconciling religious with sexual identities.[23] He also curates Queer Scotland, a blog on Scottish gay history. Community-led history projects such as Remember When and OurStory Scotland have made further invaluable contributions as well, particularly in creating spaces for communal history to be shared and discussed, as well as by gathering and preserving artefacts and ephemera.[24]

The four interviewees come from a range of cultural, socio-economic and religious backgrounds. First is Oonagh, a 48-year-old gay woman, gardener and triplet raised in St Andrews and Crail, who moved to Edinburgh as a young adult.[25] Second is Matt, a 34-year-old white Jamaican gay man who came to Edinburgh in 1995 to pursue a degree in environmental science.[26] Third is Ellen, a 64-year-old Jewish lesbian writer and editor from New York City who initially moved Scotland with her husband in 1971.[27] And finally, Jaime, sixty-four years old and gay, who grew up in the south of England and moved to Scotland in 1974 to take up a job as a sociology lecturer.[28] The original oral history research that the interviews form part of did not focus explicitly on migration but rather on notions of identity and belonging. The wider project saw interviews with LGBTQ individuals of different ages, social and religious backgrounds living in Scotland. In semi-structured interviews, they shared their recollections of queer and trans life in Edinburgh and Glasgow from the 1970s onwards. The different and changing ideas and labels around the interviewees' identities and the way these were shaped by experiences of community inclusion and exclusion were of particular interest. Questions around locality played a key role in discussing openly and secretly queer spaces, but also areas within the cities where being visibly queer and/or trans was perceived as more or less safe. While of course not representative of all migrant experiences, the four interviews introduced here offer an exemplary insight into queer migrants' homecoming to Edinburgh in the 1970s, 1980s and 1990s. All of them serve to expand our understandings of queer people's movements beyond simplified narratives of rural-to-urban migration, of queer migration to the south of the UK, and of queer-migration-as-liberation.

Hopes and fears

Which incentives and driving forces brought Matt, Oonagh, Ellen and Jaime to Edinburgh? It can be difficult to be sure of motives for any individual migrant's choices, but expectations bound up with both gender and sexuality play major roles in migration decisions and experiences. This applies to push and pull factors – both are complex and shaped by gender, racial and class contexts, meaning that individuals enter 'the urban space of the gay imaginary from very different trajectories'.[29] When it comes to queer individuals leaving their birthplaces, one common trope is that of migration from rural to metropolitan areas. Besides downplaying the existence of queer rural life, Gorman-Murray argues that 'normalising rural-to-urban migration as a "queer identity quest" overlooks greater diversity in migration patterns and experiences'.[30] Three of the interviewees here, in fact, migrated to Edinburgh directly from another city, namely London, New York and Kingston. Another long-standing trope is that of families discovering their child's sexuality and the parental home becoming a hostile and sometimes physically dangerous environment as a result. This was certainly true for Oonagh, who describes coming out to her parents: '[They] nearly strangled the living daylights out of me unfortunately. So one day I just decided that I would leave.' Jaime also describes the painful experiences and psychological trauma following his coming out to his family in the mid-1960s: '[My father] found what I'd been doing, and he was shocked but wanted to help me to be cured. [My psychiatrist] said if you can't love a member of the opposite sex, it means you're incapable of love.... I was devastated.'[31]

Simultaneously, 'apart from playing a restrictive role, the family can also offer economic, social and emotional support', which, as Thomas Wimark notes, is often a deciding factor in making transnational migration possible in the first place.[32] This may mean financially enabling a family member to travel abroad for the first time, where they are able to form early impressions of what their life in a different locality could look like. It might also mean familial financial support in the pursuit of educational possibilities that involve leaving home, with education symbolizing 'independence and freedom to discover one's sexuality'.[33] As Gorman-Murray argues, 'education, economic and sexual reasons may intermingle: as long as sexuality factors play a part in motivating migration and/or choice of destination, such displacement is a form of queer migration'.[34] There has also been some work on the role of travel in shaping the identities of queer people, such as historian Rebecca Jennings's examination of Australian and British lesbians in the mid-twentieth century.[35]

Both Matt's and Ellen's stories feature travel in the context of education, inspiring their later decisions to actually migrate. Matt first visited the UK on a school trip to attend a science conference in 1994, aged sixteen, when he first came into contact with the gay rights movement: 'That made me realize that being secretive about your sexuality and living a double life can actually be quite counterproductive, you know, and can help to perpetuate cycles of aggression, violence and misunderstanding.'[36] This experience led directly to his coming out after his return home. While his mother and stepfather took the news fairly well, reactions were stronger when news spread through the community. 'I don't want to over-dramatize these death threats, but you know, there were death threats from people. Violent words. Not so much violent action. I've never had any physical violence directed at me in Jamaica.' Ellen mentions the impact of attending a summer school at Edinburgh University as an undergrad in the mid-1960s: 'I had fallen in love with Edinburgh. I have always felt I really wanted to live on this side of the ocean. I'd never felt particularly American, I'd always felt very marginal.'[37] Rather than the childhood family, it is her birth nation she felt alienated from and ready to leave.

While Oonagh and Jaime had a lesser distance to overcome to reach Edinburgh, their act of migration was no less significant. For Oonagh, the decision to leave her parental home in the mid-1980s was confirmed by her experiences abroad as an au-pair in Germany. Upon returning, she discovered she no longer fit in: 'When I came back I thought I didn't really belong. [...] That I was really cosmopolitan and didn't want to be there, you know?' For her, the immediate pull towards Edinburgh was much more tenuous, a slip of paper torn from a magazine that she came across by chance, containing the switchboard number of Lesbian Line in Edinburgh: 'I had a little flat in Crail at the time over the harbour, there used to be a phone box where I used to go down every Sunday, and I used to phone it. And I'd always put down before anybody would answer.'[38] In Jaime's story, the idea of finding one's place through experiences as a travelling stranger is taken to its extreme, becoming the default position: 'From a very early age, the English identity is one I wanted to escape from.... Wanting to escape that identity and probably living in Scotland as an exile makes me in some ways quite happy, because I think exile is a natural position for me.' Notably, what Jaime describes here is not the notion of hoping to become more permanently at home in a new place, as discussed above. Instead, his relocation enables him to settle into a state of permanent, perfect exile which more closely corresponds to the way he thinks and feels about himself.

These life narrations serve to further expand on the simplified accounts provided by over-reliance on migration statistics – one example being matrimonial migration, described by Green as 'perhaps the most explicit example of the ways in which gender relations may cause mobility'.[39] Ellen, for example, migrated to Scotland as a married woman. She was still in New York at the time of the Stonewall uprising in June of 1969 but 'was also trying to be a very nice Jewish girl and make my mother happy. [She] had found a nice Jewish boy to marry'. Her husband's British passport facilitated their move to Scotland. Though Ellen had had 'hopeless crushes' on women by this point, she had never acted on them. She describes leaving her birthplace as key to her identity formation: 'It's really good to leave where you come from. Even if where you come from is where half the world is flocking to, to find themselves, come out, sort out their sexuality. I had to go away from New York and from my family, to be in a world where I could feel and live life differently.'[40]

The idea of queer individuals moving for the sole purpose of being more liberated to pursue their lives and relationships calls for closer examination. While some, like Ellen, migrate with their partners and without their sexuality being an immediate or obvious concern, others pursue migration choices that make their lives and relationships significantly harder. Jaime, having already met his life partner Haber, moved across the northern border to Scotland at a time when this actually meant crossing back into criminalization of same-sex activities: 'In 1967 when it was decriminalized in England and Wales, I was nineteen. I was still not able to be non-criminal. It didn't stop me, but I was still criminal for another two years' – until his twenty-first birthday because an unequal age of consent remained the law. 'When I moved to Scotland, I became a criminal again. Anything I did. That meant, gosh... even in your own home, that was criminal'. After 1980, Scotland permitted same-sex sexual encounters between consenting adults only in private, as in England. 'So, if you booked in together in a hotel, you could be prosecuted, if they suspected that something had gone on. Although it never actually stopped us doing anything. But it did make us feel strange to be coming to a Scotland where this was still criminal'. Jaime also makes a point of complicating the notion of a fixed identity, sexual or otherwise. He relates this to his ambiguous national identity as an immigrant to Scotland.

> The worst kind of hell is actually having a fixed identity. I hate people having very fixed expectation of me, and I try to flout them if possible. And I don't like to proclaim any particular identity. Whether it's national identity, or a gender identity, or a gender based around sexuality. For political purposes, I will come out concurring and saying I'm gay. But that's different from actually feeling this sums me up.[41]

Like Oonagh, he made use of magazines and newspapers to seek out vital information pertaining to his rights and safety: 'I would find that there would be something like the Scottish Minorities Group.[42] And then I would write there and say: I'm moving to Scotland and I would like to know what the legal situation is'. His partner was only able to join him permanently a few years later, in 1980, just prior to Scottish decriminalization.

Queer subcultures in a given destination, or comparable spaces queer migrants are drawn to in order to feel at home, can take on a distinct shape in their expectations. The three interviewees who crossed a national border to move to Edinburgh had clear ideas of what they were moving towards. Notably, a vibrant queer community was not explicitly at the top of that list. Much more than 'just a sort of vague sense that things would be better',[43] Ellen, Matt and Jaime all vocalized their hopes in terms of the political and social reality they wanted to live in, going far beyond queer subculture. Matt explains, 'I knew that if I lived in Jamaica, I would have to lead a bit of a double life... Very hard to live openly and safely, at the same time.... Basically, I wanted to be part of a more egalitarian society'.[44] Ellen meanwhile 'was very drawn to Edinburgh as a romantic, Scotland in general as a socialist. In those days, once upon a time, this was a place with a huge sense of a largely socialist country'. Jaime reflects on Scotland's political position within the context of the rest of the UK: 'Moving to Scotland was partly because I excluded some parts of the UK. I didn't want to get a job in the southeast of England or the midlands of England, which I regarded as rather conservative'. Matt,

Jaime, Ellen and Oonagh came to Edinburgh with a range of expectations and hopes, but all with distinct ideas about both what they were moving away from and what they wanted to move towards. Their recollections do not fit neatly into narratives around leaving intolerant families and seeking a straightforward kind of liberation.

Arrival

For most migrants, the experience of arriving in a host country is significantly more complex than the expectations outlined previously by our four narrators. Their lived reality continued to be shaped by their economic and social backgrounds and might better be described as a restructuring of previously experienced inequalities, rather than 'complete liberation'.[45] Even migrants who are objectively moving from a country with more strict anti-gay penal codes or more drastic societal sanctions placed on their identity to a supposedly more open environment can, of course, still experience a significant level of anti-gay or anti-trans violence.[46] This is very much in line with Matt's experiences of living in Edinburgh University student halls:

> There were some really negative responses…. I put up a sign in my window saying: 'heterosexuality isn't normal, it's just common'. I remember someone throwing a rock at the window. [They] wrote 'poof' across my door. And just really horrible homophobic things. The funny thing is, because I had come from Jamaica, and because homophobia to me is in a whole different league of violence, the word poof and what they'd done actually really amused me. I was like, this is as bad as it gets?[47]

While Matt gradually realized that not everyone in his chosen home was accepting of his sexuality, Jaime knew before his move that he would be crossing back into criminality. As Wimark argues, 'education and employment can also function as strategies for empowerment by focusing on one's own employment career and selecting the right place to work'.[48] Notably, while both Matt's and Jaime's migrations were tied to attending and teaching at university respectively, in some ways it was Jaime who experienced more freedom in an academic environment.

> From 1974,… I never felt I had to hide the fact that I had a male partner. So, whenever Haber came to visit, if there was a staff party or something like that, Haber would come along and I didn't have to say, this is somebody I just met on a bus…. Universities tend not to be willing to portray themselves as discriminatory. If they are, they have to do it in a very subtle way…. So therefore it was actually a very privileged place to be working.[49]

How did the interviewees perceive the mechanisms of inclusion and exclusion on the queer scene? For Oonagh, her first experiences of clubbing at Fire Island[50] on Princes Street in the mid-1980s are tied up with her first sexual experiences with women. 'It was kind of the first time that I'd ever experienced my own body, the thought

I had was sexual revolution, you know what I mean? Couldn't think of anything else! I know it sounds appalling. First time I feel alive.'[51] While Oonagh initially found what she had been looking for in Edinburgh queer venues, Matt highlights that not every queer person shared his experience as a gay man or Oonagh's as a gay woman: 'Lesbian women and gay men generally make up 99.9% of attendees at any of these events. There is very little in the way of bisexual representation. Very, very little. And the scene can be... extremely trans-phobic.'

This ties into larger issues around public safety and the safety of visibly queer people in public spaces – oftentimes in stark contrast to what Weston terms 'the vision of the city as a space of liberation from sexual restrictions and surveillance.'[52] Matt and Ellen both speak about the verbal abuse they received in the street, despite arriving decades apart. 'It tended to be random abuse shouted, with no real threat of engagement.' Matt elaborates, 'I wasn't going to stick around to find out, you know. But when I moved down to Leith, that was when I really experienced a lot more homophobia on the street.' He remembers queer visibility as generally very low at the time of his arrival in 1996, with hardly any couples holding hands or publicly kissing. He particularly recalls several 'scary incidents' after leaving a club and walking home along Lothian Road. 'One time I was physically attacked for wearing something flamboyant.... And I remember being quite shocked and horrified about that, because that had never happened to me in Jamaica. The fact that it happened to me there. I hadn't been able to defend myself, and I felt very shamed by that.'[53] For many queer Black Jamaicans in the UK as well as Afro-Caribbean migrants more generally, experiences of racism of course were and continue to be a serious safety issue when moving through public (and queer) spaces. With Matt being white, racist discrimination and violence do not factor into his story, and he focuses instead on anti-queer abuse.

In addition to a keen awareness of certain public spaces carrying more or less danger for him and a certain normalization of that danger, Matt also describes the toll this took on his personal relationships and the everyday safety measures he and his friends started taking. 'After I was attacked, my friend gave me a long coat to wear, and that was kind of my shield, it looked very bland. And it was a shield for whatever I was wearing underneath. And that was my disguise to get through town,... with a more flamboyant jacket, I'd immediately get homophobic attention. Immediately.' He remembers the awareness of the risk of imminent violence as being very pronounced within queer circles: 'There were several of my friends that at one point or another got very badly beat up. Especially in the years around when I arrived or before I arrived. Badly beat up, you know. Because they were in the wrong place at the wrong time.' Repeated experiences of anti-queer violence gradually began to change Matt's day-to-day habits. 'I was always very tactile with my boyfriends. Very tactile. Coming from Jamaica, I felt unstoppable, because homophobia over there is so much worse than homophobia over here.... People were saying horrible things, it would bounce off me because I knew there wasn't necessarily a violent edge to it.' Over time, this verbal abuse began to wear him down. 'Those public displays of affection became less and less. Just holding hands in public. Maybe a little kiss, you know. But, that's it.... No arms around each other, or a big snog in public, or anything like that.' Adding to this, Ellen's experiences exemplify the ways in which migrants often have to navigate derogatory attention aimed at more than one aspect of their person: 'There are assumptions that other people make, just as we've all had assumptions if you're lesbian or gay. I have found it much harder "coming out" as Jewish in certain contexts than coming out as a lesbian.' At the same time, she describes queer people forming unique networks that cross societal boundaries, comparing this to the ocean, with different fish inhabiting different layers of water.

> There are some Edinburgh fish who are completely unaware that there are other layers.... But one of the things about the lesbian and gay community is it cuts right through all those layers. And you discover, there are the gay lawyers, who also happen to know people who might be manual labourers. You will cross class boundaries that other people don't. In fact, was it my 60th birthday [and] we had everybody from a former Deputy Speaker of the House of Commons to a lorry driver.[54]

Of course, queerness can operate as a great equalizer for some, especially when first connecting with others in a space that requires a certain degree of anonymity. Here, networks may be forged that would otherwise be impeded by social circumstances. However, queer communities were and are far from immune to misogyny, racism, classism and ableism.

As Weston points out, it is absolutely possible for queer individuals to reach the metropolis but find themselves far from any sort of promised land and, in fact, quite isolated.[55] This was the case for Oonagh, who arrived in Edinburgh inexperienced, with only vague ideas of what queer partnerships might be like for her, and with no social support. Her first romantic relationship turned emotionally and physically abusive, which she describes as particularly surprising as 'I never thought that gay women would hit women'. Her partner's coercive control amplified Oonagh's isolation. If she spoke to acquaintances or strangers while out on the queer scene, there would be immediate physical retribution: 'When we left Fire Island we were walking down the road, she punched me so hard in the face that I just hit the shop front and my legs just went. And just slid down the shop front. And just hitting me. Broke my nose. Black eye.' Systems intended to provide support to victims of intimate partner violence failed to provide the necessary interventions, partly because they failed to recognize the dynamics of abuse in a same-sex couple. During a hospital visit after a particularly violent attack, the nursing staff only questioned Oonagh in the presence of her partner, making it impossible to confide in them. She pretended to have taken a bad fall instead. 'Somebody had said, Oonagh, we've been looking at your x-rays and everything, and there's just absolutely no way that you could have hit the curb. Would you like to talk to us? And my partner was there, and well, I was like, no, that's what happened.'

In addition to the societal blindness to issues of same-sex intimate partner abuse, Oonagh also describes incidents of systemic homophobia and violence perpetrated by members of the police. One such incident occurred when officers drove past the couple while they were in the midst of a public altercation and decided to take them both to the station, but not before driving around aimlessly for a while and subjecting them to verbal abuse: 'It was like, you fucking lesbians.... You look like fucking men.' At the station, things got worse. Oonagh describes being strip searched in a corridor without a female officer present. With the knowledge that she could not rely on institutional protection and unable to find 'anywhere you could phone, or a safe house or anything', she experienced severe depression, stopped eating and attempted suicide.

Oonagh describes losing all sense of self before finally receiving medical care, being rehoused and slowly rebuilding her life in the early 1990s. Her inability even to adequately put her experiences into words when the abuse first began has stuck with her: 'I just thought women are from heaven, just heaven-sent and everything like that. And they're supposed to love you and cherish you, so I didn't know, I was really confused.'[56] While intimate partner violence can affect anyone, Oonagh was particularly vulnerable to it by being new to both the city and the queer community. Her lack of experience and queer social ties of her own enabled her partner to control and socially isolate her, even while she was physically moving in queer spaces. Thereby, community venues that were supposed to be safe and protected spaces became physically and emotionally unsafe for her.

(Creating) spaces and places

In terms of Edinburgh's specific localities, a central question revolves around which spaces and places were frequented and shaped by the interviewees at different points in time, and how these spaces and places were queer. The Blue Moon Café, which opened in 1988 on Broughton Street, appeared to hold special relevance to nearly all interviewees. For Oonagh, it was the first place she arranged to meet up with Miles, the volunteer from the lesbian and gay helpline she had first spoken to from the public phone booth in Crail harbour. Jaime remembers the cafe for its safe, non-judgemental atmosphere: 'Blue Moon Café in Edinburgh was a major place to just go and feel that you could be together. Talk about anything… and feel that neighbouring tables wouldn't start becoming aggressive to you because they heard you talking about lesbian and gay issues for example.' For Matt, a stand-out feature of Blue Moon was its community notice board, symbolizing connections that would have been impossible or unsafe otherwise. Indeed, the cafe appears to have facilitated the meetings of a range of groups, such as the Scottish Homosexual Rights Group (SHRG) and women-only feminist groups, as well as dialogue between them, in part by encouraging patrons to share the small number of available tables.[57]

Bookshops also found special mention, both independent ones such as WordPower on West Nicolson Street[58] (a 'proper, serious, indie, left-wing alternative bookshop' in Ellen's words) and specifically queer shop Lavender Menace, which opened in 1982 in a basement space on Forth Street in Edinburgh's New Town.[59] Its later iteration, West and Wilde, was established in Dundas Street in 1987. For Ellen, bookshops functioned fundamentally as 'physical spaces for certain kinds of political culture….] There were places and spaces to go and do it in, and be it in'. For Jaime, the different localities of the queer bookshops represented changes in public attitudes towards queer people in Edinburgh. This may pertain to the change of location, from a space in immediate proximity to Edinburgh's 'gay quarter' to one in a more mainstream neighbourhood. It certainly also rings true in terms of the physical space and layout as well: Lavender Menace was literally underground in a basement space, while West and Wilde had a regular, ground floor shop front. This had an impact not only on how the respective shop was perceived by the public but also on the emotional experience of patrons.

> Lavender Menace was fabulous. It was down a basement, and in those days… you did feel that you were almost coming out by going down the basement and entering the book shop…. I felt sometimes a little sheepish about doing it. You might look around, does anybody recognize me in the street? Before you go down the basement and into the shop. West and Wilde bookshop, they moved and they took on a different name and they moved to Dundas Street. That was perhaps again a sign of the times. It was more open, it was on the ground floor, you didn't have to go down the basements.[60]

In their discussions of queer clubs and bars in Edinburgh that the interviews give a stronger sense of the complexities, inclusions and exclusions happening in and around the scene. Matt spent a significant amount of his time in (queer) techno clubs in the mid- to late 1990s, particularly at Club Joy, which he describes as 'a staple of the gay scene for over a decade', or at Tackno, a monthly club night at Club Mercado on Market Street. 'It was more of an excuse to get dressed up in really funny, tacky clothes and dance to really old, cheesy music. And it mainly had an older kind of gay crowd. But it was still really fun, and a mix of both straight and gay, but it was mainly gay at that stage.' For Matt, the distinct atmosphere and clientele of the clubs were key to finding his confidence on and off the dance floor. He describes a real blossoming of his character, adding that 'the club scene in Edinburgh I think was a really strong factor in helping to make the gay scene more mainstream. They were used to being out in clubs, where they'd see guys kissing, girls kissing, you know, there were some people who had more fluid sexualities. And therefore there was a comfort with that'.

One venue that seems to embody the growing pains of a queer community trying to keep its own safe while excluding some in the process is CC Bloom's, which first opened its doors in 1994 and can still be found on Greenside Place near the head of Leith Walk. Oonagh recalls the transformation the venue has gone through over the decades: 'CC's is slightly different now that they've cleaned up and stuff… It used to be the standing joke, it was a bit… spit and sawdust, you know. Your feet would stick to the floor and that kind of thing.' Matt vividly describes the atmosphere of scrutiny at the door.

> CC's had a very strong gay-only policy. That if you weren't a gay man, lesbian, you know, that they really didn't want a lot of you in there…. And I think it stems from the days of real violent homophobia, and the door staff had to be really strong and very prepared, because there would be occasions where you would get gangs of people outside. I was never there when this happened, but… they'd have to shut their very thick doors and call the police to get rid of these guys.[61]

While Matt himself did not experience trouble with the door staff at CC's, he remembers various friends and strangers being turned away. 'When we showed up at the door, if you weren't holding hands, or if you refused to kiss, or something like that, then they weren't being let in.' Though such practices may have grown out of a community's need to stay safe, as Matt describes, they invariably resulted in policing and excluding parts of that very community. They enforced stereotypical ideas around identities and relationships, and allowed for bias against queer and trans people in what may appear to be a mixed-sex relationship, but also against individuals who did not conform to the visual codes of queerness in that respective time and place. From around the time Matt is describing, there are also accounts of very feminine lesbian women being turned away from Edinburgh clubs and being perceived merely as 'fag hags', rather than valid members of the community.

Lastly, there remains the ever-present issue of queer nightlife clashing with mainstream sensibilities and prejudice. Oonagh recalls: 'Come out of Fire Island, and when you'd been out clubbing, and people would be really homophobic… you weren't always sure if they were going to hurt you or not. I think people's prejudices are still alive and well in Edinburgh, in Scotland, as we speak.' The naming of this early Scottish club as Fire Island, visibly linking Edinburgh's queer population to another queer community across the Atlantic, is particularly striking. It symbolizes shared international connections and histories, while simultaneously operating as code, as a straight passer-by would likely have thought very little of the club's name. While Edinburgh's queer scene was and is not as big as that of other capital cities, designated queer spaces have existed for a long time, and sometimes with a compellingly international self-image. Queer and trans people have also been instrumental in shaping more mainstream environments such as the Edinburgh clubbing or theatre scene as well as activist and political work. At the same time, community policing around sexuality and gender presentation, but also race and class, made a sense of belonging to the queer community more tangible for some and less for others.

Activism, Pride and community history

As anthropologist of sexuality, gender, race and ethnicity, Martin Manalansan points out, 'sexuality is not an all-encompassing reality but one that intersects with and through other social, economic, and cultural practices and identities'.[62] Along these lines, the element of engaging in explicitly political work in and alongside the queer community comes out most clearly in Ellen's story. After getting involved with trade union politics and joining the National Union of Journalists, she became more involved in women's liberation in the mid-1970s. She describes the political direction this gave her as a catalyst for coming out, but also for finding her voice as a writer.

Matt had his plans for becoming more openly politically involved all laid out before his move to Scotland: 'I had planned everything. I'd do that as soon as I got to Edinburgh, I wanted to meet fellow gay students, I wanted to become more politically active, I wanted to see what the gay scene was like, and all that sort of thing.' However, once he joined BLOGS, the LGBTQ student society,[63] he found that 'they were very politically active, but in a kind of more conversational, discussional kind of way'. He eventually stopped attending and instead turned to direct action, joining the efforts to repeal Section 2A by defacing political propaganda defending it along with other community activists. He describes this as a unifying experience, saying that 'I think… people definitely came together a bit more during that time…. The law got wiped out. It was great'. This experience, for him, is directly linked to his estimation of Scotland and its prospective independence. 'It was the first Act of the Scottish Parliament. I feel so positive about that. And I'm much more pro-Scottish nationalism now, because of that great start. I think if that hadn't been done, I'd be a lot more sceptical and a lot more worried about what Scottish independence could mean for the gay community and for myself.'

Meanwhile, Ellen describes being involved in various forms of political work prior to her move to Scotland but says that her coming out and subsequent involvement in a lesbian-feminist group coincided with her most focused activist work. But even at this time, she was 'not particularly directly involved', adding that joining the Section 2A demonstrations from 1988 onwards was just something that everyone did. Rather, she highlights the importance of facilitating slow, subtle change through creative work: 'A lot of people have said "I loved such-and-such of your novels, that was my coming-out book". I think that is a kind of activism. It's not like I was campaigning that people should define themselves. It was more to be there and help be part of a set of cultural stories that hadn't previously been available.'[64]

And while Oonagh gives a humorous account of not getting involved in activist work and instead setting other priorities for herself, she does so not without a hint of guilt, as though political involvement were to be expected: 'About gay rights … ? No, not really. My sexuality … [I] might have taken that a bit too far, but I think I was more interested in that, you know. That sounds terrible. Maybe now, I'd be more switched on obviously, darling, you know'.

A further keystone of shared community history is Pride. Both Matt and Jamie recall their experiences of attending Edinburgh Pride marches. For Jaime, attending the first-ever Pride march in Scotland in June of 1995 was a seminal moment, bringing together more than 3,000 people.[65] It pushed him from being a spectator to becoming a visible participant in the march: 'Pride meant going through the streets. It meant that people would begin to identify you, would see you, see you marching, and thinking: Oh, he's gay. And that was a very out thing to do.' He recalls watching from the far side of the railings on the Mound as the march approached.

> I felt I was caged, and they were the free ones…. I followed along on the pavement, and when it got up to George IV Bridge, I suddenly thought: Here I am walking along the pavement, and they're walking along in the middle of the street. This is silly. So I actually began to join it. Just before it got to the Meadows, I was there in the march itself and… for me that was quite significant. This was me identifying that way. It was joyful.[66]

Matt describes joining Pride celebrations in the Meadows and being especially happy about seeing families with children there, as well as a generally mixed crowd: 'I thought, wow, this is the gay community. Because of course when you went to clubs, you'd see guys and girls, but they were all young, or of a certain age, with a few exceptions. You went to bars, they tended to be male-dominated. There was never a sense of community.'

Both Ellen and Jaime eventually turned their attention to not only making but also recording queer and trans history in Edinburgh. In 2000, Jaime and his partner Haber founded OurStory Scotland, a charitable organization collecting and archiving LGBT stories from across Scotland, which was a form of activism as well: 'You had to spell it out. You would go to meetings and you would say: "I am looking at the stories of... and you would have to say: lesbian, gay, bisexual, transgender". And you then looked around for whether people would be flinching.' OurStory has since collected oral histories, artefacts and images from across Scotland and prepared them for archival deposit as well as facilitating exhibitions, dramatic performances and storytelling sessions, such as a series of group recordings at Edinburgh University between 2012 and 2015.[67] A few years after the beginnings of OurStory, Ellen became involved in Remember When, a 2003–2006 Heritage Lottery-funded project, as one of three part-time staff who worked with a group of volunteers to assemble an exhibition of artefacts of Edinburgh's queer history. The project culminated in an exhibition at the City Art Centre on Market Street, next to Waverley Station, as well as a volume documenting the exhibition, *Rainbow City*, published through WordPower Books. It includes seven 'LGBT paths', short self-guides walking tours exploring various queer Edinburgh localities through the centuries.[68]

Jaime's and Ellen's work illustrates the ways in which spaces may be queered through the making, but also through the sharing, of communal histories. The telling of events and experiences of the (queer) past in close proximity to the places and spaces where they originally took place can be an affirming experience for the narrator. But it can also foster a more concrete sense of shared history in queer listeners who were not around or even alive at the time of the events in question, allowing them to view an inconspicuous building or street corner they pass by every day with new eyes, walking in others' footsteps while adding their own.

Conclusion

As (particularly queer) migration research has highlighted, migrating can allow for individuals to grow into themselves and into a community in ways that were not available to them in their place or country of origin. At the same time, the expectations individuals carry concerning their chosen home, and their evaluation of the reality they are confronted with, are fundamentally shaped by both what they sought to find and what they sought to leave behind. The interviewees' previous experiences – spanning a range of familial, class, religious and political environments – allow them to interrogate and reflect on their distinctly Scottish communities and experiences at different points in time over the course of the 1970s to the early 2010s. In doing so, their voices also provide a window into the changing landscape of Scottish LGBTQ communities, rich in detail and wit. They describe a Scotland rapidly evolving in terms of civil rights, visibility and acceptance of queer and trans people, while at second glance, things are perhaps not as egalitarian as expected, but rather more complex. Individual and communal identities are tightly intertwined and play out across Edinburgh's queer meeting places, cafes, clubs and unique bookshops. Meanwhile, activists struggle to bridge racial and class divides, and communities face issues including gender inequality, trans exclusion, gender-based and intimate partner violence. While these issues are by no means unique to Scotland – they find their parallels in the history of many queer communities in Europe[69] and globally – they add a Scottish perspective to the conversation around queer localities in the UK and beyond. As for the situatedness of sexuality within local circumstances, it is crucial to remember, as Manalansan asserts, that the reverse is also true: 'Recent works on sexuality and migration, particularly those that document queer sexualities, have emphasized not only the viability and importance of sexuality as an object of study, but also pointed to its constitutive role in the formation and definitions of citizenship and nation.'[70] In this sense, queer sexualities may also share a role in shaping their locality. Certainly, Oonagh's, Matt's, Ellen's and Jamie's accounts from Edinburgh serve to complicate and expand narrative tropes. Queer migration need not only be conceptualized as rural-to-urban or from Scotland to England. And while London, as the stereotypical metropolis, does have its charms, as Oonagh puts it, 'I quite like to visit, but I don't ever want to live there'.

As for the argument that (transnational) migrational movements by non-cisgender, non-heterosexual individuals serve to enable queer practices and identities, the interviewees' narratives suggest that their migration to Edinburgh facilitated more than just a one-time shift into a new identity. Instead, Jaime reminds us that arriving in the right locality can also bring the freedom to continuously resist a fixed identity. We are further reminded that arriving in a new home that we associate with greater personal freedom can change us in unexpected ways. Matt puts a sharp point on this when describing how his outgoing, affectionate nature was dampened over time by repeated experienced of societal pressure and hostility. This realization stands in stark contrast alongside his narrative of a Scotland that was extremely homophobic in the 1970s, before his arrival, but that changed rapidly and consistently for the better in terms of gay rights, visibility and acceptance.

What can we make of the essence of queer life in Edinburgh? What are the local specificities that characterize queer community life there, in the eyes of Ellen, Jaime, Matt and Oonagh? Overall, the idea of one shared queer community remains a term of convenience that feels most tangible in moments where different networks come together to pursue a specific shared goal. One example both Ellen and Matt bring up in this context are the demonstrations against militant homophobic evangelist Pat Robertson, who was lining up to become a business partner with the Bank of Scotland in 1999. At the same time, Edinburgh is small enough that many shared histories do overlap, as exemplified by Ellen's metaphor of the city as an ocean. From this vantage point, queer movement across boundaries and borders is an essential element of daily Edinburgh life that continues long after migration. Either way, queer migrants to Edinburgh continue to play a crucial role in shaping the city and its physical, social and political spaces.

Notes

1   Queer is used throughout the chapter to denote non-heterosexual and/or non-cisgender lived experience. This is intended to include lesbian, gay, bisexual and trans individuals, while leaving space for less fixed identities. Interviewees' self-labels are, of course, retained.

2   Section 28 (2A in Scotland) of the Local Government Act 1988 contributed to the isolation and alienation of queer adults, as well as preventing adequate education, protection and support for queer youth.

3   Nancy L. Green, 'Changing paradigms in migration studies: From men to women to gender', *Gender & History* 24, no. 3 (2012): 782.

4   Ibid., 784.

5   Richard Mole, 'Sexualities and queer migration research', *Sexualities* 21, no. 8 (2018): 1.

6   Martin F. Manalansan, 'Queer intersections: Sexuality and gender in migration studies', *International Migration Review* 40, no. 1 (2006): 225.

7   Ibid., 226.

8   Andrew Gorman-Murray, 'Intimate mobilities: Emotional embodiment and queer migration', *Social & Cultural Geography* 10, no. 4 (2009): 442.

9   Ibid., 443.

10 Anne-Marie Fortier, 'Making home: Queer migrations and motions of attachment', in *Uprootings/ Regroundings: Questions of Home and Migration*, ed. Sara Ahmed, Claudia Castaneda, Anne-Marie Fortier and Mimi Sheller (London: Berg Publishers, 2003), 117.

11 Kath Weston, 'Get thee to a big city: Sexual imaginary and the great gay migration', *GLQ: A Journal of Lesbian and Gay Studies* 2, no. 3 (1995): 255.

12 Bob Cant quoted in Fortier, 'Making home', 120.

13 Ibid., 120.

14 See Cindy Patton and Benigno Sánchez-Eppler (eds), *Queer Diasporas*, Series Q (Durham: Duke University Press, 2000).

15 Fortier, 'Making home', 118.

16 Ibid.

17 Ibid., 123.

18 See Bob Cant, *Footsteps & Witnesses: Lesbian and Gay Lifestories from Scotland* (Edinburgh: Word Power Books, 2008); see Bob Cant, *Invented Identities? Lesbians and Gays Talk about Migration* (London: Cassell, 1997).

19 See Amy Tooth Murphy, '"I conformed; I got married. It seemed like a good idea at the time": Domesticity in postwar lesbian oral history', in *British Queer History: New Approaches and Perspectives*, ed. B. Lewis (Manchester: Manchester University Press, 2013), 165–87.

20 See Brian Dempsey, *Thon Wey. Aspects of Scottish Lesbian and Gay Activism 1968 to 1992* (Edinburgh: Outright Scotland, 1995).

21 See Roger Davidson, 'The Cautionary tale of tom: The male homosexual experience of Scottish medicine in the 1970s and early 1980s', *Journal of Scottish Historical Studies* 28 (2008): 122–38; see Roger Davidson and Gayle Davis, 'Sexuality and the state: The campaign for Scottish homosexual law reform, 1967–80', *Contemporary British History* 20 (2006): 533–58.

22 See Grant Anderson, 'Non-Conforming Gender Geographies: A Longitudinal Account of Gender Queerness in Scotland', PhD thesis, University of Glasgow, 2019.

23 See Jeffrey Meek, *Queer Voices in Post-War Scotland: Male Homosexuality, Religion and Society* (New York: Palgrave Macmillan, 2015).

24 Some of this material can be found at https://livingmemory.org.uk/rememberWhen/ and https://www.ourstoryscotland.org.uk/ respectively (accessed 10 May 2021).

25 Oonagh's interview by the author was recorded in December 2012 at her home in Leith, Edinburgh.

26 Matt's interview by the author was recorded in July 2012 at the offices of Positive Help in New Town, Edinburgh.

27 Ellen's interview by the author was recorded in June 2013 in Made in France Café in Bruntsfield, Edinburgh.

28 Jaime's interview by the author was recorded in August 2012 at his home in the Edinburgh West End.

29 Weston, 'Get thee to a big city', 269.

30 Gorman-Murray, 'Intimate mobilities', 444.

31 Interview with Jaime.

32 Thomas Wimark, 'The impact of family ties on the mobility decisions of gay men and lesbians', *Gender, Place & Culture* 23, no. 5 (2016): 664.

33 Ibid., 669.

34 Gorman-Murray, 'Intimate mobilities', 443.

35 Rebecca Jennings, '"It was a hot climate and it was a hot time": Lesbian migration and transnational networks in the mid-twentieth century', *Australian Feminist Studies* 25, no. 63 (2010): 31.

36 Interview with Matt.

37 Interview with Ellen.

38 Interview with Oonagh.

39 Green, 'Changing paradigms in migration studies', 791.

40 Interview with Ellen.

41 Interview with Jaime.

42 The Scottish Minorities Group (SMG), founded in 1969, eventually became the Scottish Homosexual Rights Group (SHRG), playing a key role in the campaign for decriminalization.

43 Weston, 'Get thee to a big city', 261.

44 Interview with Matt.

45 Claudia Fournier, Louise Hamelin Brabant, Sophie Dupéré and Line Chamberland, 'Lesbian and gay immigrants' post-migration experiences: An integrative literature review', *Journal of Immigrant & Refugee Studies* 16, no. 3 (2018): 332.

46 Ibid., 341.

47 Interview with Matt.

48 Wimark, 'The impact of family ties on the mobility decisions of gay men and lesbians', 669.

49 Interview with Jaime.

50 Fire Island's name was, of course, a reference to Fire Island Pines, a town on Fire Island, a barrier island off the New York coast. Fire Island (and the adjoining Cherry Grove) gained a reputation as the United States' first gay and lesbian town from the 1920s onwards.

51 Interview with Oonagh.

52 Weston, 'Get thee to a big city', 267.

53 Interview with Matt.

54 Interview with Ellen.

55   Weston, 'Get thee to a big city', 267.

56   Interview with Oonagh.

57   Ellen Galford, Ken Wilson and Remember When Project, *Rainbow City: Stories from Lesbian, Gay, Bisexual and Transgender Edinburgh* (Edinburgh: Word Power Books, 2006), 64, 111.

58   WordPower first opened in 1994. In 2017, it was replaced by Lighthouse Books, an independent, political community book shop that continues to house WordPower Books, the publisher. The author lived above WordPower during her time at Edinburgh University.

59   James Ley's play *Lovesong to Lavender Menace*, which pays homage to the shop's role for queer communities, premiered at the Royal Lyceum Theatre in 2017. The name Lavender Menace was, of course, chosen in reference to the term coined by Betty Friedan in 1969 in trying to distance herself and the 'straight' women's movement from any association with lesbian and queer women. The term was subsequently reclaimed by lesbian feminists protesting their exclusion from the women's movement.

60   Interview with Jaime.

61   Interview with Matt.

62   Manalansan, 'Queer intersections', 243.

63   The student society BLOGS still exists today, but has recently been renamed PrideSoc.

64   Interview with Ellen.

65   Galford, *Rainbow City*, 74. Even though no direct commemoration of the Stonewall uprising is recorded for Edinburgh's first pride parade, it may be seen as a further indication of transatlantic queer cultural influences.

66   Interview with Jaime.

67   Alva Träbert, 'Scottish storytelling sessions: Queer history, community and archives', Notches: (Re)marks on the History of Sexuality, 29 March 2016: https://notchesblog. com/2016/03/29/scottish-storytelling-sessions-queer-history-community-and-archives/ (accessed 5 May 2020).

68   Galford, *Rainbow City*, 124–39.

69   Jennifer V. Evans and Matt Cook (eds), *Queer Cities, Queer Cultures: Europe since 1945* (London: Bloomsbury, 2014).

70   Manalansan, 'Queer intersections', 224.

2

'He had a pair of shoulders like the Tyne Bridge': Queer evocations of the North East and the legacy of *Out on Tuesday* and *Out*

Gareth Longstaff

Introduction

The relationship between queer life in the 'North' and 'South' of England has produced some powerful narratives of queer experience aligned to the citizens of both locations. I am one of those citizens. I was born in Newcastle upon Tyne in 1979 and lived there until 2001. In 2001 at the age of twenty-two I moved to London and lived there for several years. In 2009 I moved back to the city of my birth and have lived here ever since. Yet I find myself back in London a lot, and because I am not from there, I find that I romance and obsess with it as a city, I magnify its allure, and I know that one day I will return to it. Like an old friend, a nostalgic object or an evocative memory, London pulls me towards it when I am in Newcastle, just as Newcastle beckons me back when I am in London.

As I move between these places, I feel personally connected and disconnected to each and like many queer people who have long sought pleasure, belonging and freedom away from the constraints of local and regional life, this has informed my queer movements towards the capital.[1] The Northern queer migrant and more specifically those of us from the North East who drift to cities like London have formed agile and affective ways of connecting and incorporating our regionality into the capital's diasporic culture and geography. Yet, just as London tenders the potential of a new life, one that can be cultivated beyond the confines of regional indigeneity, this is not the reality of how London is experienced by those of us who are drawn to it. Rather, it is a space that simultaneously weakens *and* amplifies regionality so that 'when we look askance, take our cues from everyday lives and memories [and where…] we don't find a homogenous, singular and collectively comprehended gay London', we find its essence.[2] London may be more usefully marked out as a queer city with local and regional micro-geographies, and because the regional queer person moves to and adapts in London, they do so by negotiating, assimilating and appreciating their regionality afresh. It is also in this setting that new queer relationships between regionally displaced individuals and geographies develop.

These movements of the queer individual from region to capital city and 'closet' to coming 'out' for many also involve the sort of bildungsroman journey and narrative of self-realization that happens when a previously provincial and repressed 'life before' is abandoned so that an out and autonomous 'new life after' can emerge. Yet, these movements between the North and South are not as clearly defined and polarized as a 'life before' and 'life after' might suggest. Queer migrations, intersections and possibilities of movement between the assumed confines of a regional context and the freedom of a metropolitan city configure queer regionality in relation to a mythical or utopian construction of London that 'represents not only "out" sexuality but a hegemonic geography of centre and margin, [always] figuring the north as marginal, uncivilised and unliberated'.[3] In this chapter some of these issues and exchanges between the North (with a focus on Newcastle upon Tyne) and South (with a focus on London) are guided by my personal and academic relationship with Channel 4's first gay and lesbian magazine-style TV programme *Out on Tuesday* (1989) and later *Out* (1990–4).[4] The chapter aims to both explore and contextualize the representational, political and affective dimensions of queer regionality and experience, and I use the programme as a pivot to consider how processes of ordinary and everyday affects and the evocation of personal and impersonal pasts permeate queer movement, community and regional experience. More specifically one thirteen-minute report on the programme, *Girls in Boy Bars,* connects these ideas to queer regional lives and desires in Newcastle upon Tyne and the shifting configurations of how social class, gender and sexuality are expressed.[5] In this report, the articulation of queer desire and a regional self are both preceded and connected to how that self is marked out, mapped and mediated as a queer body from both inside and outside the queer community of the North East. In this way my broader consideration of both *OOT/Out* and the specific people in *Girls in Boy Bars* as 'an engaged and affectively involved demographic' also explores political and personal meaning through an engagement with regional queer space and my own identifications with queer indigeneity and displacement.[6]

This chapter also seeks to 'make personal experience [into] meaningful cultural experience'[7] by considering how both *OOT/Out* and *Girls in Boy Bars* connect to three autobiographic and auto-ethnographic moments in my own queer life. These take place in 1991, 2006 and 2020 and reveal the extent to which the queer self is simultaneously a socio-political as well as an individual construct. Each gesture towards Sara Ahmed's work on queer 'orientations' as ways of being that 'involve different ways of registering the proximity of object and others [... and] shape not only how we inhabit space, but how we apprehend this world of shared inhabitance, as well as "who" or "what" we direct our energy toward'.[8] These memories and reflections also function as 'personal experiences that stem from, or are made possible by, being a part of a culture and/or from embracing a particular cultural or personal identity'[9]. The subsequent analysis of both *OOT/Out* and *Girls in Boy Bars* considers how my own regional queer identity and the identities of others rely upon 'how we become oriented in moments of disorientation that we might learn from what it means to be orientated in the first place'.[10] In this account, there are moments of the familiar and unfamiliar, new and old, here and there, and like many queer lives and experiences they are connected to how we are all continually 'losing our way as well as finding our way' in the memories, feelings and impressions of our queer pasts, presents and futures.[11]

Summer 1991, Newcastle upon Tyne, England

My name is Gareth. I have just turned twelve. Six months earlier I received a red portable TV for Christmas, and it has transformed my world. I do not know it yet, but the first TV that I can personally control and watch alone will come close to what Sherry Turkle has positioned as an 'evocative object'.[12] It becomes my 'companion in life experience' and connects my social, erotic and at times traumatic desires to those of the programmes I watch alone in my bedroom.[13] On Channel 4 I watch an American sitcom called *The Golden Girls*, which really makes me laugh and instils an early sense of what camp humour and queer modes of community and affinity might be. *The Golden Girls* will never leave me, its one liners and sentiments on friendship, family, age and loss becoming a way for me to understand, draw strength from and feel safe. Consequently, it is not only the TV but the programmes it transmits and the channels it broadcasts them through that yield 'emotions and ideas of startling intensity' and in part affirm who I am from that point on.[14]

At twelve I am also discovering my body and my desires. I find myself gazing at a boy in the year above me at school. He wears a Morrissey t-shirt that I can see under his thin white school shirt, and with his floppy blonde curtains of hair and tortoiseshell spectacles, I ache as he walks past me in the corridor. He never seems to notice me. He triggers sexual and bodily longing in me which I now know as gay desire, yet at the time I find myself wondering why I find this boy so fascinating and why his body, his clothes and his hair make me feel elated, sick, excited and uncertain all at once. In 1991, I am not yet ready or able to articulate this but the programme that precedes *The Golden Girls*, and which intrigues, arouses and helps me to shape this desire is called *Out*. It functions as a compelling, surreptitious and enigmatic object that orients and situates my closeted young life and also becomes the trigger for my desire and fascination with London. A report that resonated and navigated some of my early longings for the city was 'Pride '91'. This is a record of the 1991 London Lesbian and Gay Pride march on 29th June 1991, and it is set to Ravel's *Bolero*. Looking through the work and archives of the programme, I can accurately date the time I watched the original broadcast to 3rd July 1991.[15] I remember the intensity of the sunshine, the striking young guys in 'Queer as Fuck' t-shirts laughing, dancing and shouting in the streets. As my parents and little brother sit downstairs, I 'watch television furtively without the possibility of discovery' and begin to imagine that all queer people in London 'were in the foreground for all to see'.[16] Within the reports and films of *OOT/Out* I 'scanned ruthlessly for representations of… kin in secluded privacy during… my] formative years'[17] and it was queer London and the possibilities that it seemed to offer that drew me in again and again. It sounds like a very well-worn cliché but in my suburban bedroom in Newcastle upon Tyne it was at this moment (and countless others just like it) that queer life and London became tangible and somehow possible through its intangible and impossible distance from my own.

Summer 2006, London, England

I have just turned twenty-seven. I am a gay man. I live in New Cross, South London, and while life is not exactly how I imagined it would be in 1991, it is good. I am uninhibited, skint and optimistically queer. During the 1990s I grew and formed my desires for men through that red TV in my bedroom, and until I left home in 1997 and came out the following year, it was my main point of access and reference to queer experience. By the late 1990s and into the early 2000s I had somehow forgotten about *OOT/Out* but now and then an encounter or conversation brought me back to it. In late 2005 I buy *The Best of Out and Out on Tuesday* on VHS for 50p in a charity shop in Greenwich. The video cassette is damaged, and I do not own a video player, but I keep it and place it somewhere on my bookshelf. Around this time my PhD supervisor suggested that I apply to take part in a summer-long project to document, catalogue and archive the programme to celebrate the twenty-fifth anniversary of Channel 4's 1982 inception, and as I tell him about how I used to watch it in the isolation of my bedroom, I have no idea where it is going to take me next. I send off my application and by June I have started work at the BFI on Stephen Street. This was no longer my bedroom in the early 1990s.

At the BFI I was working through crates of hastily labelled VHS tapes of the programme which had shaped my queer desires fifteen years before. I read and re-read Joe Brainard's 1975 book *I Remember*. In it Brainard begins each new entry with these two words and creates an organizing principle to mobilize and open up latent and forgotten memories. Many of his entries are textured by gay male desire, such as 'I remember sexual fantasies of old faded worn and torn blue jeans and the small areas of flesh revealed. I especially remember torn back pockets with a triangle of soft white bottom showing'.[18] These coalesce with my own experiences, and I begin to use his method of remembering to catalyse a memory I had forgotten. Here the personal memories of Brainard that were not mine reverberated with my own personal ones. As I wrap myself in Brainard's remembrances of the 1950s and 1960s, my own memories of the 1980s and 1990s resurface and within them *OOT/Out*. At once an exercise in self-analysis, self-reflection and self-indulgence, this is also a way to try and map out and understand the protean ways that day-to-day experiences simultaneously undo, disappear and return. At this time, I begin to realize that remembering is also a way of forgetting. More so than anything this was and still is clearly embedded in the report *Girls in Boy Bars*, which I first encounter again on Thursday 22nd June 2006.

I vividly remember having grabbed some lunch on Tottenham Court Road and making my way back to a windowless grey room at the end of a long corridor to catalogue the eighth and final episode of series one. The June swelter made me tired but the expectation and anticipation of not knowing what would appear in the next episode of the series woke me up. As I played the VHS cassette, I immediately recognized that week's presenter, the comedian Julian Clary. In his introduction outside a gent's toilet, he campily asked, 'why would a straight woman go to a gay bar... how would I know about it, I'm neither heterosexual nor female, quelle surprise', which made me laugh. And then unexpectedly the scene cut to an image of the Tyne Bridge, and without any signalling or introduction, a report about the relationship between straight women, gay men, lesbians, drag queens and misogyny played out in my hometown. This was Newcastle upon Tyne in 1989 and, thinking back to myself in 1991, I began to understand that *OOT/Out* and the extracts of queer life it contained held the potential 'to preserve and produce not just knowledge but feeling'.[19] *Girls in Boy Bars* presented me with an aspect of queer experience in people I recognized. I felt moved, compelled, lost and found. From the late 1990s onward, I had socialized (and continue to do so) on this very 'gay scene'; I danced in Rockshots nightclub and met some of my best friends in bars like the Courtyard. I knew people in the report. Others I didn't know, but I wanted to know more about them. Here my own regional and migratory position was textured with 'nostalgia, personal memory, fantasy and trauma' and my own fundamental archive of emotion allied to experiences of being queer and the importance of *OOT/Out* began to grow beyond the conventions of cataloguing the show and its contents.[20]

Summer 2020, Newcastle upon Tyne, England

I have just turned forty-one. There is a global pandemic and I listen to Taylor Swift's *Folklore* endlessly and intently as I write this. Another evocative object for my collection and my archive of memories and affects. I wonder where that red portable TV went and long for it. The VHS cassette of *The Best of Out and Out on Tuesday* is on the bookshelf behind me. Almost three years earlier, in December 2017, I spoke at the 'Queer Localities' conference at Birkbeck in London and the paper that I give is now this chapter. It is here that I first speak publicly about how the contours of *OOT/Out* and my life intersect, and since this moment my work and ideas around them have developed as a kind of 'ordinary affect'.[21] In this way, and as I start to write more about the programme and the objects and ideas attached to it, I find that my account is 'not the kind of analytic object that can be laid out on a single, static plane of analysis'; rather, it is framed by 'a problem or question emergent in disparate scenes and incommensurate forms and registers; a tangle of potential connections' that constitute how a regional queer life can be affected and evoked through movement and desire.[22] It is also here and within this chapter that my own evocations, memories and experiences of queer regionality connect with *OOT/Out* and how *Girls in Boy Bars* has guided them.

Out on Tuesday and *Out* – Who are you? Who am I?

Beyond the regional, auto-ethnographic and affective dimensions of this report and *OOT/Out* it is also important to position some of the ways in which the programme documented, explored, discussed and in many respects sought to empower queer identities for British audiences. The programmes looked at gendered and sexual relations in the context of identity, lifestyle, aesthetics, personal politics, physical and mental health, history, desire, rites of passage and did so in the context of regional, national and also international experience. For around five and a half years it ran for a total of forty-four episodes with an average audience of just over 1 million. *Out on Tuesday* ran for eight episodes and over one series between 14th February and 4th April 1989, and the following year the programme was moved to a Wednesday night slot and renamed *Out* running for a further four series. The first three were commissioned at ten episodes each, while the fourth only ran to six with the final episode broadcast on 14th September 1994. The programme was embedded in the ethos of Channel 4 and its position as both 'a product of 1970s social democratic consensus politics [… and] 1980s right-wing free market dogma'.[23] Leaning into the importance of the 1980 Broadcasting Act and its aim to 'encourage innovation and experiment in the form and content of programmes', the programme worked in sync with the channel's approach to not making TV programmes itself but commissioning 'independent production companies to make them' as well as buying in 'ready-made films and programmes from home and away'.[24] The production and format of the programme also connected to Channel 4's approach to TV that was 'made by a minority, for a minority and on the minorities channel'.[25] Yet at the time the programme may have also been 'calling to those in the know, to the converted' and, most obviously, to those in London with the appropriate access to queer culture.[26] Indeed, Channel 4 widely promoted the series in the gay and lesbian press which gave an informed and metropolitan edge to the overall disposition and stylization of its content.

Abseil Productions and later Alfalfa and Limehouse were the main companies used to produce and edit content for the programme and all were based in London. Abseil was 'a company named after the spectacular coup by a small group of lesbian women, who abseiled into a working session of the House of Lords in 1988 to demonstrate against section 28 of the Local Government Act'[27] and related to TV as 'political, liberal, vaguely left of centre, community-oriented, experimental, even arty, and willing to tackle "difficult" adult themes, notably sex and sexuality'.[28] We see elements of this in how the programme was ambiguously shaped and presented as a magazine show. On the one hand it often followed a conventional magazine format by including pieces with an emphasis on 'serious current affairs coverage with lighter entertainment and consumer affairs' and on the other it offered its audience reportage with a breathless and diffuse edge which could 'be dipped into and wandered out of'.[29] In the programme we also find a self-referential and postmodern tone where 'capacious miscellanies that covered many different topics for many different types of people' were produced and explored.[30]

As well as this there were technical devices, including reporter-led narration and the lack of an interviewer that invited audiences to navigate and situate their own identifications and desires in relation to the segments, reports and films assembled into each episode. In an endnote to his 2009 chapter on lesbian and gay magazine programming on British television, Gregory Woods cites and supports Colin Richardson's claim that the programme was not a 'proper' magazine programme because 'it had no studio audience, no common presenter across a whole series and was pre-recorded; also, many of its individual items were too long'.[31] Yet couldn't this now be positioned as a crucial and empowering queer feature of the show in that it allowed the individual viewer to interpret and assert their own position in terms of those regional and local experiences that many of the reports such as *Girls in Boy Bars* attempted to incite and articulate. In this way the context of *OOT/Out* and its lack of an organizational structure or format allied to the magazine programme further empowers and catalyses how queer affects, memories, and narratives are expressed and interpreted through it. More so, and in terms of the absence of coherent themes and linearity, the programme still feels unpredictable, uneven and irregular, and in many ways, this is its queer appeal.

This indefiniteness resulted in a rare blend of TV and culture that Amy Villarejo refers to as the 'presence of *critical cultural studies on TV!*'[32] which also worked to centralize politicized modes of resistance, activism and the portrayal of queer lives across Britain. The chaotic essence of how queerness was reported and mediated situate a programme that is 'a jumble of bits and pieces which would not attempt to construct some totalising world view but would allow the viewer almost complete freedom to make whatever meanings they wanted (or even none at all)'.[33] This in itself yields much of its queer resonance around aspects of regionality and locality. Yet the content speaks to and is informed by these issues in an accessible and ironic way with innovative, fresh and often disparate elements each week. Guest 'commentators' such as Bea Campbell, Ian McKellen, Simon Fanshawe, Richard Coles, Audre Lorde, Simon Callow and the Geordie lesbian presenter 'Hufty'[34] appear throughout the first two series. Contemporary topics such as post-communism, queer fostering, Section 28 and HIV/AIDS are interspliced with short films on Gay Pride, Eurovision, Hollywood camp, gays and lesbians in the UK Jewish community, and homosexuality in Nazi Germany. Many of these reports and films consider queer lives beyond the UK as they begin to situate and consider how those lives are then remapped and reconfigured into a UK context.

This diffuse content is detailed and explored in an acerbic critique of the programme by Colin Richardson.[35] He groups the content of the programme into categories of 'Personal and Identity Politics; Lesbian and Gay Rights; Lifestyle; History; Fiction; and News' but also stresses that because the programme did not belong to a specific TV genre, it generated a kind of 'cumulative, subliminal impression' of queer life.[36] While it is both rigorous and comprehensive, twenty-five years later Richardson's work needs to be reassessed to consider questions of queer regionality and locality. For example, the assertion that the series presented queer life as 'not so much a *real* way of life as an *ideal* one' as well as his claim it was the programme's 'openness to a multiplicity of readings that thwarted *Out's* attempts to position and direct its viewers' seem unfounded when we view the reports retrospectively and more so through the prism of regional queer experience.[37] For instance, in *Girls in Boy Bars* we see that both the cultural heritage of the North East and the 'gay scene' in Newcastle upon Tyne inform the experiences of the participants. Here we find a well-established 'gay scene' and its conversant inhabitants negotiating issues of misogyny, homophobia and gender politics in relation to social class, industry and the economy. The nuances of queerness and locality in the North East are shrewdly and perceptively conveyed and connect to a group of people who understand this 'scene' and the opportunities it offers for inclusivity and pleasure as well as conflict and exclusion in a regional context.

Similar examples of this include films such as *Khush*, where the lives of South Asian lesbians and gays in UK are carefully unpacked. Also, in the final series, we find a '*News From...*' feature where regional life in Dublin, Edinburgh, Blackpool, Manchester and London are connected to modes of queer experience. Richardson also seems to suggest that the programme somehow failed to confront how this queer experience was defined by systemically heteronormative and homophobic structures because its content was not 'addressed out at them (challenging) but inwards to us (questioning)' as queer and out viewers.[38] Yet, for closeted viewers, and for regional queers who watched (and appeared) in the series, the public and televised acts of self-nomination and empowerment were challengingly bold, varied and at times subversive. They allowed for queerness to be visualized through regionally familiar encounters with individuals and communities and did so by exploring the mutability of queerness, locality and the self.

Caroline Spry, who was the assistant commissioning editor for independent programmes at Channel 4, was 'assigned the task of overseeing *Out's* transition from drawing board to small screen', and as a result she became the '*de facto* commissioning editor for lesbian and gay programmes'.[39] In a 2020 interview[40] that I conducted with her, Spry remarked that 'Channel 4 is strange about its history... a lot of the politics and ethics that connect to the first 10 years of Channel 4 are now very difficult to find', and that while the production and distribution of the programme was 'deeply politically informed in terms of a department and a staff', this did not come without its problems. Spry also acknowledged that the programme connected to the founding chief executive of Channel 4 Jeremy Isaacs and his 'vision for access for unheard voices and an approach of direct speech from people not usually heard on the channel, as well as his notion of radical pluralism'. In a biographical account[41] of his time at Channel 4, Isaacs mentions how 'the stewardship of Caroline Spry' and the 'journalistic magazine format' of *Out on Tuesday* created a space where gay people encountered a sense of 'self-awareness and self-confidence' through the representation of other gay people who shared their 'individuality,... pursuits and aspirations, [... and] common difficulties'. While this kind of account presents an optimistic sense of gay life and experience, when I discussed this with Spry she offered a counterpoint to Issacs's perspective by also emphasizing that the show 'always felt very metropolitan with young gay and lesbian people working together in London in a rather mad, nebulous, and chaotic way, and with voices from all over the place... a kind of sense of "everything" which at the same time still provided a quite specific glimpse of contemporary gay experiences'.

Spry left Channel 4 in 1995 and reflects on the fact that it was entirely her decision to end the series. She says that 'it was clear that the channel was changing in 1994... it started to become a different creature'. This was also to do 'with the changing social and cultural face of TV and I think that post-*Out* we see a shift to lifestyle-based TV where political content seemed to dissipate and disappear'. In contrast and looking at the programme in terms of regional queer experience, she also restates that 'it was a very metropolitan series with a London bias which neglected some of the regional programming that underpinned the channel's ethos so that in the end and in terms of class and regionalism – we didn't quite get there'. This suggests that the values and narratives allied to the modes of production and consumption which define *OOT/Out* and how they align to regional queer experiences are inherently complex. Here there are ideological gaps between the metrocentric life of young and queer creatives producing and editing a cutting-edge TV programme in London and the regionally informed content it contains in a report such as *Girls in Boy Bars*. The programme also raises questions around the authentic experiences of queer regionality in a city like Newcastle upon Tyne and the re-mediation of it as televisual content in London. Yet the fact that reports like *Girls in Boy Bars* were even produced and broadcast indicates that localized queerness and regional difference were just as crucial and perhaps more reflective of how everyday queer life was experienced beyond London. More than any other *OOT/Out* report *Girls in Boy Bars* captures the programme's emphasis on distinctive aspects of regional queerness and how it is evoked. In the report the parameters of queer life which are coded around the localized familiarity and to an extent ordinariness of this 'gay scene' convey modes of queer politics and experience that still feel relevant. Here the incisive and sharp observations of the various participants are articulated via an awareness of how subjugated and marginalized modes of queer life are experienced in a regional setting. These accounts also often address the politics of misogyny, homophobia and heteronormativity through moments of personal experience and testimony.

Girls in Boy Bars: Situating and Evoking Queer Regionality

Girls in Boy Bars captures the Newcastle 'gay scene' of 1989 and in it the North-east is constructed through a compound of community, humour, acceptance and discrimination allied to discourses of regional and working-class life. Through informal interviews participants use personal narratives, reflections and recollections, and a focus is placed on the cultural and social relationship between gay men and straight women in the bars and clubs of this 'scene'. In the late 1980s and early 1990s a decline in employment in shipbuilding, coalmining and factory labour, and the subsequent move to tertiary-based modes of production in the North East meant that how sexuality and sociality were being articulated there was always qualitatively different to how they were understood and mapped in London and elsewhere. Yet this difference does not mark the city's or the region's move away from practices of class-based socializing and queer life. Instead, it places a new queer texture and emphasis on them. The report is also connected to and precedes changes to the cultural geography and queer night-time economy of the city. In 1989 the gay 'boy bars' in Newcastle that these queer citizens visited were still very much 'geographically isolated and culturally marginalized from the mainstream', and the advancement of post-industrialization during the 1990s and into the 2000s was still to come.[42] In 1999, Newcastle City Council announced it was actively seeking to develop a 'gay village' and that its development was to be part of wider ongoing gentrification and rebranding of Newcastle as a cosmopolitan city, in attempts to shake off its 'hard drinking "laddish" identity'.[43] This gave rise to the emergence of a 'Pink Triangle' that was at once 'geographically isolated and culturally marginalized from the mainstream of Newcastle' but because of its proximity to the main railway station gradually became a space that remained accessible and one that has gradually grown into a favoured destination for both the city's gay *and* straight night-time economy users over the last twenty years.[44]

The Pink Triangle, the content of the report and more broadly the evolution of queer life in Newcastle since 1989 are contoured by some of these tensions. Marc Lewis (1994) provides a unique account of the commercial gay scene in the city in the early 1990s and uses the premise that Newcastle is 'always on the margins'[45] to trace the distinctness and difference of Newcastle's queer geography and people. He situates the North East as a geographically isolated region 'being some 430km from London',[46] yet more significantly it is also 'isolated from national social trends in that a majority of the region's people demonstrate a tenacious working-class culture'.[47] Newcastle as a queer space is demarcated by these narratives of class, local community and regional experience, yet amidst these modes of belonging, inclusion and empathy there remains an element of homophobic apathy, exclusion and isolation. In this way Newcastle's geographical, economic, cultural and queer conditions of isolation and/or marginalization seem more unusual considering its broader reputation as a hedonistic, friendly and safe city. Here is a city that simultaneously negotiates, affirms and negates queer life through the markers of its industrial and working-class heritage and arguably its "gay scene" is defined by and retains a' decidedly working-class character compared to other major British cities'.[48] For the uninitiated its bars, clubs and streets can seem edgier, rougher and tougher and, in contrast to those scenes we find in London's Soho or Vauxhall, Newcastle's queer space and community requires 'the development of a different physical and psychological symbolic world so that a separate cultural identity can be created and maintained'[49] and embodied through a distinctly queer North-eastern or queer 'Geordie' self.[50] Here the sexual and social structures, ideologies and formations allied to queer lives in Newcastle and the North East are unwrapped as productively ambiguous constructions that simultaneously 'look to'/'resent'/'envy' and 'pity' the modes of cultural capital that a city like London has produced. In this way the queer North East is situated within a purview of enigmatic cultural change and contradiction.

More so and since the *Girls in Boy Bars* report was first broadcast, the commodification and visibility of queer culture in Newcastle has also connected to what might be best called a surplus of 'leisure, services, culture and tourism to re-develop and re-brand the post-industrial city as a cosmopolitan place that is desirable to visit'[51] and thus 'negotiated the transition from an industrial to a post-industrial or, more accurately, neo-industrial economy, in which the effects of globalisation are manifest at economic, social, political, and cultural levels within the locality'.[52] Yet, the 'girls' and 'boys' in these bars are not yet aware of this and their queer experiences are informed and empowered by a distinctly and at times stubborn regional outlook that does not seem to need or rely on values, opinions and geographies other than their own. For example, Stuart introduces himself with a thick Geordie lilt by asserting, 'I'm gay and I go out with girls', while his straight female friend Davina asserts, 'Hi I'm Davina and I'm not a fag hag', later stating that the term 'fag hag' is 'horrendous… I am not a fag hag I'm Stuart's friend'. In these bars and on this distinctively local 'scene', men self-identify as gay via an identification with a straight woman, and straight women are able to take cover and negotiate their own desires by being out with gay men. While the practice of straight girls going out and socializing with gay men is in no ways unique to this region, these bars appear to be more integrated, accessible and mixed than those in London and here the local community seem to have created and sustained their own queer codes and rituals associated with how gendered and sexual minorities socialize.

These forms of queer relationality are delineated and negotiated throughout the report, and, in an era where queer representation has been transformed and repositioned through excessive commodification, celebrity culture, self-promotion and self-representation, it is difficult to grasp just how this kind of report 'splinters the monolithic TV image that usually represents us'[53] both as queer[54] and more so as regionally queer. In this way *Girls in Boy Bars* can be situated within an ongoing context of enigmatic cultural change, and by using the testimonies of ordinary people like Davina and Stuart, it seems to capture how strands of regional life coalesce with broader forms of gender, individuality and sexual politics. In turn and in the report the North East is used as a space to consider and unpack some complex layers of personal and political experience. For those who watched that night in 1989 (and for those like me who have watched since) the testimonies and personalities in *Girls in Boys Bars* assertively articulated themselves on a range of queer issues which underpinned their 'scene'. Of course, this queer world existed before the production team from London arrived, but in its final format as a short film, we get a sense of a 'scene' that captures a distinctly personal and local perspective on broader political issues of queer affirmation, friendship, belonging and conflict.

In the opening shot of the report, the sounds of shipping horns signal the precarity of heavy industry and the closure of the shipyards on the River Tyne. Local drag queen Miss Greta LaMore then introduces the report in a profuse and wryly camp Geordie accent: 'Good evening, bonsoir – my name is Greta LaMore (Miss).' Here the quick-witted codes that Greta used to both endear and often offend audiences in Newcastle resonated with me poignantly and affectively. Yet to the uninitiated the nuances of Greta's persona may well fall flat, fail to affect and pass them by in the brevity of the report. Almost immediately this identification with Greta requires a level of local queer knowledge in order to recognize and position her as a local drag legend with a repertoire that cites aspects of working-class life in the region. Greta's later responses to the off-camera prompts build on this via the discourse of queer regional life and working-class heritage. When asked, 'Does Drag degrade women?' Greta responds, 'I think women degrade drag... have you seen them, they come in here, I've never seen so much acrylic and crimplene in my life', and 'you can get an auld boiler like me, I put on a cloth cap and just stand on the stage with a bit of slap on... and I'm fabulous'. Here the reference to a 'cloth cap' alludes to the heritage of masculinity and labour in the region and perhaps more so working men's clubs where many North East drag acts such as Greta regularly appeared (and continue to appear). Greta's seditious reference to an object that signifies and symbolizes working-class pride and masculinity indicates both an affinity and an indifference to it. Here the ordinary and evocative contours of regional experience and an awareness of what the cloth cap symbolizes allow Greta to articulate how queerness and working-class life intersect. These kinds of references and allusions to class are underpinned by Greta's own experiences of regionality but not confined by it, and in this way, they undermine the kinds of narratives that privilege and place emphasis on the cultural superiority of London and its allure. More specifically and because the embodied and lived experiences of the participants like Greta are regionally expressed, they affirm an implicit sense of autonomy and agency that is empowering because it is expressed from a regional perspective.

Some of the most engaging aspects of the film explore conflict and differing perspectives on the scene. While the 'scene' is diverse we hear that lesbians do not mix easily with gay men and the politics of drag, misogyny and masculinity are continually challenged and upturned. The familiarity of this 'scene' allows for confrontational encounters to occur, and alongside Greta Lamore, the participant who stands and speaks out most is a local lesbian called Debbie Burton. She initially mocks her own lack of success in pulling straight women, stating that 'they took the tabs, took the drink and buggered off basically', and then goes on to recollect how she was thrown out and barred from local club 'Rockshots' by a male bouncer because she 'thumped' a drag queen for throwing a nappy covered in tomato sauce into the crowd. Here Burton contests and questions the discriminatory and offensive actions of the drag queen and the disrespectful use of menstruation to get what she refers to as 'a cheap laugh'. In marked contrast to others in the report she uses the setting of the 'gay scene' differently. It is in the public space of 'Rockshots' that her direct actions and radical protest are possible and where her local reputation as an outspoken local lesbian is initiated. Debbie self-reflects on this and seems to fully understand and exploit the potentials for dissidence that exist from inside her own queer community and locality. As she is ejected from the club, she imitates the gruff Geordie bouncer's voice: 'divvn't botha comin' back', meaning 'don't bother coming back', and seems to use the Geordie accent as a way to frame his normative and dominant masculinity. She then recollects that returning the next week wearing a wig to gain entry she 'felt like I had a bag of coal on me head', as she describes her fear and amazement on encountering the same bouncer. In a similar way to Greta and her reference to the cloth cap, Debbie combines the performativity of the wig with the image of a bag of coal. Here the long and proud mining heritage of the North East is ironically used by Debbie as a way to self-define and tether herself to the region and its narratives of working-class life.

She goes on to claim that 'He had a pair of shoulders like the Tyne bridge... and filled out the whole of the doorframe'. Here the Tyne Bridge as another powerful symbol of local pride and belonging is personified through a forcefully masculine and working-class culture exemplified by the bouncer. This ideological image of the straight white Geordie man with shoulders as broad and sturdy as the iconic bridge that straddles the Tyne is, like the bag of coal, a paradoxically persistent and reductive regional representation and one which allows Debbie to navigate her sardonic queerness. Just as he asks her, 'are ye coming in pet?', he adds, 'How I na your face?' Debbie responds, 'dos café con leche por favour' as he mumbles 'aye, ah gan on gerrin', which she knowingly translates as 'go ahead young lady'. Once back into Rockshots she ripped off the wig yelling, 'Thank Christ for that' running onto the dancefloor 'before he could catch is'. In Debbie's account the North East is emerging as a space where previously 'heavy industries associated with the shipyard and the pit,… have now been further fragmented and splintered' and this has also defined how the social, sexual and gendered bodies align to the 'transformation of a region relinquishing its strong industrial base'.[55] The Tyne Bridge, the cloth cap and the bag of coal as symbols of an older and familiar North East are spiritedly sabotaged and connected to a socio-economic move away from the 'traditional "masculine" infrastructure' of the region and its 'monochrome representation as a bleak post-industrial outpost'[56] towards something far queerer. Through the stories and testimonies of people like Debbie we begin to see how the nuances of queer regionality and resistance both inform and enhance the experiences of this local queer community. More broadly, *Girls in Boys Bars* and the forms of regionality and community it evokes upturn Colin Richardson's claim that the content of *OOT/Out* presented 'an enclosed narrative; a ring-fenced portion of the schedule [… where] we were left talking to ourselves'.[57] Rather, the report explores and affirms how queer individuals were talking from both inside *and* outside their communities and regional setting. By using this 'gay scene' to position what queer life, politics and experience meant in relation to much broader hegemonic structures of dominance and discrimination, we see how *OOT/Out* and *Girls in Boy Bars* documented and facilitated a simultaneously regional and political space. In this setting queer people moved beyond the discourse of their genders and sexualities, and arguably did so in ways that placed a fresh emphasis on their own self-defined experiences and identities as regional queer citizens of the North East.

Conclusion

Since that June afternoon in 2006 at the BFI I think I have watched *Girls in Boy Bars* hundreds of times. Every time the assemblage of regional queer lives, personas and desires resonate with me in a different way and even now they continue to do so. My move back from London, my need to get back there, my home in Newcastle and my own personal memories all resonate and cling to that report as a queer object that locates, comforts and perplexes me. In it the Newcastle 'gay scene' emerges as a space where ideas, opinions and relationships were (and indeed still are) in a constant state of change, interspersing regional experience, community space and sociality through contingent processes of how these queer people spoke, thought, lived and desired. When I first saw it I longed for home and wondered how I might connect this understanding of Newcastle upon Tyne and the North East to life in the capital. It struck me that this report was in some way a kind of lost thread and record of ordinary and regional queer life – an incisive and astutely made film that had been produced and filmed in Newcastle upon Tyne but then mapped into the broader landscape of queer life in other UK cities and then edited, marketed and to an extent commodified in London. Here the content of the film itself became less relevant, and as I watched again what resonated and affected me most were the participants' ways of orienting, evoking and speaking of the spaces they were in and the regional queer lives they were living.

Both *OOT/Out* and *Girls in Boy Bars* are tethered to the past but what they catalyse and inform in relation to contemporary queer life and desire remain relevant. In this way the report and more crucially *OOT* and *Out* should function as a decisive archive for queer lives in Britain and how they are dispersed and appropriated. In many of the *Out* and *OOT* reports the content is still daring, intelligent, controversial and one might say retrospectively queer, none more so than in *Girls in Boy Bars*. It is an attempt to use the televisual medium to speak to queer people in ways which are simultaneously direct, ironic, perceptive and inclusive. More so and when these complex modes of address and interpellations are framed through a regional and local lens, they indicate that 'the people on *Out* weren't *other* people; in a sense they were me'.[58] Yet how a regional queer life might have been evoked and constructed as personal and unique is, of course, like the televisual forms and structures used to proclaim them, a form of mediated representation for an audience. Nonetheless, these collective and subjective memories, experiences and realizations have the capacity to shift with those audiences and renegotiate the programme's meaning and place in British queer history. Just as social relations change over time and space, and as lives move on, locality and regional identity will continue to be of significance. In this way how *OOT/Out* is interpreted and encountered also changes and adjusts to reflect how the contours of queer locality, regionality and displacement are experienced by queer people.

Notes

1   This kind of queer narrative is articulated in a number of texts and most notably in the introduction to Matt Houlbrook's *Queer London* (2005), 1–13. Here, Houlbrook presents us with 'Cyril's Story', which functions as a compelling allegory and speaks to how these kinds of tensions are aligned to the pursuit for a queer life beyond the confines of a regional setting. This kind of desire for movement away from those regional spaces and narratives of homophobia, the closet and normativity are also captured in Bronski Beat's 1984 song *Smalltown* Boy.

2   Matt Cook, 'Capital stories: Local lives in queer London', in *Queer Cities, Queer Cultures – Europe since 1945*, ed. Matt Cook and Jennifer V. Evans (London: Bloomsbury, 2014), 51.

3   James Knowles, 'Hypothetical hills': Rethinking northern gay identities in the fiction of Paul Magrs', in *Territories of Desire in Queer Culture – Refiguring Contemporary Boundaries*, ed. David Alderson and Linda Anderson (Manchester: Manchester University Press, 2000), 135.

4   From this point on the programme is referred to as *OOT/Out*.

5   This was first broadcast on 8 April 1989 and drew in the largest of all *Out*'s audiences, with 1.576 million watching the programme that night. For a more detailed information on the viewing figures of both *Out on Tuesday* and *Out* see Colin Richardson, 'TVOD: The never-bending story', in *A Queer Romance: Lesbians, Gay Men and Popular Culture*, ed. Paul Burston and Colin Richardson (London and New York: Routledge, 1995), 241–4.

6   Glyn Davis and Gary Needham, 'Introduction – the pleasures of the tube', in *Queer TV: Theories, Histories, Politics*, ed. Glyn Davis and Gary Needham (London and New York: Routledge, 2009), 8.

7   Tony. E. Adams, *Narrating the Closet: An Autoethnography of Same-Sex Attraction* (Walnut Creek, CA: Left Coast Press Inc, 2011), 159.

8   Sara Ahmed, *Queer Phenomenology: Orientations, Objects, Others* (Durham and London: Duke University Press, 2006), 3.

9   Adams, *Narrating the Closet*, 159.

10 Ahmed, *Queer Phenomenology*, 6.

11 Ibid., 20.

12 Sherry Turkle, *Evocative Objects – Things We Think with* (Cambridge, MA: The MIT Press, 2007).

13 Turkle, *Evocative Objects*, 5.

14 Ibid., 6.

15 Note that Colin Richardson's work is the most rigorous and comprehensive account of both *OOT* and *Out*. At the time of writing the author's own archival records and cataloguing from the BFI in 2006 remain his own and are unpublished. There is also a comprehensive account of each episode of the programme that has been catalogued and documented by Caroline Spry. Events such as 2019's 'Remembering Channel 4's Out on Tuesday: Queer Spaces in Public Service Television', which took place at Birkbeck, considered this and indicate the renewed interest in the programme and its legacy. See link here http://blogs.bbk.ac.uk/bimi/remembering-channel-4s-out-on-tuesday/ (accessed 3 November 2020).

16 Richardson, 'TVOD: The never-bending story', 229, 234.

17 Davis and Needham, 'Introduction – the pleasures of the tube', 6.

18 Joe Brainard, *I Remember* (Widworthy Barton: Notting Hill Editions Ltd, 1975), 41.

19 Ann Cvetkovich, *An Archive of Feelings: Trauma, Sexuality and Lesbian Public Cultures* (Durham and London: Duke University Press, 2006), 241.

20 Cvetkovich, *An Archive of Feelings*, 245.

21 Kathleen Stewart, *Ordinary Affects* (Durham and London: Duke University Press, 2007).

22 Stewart, *Ordinary Affects*, 4.

23 Richardson, 'TVOD: The never-bending story', 217.

24 Ibid., 217.

25 Ibid., 220.

26 Ibid., 230.

27 Gregory Woods, "Something for everyone" – lesbian and gay "magazine" programming on British television 1980–2000', in *Queer TV: Theories, Histories, Politics*, ed. Glyn Davis and Gary Needham (London and New York: Routledge, 2009), 111.

28 Richardson, 'TVOD: The never-bending story', 217.

29 Woods, 'Something for everyone', 114.

30 Ibid., 111.

31 Ibid., 119.

32 Amy Villarejo, 'Ethereal queer – notes on method', in *Queer TV: Theories, Histories, Politics*, ed. Glyn Davis and Gary Needham (London and New York: Routledge, 2009), 54.

33 Richardson, 'TVOD: The never-bending story', 223.

34 Note – Hufty features in several reports and is notable for the emphasis that she places on her regionality and lesbian identity. I am hoping in future work to both interview and archive her work and its importance in relation to queer identities in the North East.

35 Richardson, 'TVOD: The never-bending story', 216–48.

36 Ibid., 226–7.
37 Ibid., 228.
38 Ibid., 228–9.
39 Ibid., 220.
40 Caroline Spry – Interviewed by Gareth Longstaff, 19 June 2020, via Zoom.
41 Jeremy Isaacs, *Storm Over – A Personal Account* (London: Weidenfeld and Nicolson, 1989), 134.
42 Mark Casey, 'De-dyking queer space(s): Heterosexual female visibility in gay and lesbian spaces', *Sexualities* 7, no. 4 (2004): 450.
43 Casey, 'De-dyking queer space(s)', 450.
44 Ibid., 450.
45 Marc Lewis, 'A sociological pub crawl around gay Newcastle', in *The Margins of the City – Gay Men's Urban Lives*, ed. Stephen Whittle (Aldershot: Arena – Ashgate Publishing House, 1994), 85.
46 Lewis, 'A sociological pub crawl around gay Newcastle', 85.
47 Ibid., 85.
48 Ibid., 88.
49 Ibid., 88.
50 For a socio-cultural account of the history, discourse and representation of the 'Geordie', see – Robert Collis and Bill Lancaster (eds), *Geordie – Roots of Regionalism* (Edinburgh: Edinburgh University Press, 1992).
51 Carl Bonner-Thompson, 'The meat-market': Production and regulation of masculinities on the Grindr grid in Newcastle upon Tyne, UK', *Gender, Place and Culture* 24, no. 11 (2017): 1613–14.
52 Anoop Nayak, 'Last of the "Real Geordies"? White masculinities and the subcultural response to deindustrialisation', *Environment and Planning D: Society and Space* 21 (2003): 10.
53 Richardson, 'TVOD: The never-bending story', 221.
54 For a more detailed account of the history and mediation of gay and queer identities and lifestyles on British TV, see Sebastian Buckle, *Homosexuality and the Small Screen: Television and Gay Identity in Britain* (London: Bloomsbury, 2018).
55 Nayak, 'Last of the "Real Geordies"', 9.
56 Anoop Nayak, 'Displaced masculinities: Chavs, youth and class in the post-industrial city', *Sociology* 40, no. 5 (2006): 817.
57 Richardson, 'TVOD: The never-bending story', 234.
58 Ibid., 236.

3

Sectarianism and queer lives in Northern Ireland since the 1970s

Sean Brady

In October 2019, nearly three years after the collapse of power-sharing and of functioning devolved government in Northern Ireland, the Northern Ireland Assembly was briefly recalled by unionist parties. The trigger for the petition to recall the assembly after its rancorous collapse, and in a period of intense positioning and negotiations over Brexit and the UK's Withdrawal Agreement with regard to Northern Ireland, was a campaign led by the Democratic Unionist Party (DUP) to restore the devolved assembly with the single purpose of blocking UK legislation imposed by the Westminster parliament that would legalize same-sex marriage and decriminalize abortion in the province. In one of the most remarkable political events, certainly to the outside world, the assembly at Stormont was recalled in this episode and attempts were made to introduce a new bill, the Defence of the Unborn Child Bill, in order to block marriage equality and access to abortion in Northern Ireland.

It took the campaigns of Labour MPs Stella Creasy and Conor McGinn to create cross-party consensuses in the House of Commons at Westminster, on the issues of abortion and same-sex marriage respectively, for the UK government to make the highly unusual move of imposing legislation on Northern Ireland to bring the province in line with the rest of the United Kingdom. In the absence of devolved government in Northern Ireland, MPs in the Commons voted overwhelmingly in favour of this extension to the UK government's legal powers to resolve, once and for all, two of the most socially divisive issues in the province today. Even as the High Court in Belfast ruled in early October 2019 that Northern Ireland's near-total criminalization of abortion breached the UK's human rights commitments, the DUP and other unionist parties nonetheless pressed ahead in their attempt to recall the assembly to block Westminster.

All of Northern Ireland's political parties, irrespective of the sectarian divide, hold and have held and promoted reactionary and socially conservative attitudes in recent decades. Social progressivism in the Northern Ireland context had been limited, in many respects, to efforts at cross-sectarian community building rather than issues of LGBTQ equalities, women's reproductive rights or multiculturalism. In many respects, LGBTQ equalities and women's bodily autonomy have been inextricably entwined, in both Northern Ireland and the Republic of Ireland, due to the overwhelmingly religious orientation of politics and society in both jurisdictions. So why does Northern Ireland differ so sharply in social attitudes to the rest of the UK? Also, why were marriage equality and women's reproductive rights not already enshrined in law in Northern Ireland, given that it is an intrinsic part of the UK and, until 2021, part of the European Union?

Religion, regionality and homosexuality

As a 'queer locale', Northern Ireland is rarely considered by scholars; and yet, the cultural and social specificities of the province have long created a hostile environment for LGBTQ people. Society, culture and politics in the province are riven with religious sectarianism and legacies of violence. Even among those who are religiously non-practicing, the 'habitus' of religion and sectarianism in Northern Ireland remains deeply ingrained.[1] Unlike in Britain, the non-religious cannot be labelled 'secularists', as religiously based sectarianism defines social existence for practically everyone. Northern Ireland is by far the most religiously observant part of the UK today. The divisions in society are also generational. The contemporary rise in conservative evangelicalism and fundamentalism in some sections of the Protestant community in Northern Ireland, particularly among younger Protestants, exacerbates the sectarian divide. Notable is the role of Premillennialism, the eschatological belief in the physical 'second coming' of Christ, the 'rapture' and Christ's rule on earth before the 'millennium'. The inherently Premillennialist (and vehemently anti-Roman Catholic) theology and rhetoric in Ulster Protestant fundamentalism, such as that of the highly politicized Free Presbyterian Church of Ulster, tends to evaluate political conflict, and the woes and necessary defence of Protestant Ulster, through biblical discourse.[2] In some respects, it is a helpful analogy to think of politics in Northern Ireland in a similar light to the syncretism between fundamentalist religion and Republican Party politics in the United States in the last three decades.[3]

Northern Ireland's regional divisions and dimensions further affect the realities of queer lives in the province. First of all, there is a division between urban and rural, in that urban centres such as Belfast and Derry have at least offered queer people some spaces and organizations that promote their rights and facilitate befriending and the ability to meet. As we shall see from the evidence from Cara Friend's archive, being queer in Northern Ireland's rural areas historically has been an even more isolating and hostile experience than for queer people in its urban centres. Also, there are further historical divisions east and west of the River Bann, which cuts across the north of the province. Before the imposition of direct rule in 1972 at the height of the Troubles, the Ulster Unionist power bloc in the (then) Parliament of Northern Ireland at Stormont gerrymandered constituencies west of the River Bann, where there were more Roman Catholics, in order to maintain Ulster Unionist majorities and hegemony.[4]

The religiously orientated sectarian communities in Northern Ireland are antithetical and violently inimical towards each other across these geographical and community divides. However, they have shown remarkable levels of accord when it comes to hostility towards social issues such as homosexuality, marriage equality legislation for same-sex couples, women in mainstream political life and the decriminalization of abortion in Northern Ireland. Most significantly, devolved law, such as family law in Northern Ireland, is used by religious fundamentalists in the province to 'defend' the socially conservative status quo and to 'resist' developments in family law including marriage equality elsewhere in the UK. One reason for this alignment is that Northern Ireland's sectarianized communities are, in themselves, competing and conflicting hegemonies of masculinity and male dominance.[5] The volatile cultural amalgam of male-dominated and widespread male-only associational culture, both Protestant and Roman Catholic; the primacy of organized religion and the male-only Orange Order in the history of the province; and the bitter divisions and deep social and gender conservatism on both sides of its sectarian divide pose 'the question forcibly' of why questions of sexualities, gender, men, masculinities and religion have not been 'an integral part of the analysis of Northern Ireland's history, society and culture'.[6]

One of the surprising features of the scholarship of Northern Ireland, irrespective of scholarly discipline, is that questions of sexualities, masculinities and gender, or for that matter the centrality of religion in its ethno-nationalist conflict, are not much considered. Scholarly questions of homosexuality and the conditions for LGBTQ people barely exist in the Northern Ireland paradigm despite the existence of organized LGBTQ organizations for nearly half a century. Practically none of the burgeoning developments in historical studies of gender, masculinities and sexualities in Britain, for example, have affected or penetrated the historiography of Northern Ireland.[7] As the sociologist and criminologist Fidelma Ashe argues, scholars of Northern Ireland typically have ignored its gendered dimensions. Thus, men's dominance in the politics and society of the province, both historically and today, 'has been framed as normal and natural'. Priority has been given to 'inequalities relating to ethnonationalist identities', resulting in the marginalization of other identities,[8] such as sexual difference. Male dominance, along with a conservative and narrow historiographical tradition, and a society and politics that to this day is, by and large, hostile to equality rights for LGBTQ people, has meant that scholarly questions of homosexuality in Northern Ireland have been neglected and ignored. Such silence has been part of the particularity of Northern Ireland as a queer locale. Silences pervade aspects of scholarly questions of homosexuality in the rest of the UK too, as can be seen in Louise Pawley's chapter on Brighton and Alan Butler's chapter on Plymouth in this volume. But unlike the scholarly field in Britain, comparatively Northern Ireland has received barely any attention.[9]

LGBTQ life in Northern Ireland

LGBTQ people in Northern Ireland, and most especially in Belfast since the 1970s, have been organizing themselves in a manner commensurate with LGBTQ groups in other Western societies. Although the LGBTQ community was and is small in size and predominantly confined to the few urban centres in the province, such as Belfast, Derry/Londonderry and Colraine, activists adapted ideas emerging elsewhere. Such an example was Cara Friend, set up in October 1974 in Derry/Londonderry as a befriending organization for LGBTQ people across Northern Ireland. It was founded by individuals closely involved with the creation of the Northern Ireland Homosexual Law Reform Committee in the same year, as well as the foundation of the Northern Ireland Gay Rights Association (NIGRA) in 1975 in Belfast. It took as its model existing 'gay befriending and information organisations elsewhere', including FRIEND, a national gay befriending organization in England and Wales, the 'London Gay Switchboard, London Icebreakers, Parent's Enquiry, Telafriend in Dublin, and the Albany Trust'.[10] Due to lack of funds, however, Cara Friend did not have a telephone for the first few years of its existence – which of course is manna for the historian, as many clients were moved to write letters describing their experiences living with their homosexuality in Northern Ireland.

Not only were Cara Friend and its concomitant organization NIGRA targets for the DUP's notorious 'Save Ulster from Sodomy!' campaign but Cara Friend's male voluntary organizers and befrienders were also subjected to raids and arrests between January and June 1976 by the Royal Ulster Constabulary (RUC). The continued criminality of all male homosexual sexual acts in Northern Ireland until 1982 gave the police justification for such actions. For Cara Friend, which after October 1975 received a modicum of funding for its activities from the Department of Health and Social Services in Northern Ireland,[11] these raids were a particularly worrying development, as its function, advertised in newspapers such as the *Belfast Telegraph*, was to act as a confidential service for LGBTQ people.[12]

Cara Friend highlighted that it was its male volunteers who were arrested, as 'female homosexuality is not illegal'. The RUC submitted Cara Friend's volunteers to threats – such as revelation of sexual orientation to employers and families – in attempts to 'obtain statements concerning the personal sexual relationships of those being questioned'.[13] Fortunately, 'because of the safeguards employed by Cara Friend no confidential Cara Friend information was passed into the hands of the police', but these events created huge concern among Cara Friend's organizers: the RUC's harassment 'caused great fear and mental anguish among many gay people in the Belfast area including many who had nothing to do with [Cara Friend]'.[14] The raids received press attention both within Northern Ireland and also in British and Irish newspapers.[15] Furthermore, in the first half of 1976, the RUC raided the homes of members of the Students' Gay Liberation Group at Queen's University Belfast, and also the homes of key organizers and campaigners within NIGRA. In total, twenty-two men associated with Cara Friend, NIGRA and the Students' Gay Liberation Group were arrested, and had their private documents seized, as the RUC were looking for evidence of criminality in order to shut down these organizations.[16]

In the end, none of the men involved were prosecuted, though according to NIGRA this was 'a political rather than a judicial' decision, as the Attorney General for Northern Ireland eventually became involved in these cases (a highly unusual development).[17] But the RUC raids and the vociferous 'Save Ulster from Sodomy!' campaign intensified the deep sense of precariousness experienced by legitimate organizations intended to improve the lives of LGBTQ people in Northern Ireland, and exacerbated the huge difficulties faced by the organizers and volunteers at Cara Friend, and their clients in this period.

The 'mental anguish' described at the time of RUC raids of LGBTQ people and their organizations is reflected across Cara Friend's correspondence from clients, which are further pervaded by emotions of religious guilt and shame. One letter, from a young man of nineteen, stated that 'because of my Christian beliefs I have to resort to masturbation and this means I neither get support or company from people like myself'.[18] Another man, aged twenty-seven, informed the Cara Friend volunteers that 'knowing the situation in Ulster I suppose it is best to point out that I am a Roman Catholic'.[19] The declaration of religion and community is common throughout Cara Friend's huge cache of redacted correspondence. The Troubles were themselves a barrier to meeting other people. One man from Enniskillen stated:

> I am 21 and very lonely. I don't like going to Belfast because of the 'Troubles' please reply to the address below (which is where I work) as soon as possible. Unfortunately I cannot give my home address as there is a danger of my letters being opened.[20]

A 31-year-old man was moved to contact Cara Friend having watched a programme on homosexuality on the television: 'As I am a Christian and have never been attracted to girls I saw a programme on TV where this man said he was gay but was also a Christian. You see I lead a very lonely life'.[21] Another letter came from a man enquiring about gay Christian meetings. He did not hold strong religious views but was afraid of the potential for violence he encountered in Belfast's gay bars:

> I am 24 years old and live with my parents, although I am not what you would call a Christian in the sense of the word, I do believe in God. I would like to meet people like myself in the religious gay Christian fellowship. I usually go to a gay disco in Belfast but I do not seem to fit in with it, and I have lost all faith in people after I was beaten up by a person at the disco and assaulted with an iron bar.... Are people in the Religious Fellowship different from what I have found [in] other people?[22]

Gay bars were not generally associated with violence, but this young man reveals the extent to which the context of violence more broadly in Belfast was reflected even in a supposed 'safe space' for LGBTQ people.

Cara Friend volunteers, who would meet up with correspondents, were also required to keep records of their meetings. In response to meetings with a young male Protestant, the volunteer reported:

> [he] has to a large extent gotten over his religious difficulties although still devout. The difficulty now is meeting other people, as he does not like large crowds, [and] is afraid of being found out. He has not turned up [to our last meeting] although he replied to my letter with regard to some reference I made to religion.[23]

A man in his thirties from Carrick was reported to be having 'difficulties with some very close Christian friends who have pestered him to find out what was "wrong" with him and then being shocked when he declared himself to be gay!' The volunteer added with resignation that the client was problematic to deal with as he presented with 'the usual fundamentalist difficulties that is [*sic*] very difficult to argue with'.[24] Report entries such as 'Mother has cancer, family are born-again Christians – they guilt trip him';[25] or "[he] is a Christian living at home with his parents. His Christianity has created problems in dealing with his sexuality";[26] or "[he] is a Christian and gay, & closeted, interested in meeting other gay Christians"[27] represent the kind of issues around religion and clients' homosexuality and illuminate the range of 'fundamentalist difficulties' the volunteer was referring to. Another volunteer's report commented, on meeting with a male client in his thirties, that '[he] has been living a "good" Christian celibate life due to his erroneous belief that Christianity and homosexuality don't meet. But there's hope for him yet… Praise the Lord … Had a short chat re: the Biblical position regarding homosexuality'.[28] The problems created by religious guilt not only affected clients seeking help for their sense of desperation and isolation. It is also clear from their comments that Cara Friend's 'out' lesbian and gay volunteers were as deeply affected themselves by the religious scene in Northern Ireland as their clients. It also became necessary for the service to provide specialist denominational help because gay clients troubled by religious issues often requested that they discuss their problem with volunteers from their own side of the religious divide.

While the vast majority of clients who contacted Cara Friend were men, women did contact the service, and Cara Friend developed its own women's volunteer networks. The Cara Friend annual report for 1976 suggested that 'the low percentage of women who contact Cara Friend is partly, we think, due to the general oppression of women's sexuality; many gay women may also get married since this is easier than trying to find a female partner'.[29] But the few letters from women that do give details about their lives reveal an even greater sense of isolation, ambiguity and religiously orientated guilt about their sexual feelings than the male correspondents. A young woman from Donaghdee wrote:

> I have never been able to approach other girls or talk to anybody as they probably would be shocked and appalled. I brought the subject up in front of my parents and they thought that homosexuals should be shot so I decided not to tell them that I was. I have nobody to talk to about my problem, and sometimes I get that frustrated and lonely I want to be dead. I have tried to do that and couldn't even do it properly.[30]

It is significant that most of the women that contacted Cara Friend were married (as indeed were a good deal of the male correspondents). One report noted that '[She] is married with three children. Had been having a relationship with a woman for two years but has ended recently. Basically she just wanted someone to talk to and seemed very glad we were here'.[31] Another report noted that '[She] has been married for seven years – has two kids and is not sure if she is gay or not. Says sex with her husband means nothing… Has thought of having sex with other women but feels because of religious upbringing that she would never be able to actually <u>do</u> it'.[32] Nonetheless, the organizers of Cara Friend stated that women, once they contacted the service, were far more likely to 'follow up' after first contact with a befriending meeting and networking than most of the men. As the first annual report stated, 'where a year ago there were very few gay women in contact in Belfast, there is now an established Sappho group, many of its members having made contact through Cara Friend'.

Issues of gender variance do appear occasionally in the service's files, but these individuals were arguably the most isolated of all Cara Friend's correspondents and clients. In the annual reports from the early years of the service, issues of gender variance did not even have a category in the breakdown of the kinds of clients who contacted the service. One individual, who did not disclose whether they were cross-dressing male to female, or female to male, wrote: 'I am a transvestite and am eager to meet other people like myself. Is there any place where people like me frequent or could you put me in touch with someone?' Cara Friend put this individual in touch with 'some transvestites' who were running their own 'TV/TS group' ('transvestites and transsexuals') in Belfast.[33] Another individual wrote:

> I am in total desperation of my plight. For ten years now I have been very attracted to other men and I also have an uncontrollable urge to dress up in women's clothes. I hope you can help me as it has got to the stage of me contemplating suicide. Could you please reply to my work address as I would not want my wife and children to find out about this.[34]

Whether lesbian, gay, bisexual or transgender, Cara Friend, with very few resources and a small number of highly dedicated volunteers, provided a lifeline of contact and information for LGBTQ people in the province, a service it continues to provide to this day.

Save Ulster from Sodomy!

Northern Ireland is unique in Europe for the intensity, and also the repeated historical cyclicality, of popular evangelical revivals among its many Protestant denominations. Many Ulster Protestants are not only premillennial in belief, emphasis and worldview but regard Ulster as the new Jerusalem, and the last bastion of true Christianity in what they regard as an apostate, amillennial and atheist Europe. Emotions of guilt for the evangelical premillennialists were, and still are, characterized by actions and feelings of shame for what they regard as toleration of sin, especially sexual sin, within society. After all, they expect the Second Coming imminently. For Ulster's premillennial 'ultras', the 'Save Ulster from Sodomy!' campaign of the 1970s accorded well with this worldview. It is impossible, in either urban or rural settings, not to be confronted with moralistic biblical exhortations as many Protestant evangelical denominations use billboards, advertising on public transport and vocal 'crusades' in public spaces to target LGBTQ people. No LGBTQ individual, then or now, can avoid this form of evangelizing in Northern Ireland and being subject to some form of hostile moralistic evangelically inspired messaging is a daily and ubiquitous negotiation throughout the locale.

Targeting LGBTQ people and their organizations would, in this set of beliefs, induce the 'End Times' and hasten the Second Coming of Christ. Of course, not all of Ulster's Protestants either participated in evangelical revivals or joined in directly with the 'Save Ulster from Sodomy!' campaign (Figure 1).[35] Although evangelically inspired campaigns in Northern Ireland have at their root an intense and virulent hostility to the Roman Catholic Church and to Catholics, campaigns such as 'Save Ulster from Sodomy!' and also the continued illegality of abortion in the province until March 2020, paradoxically, were given tacit, and sometimes explicit, support by the Roman Catholic hierarchy and by other, more moderate, Protestant denominations in the province. Patriarchy, the heteronormative family and the dominance of men and traditional gender relations explain to some extent the 'coming together' of historically opposing forces on questions such as LGBTQ rights or women's rights over their own bodies. In direct corollary with its religiosity, Northern Ireland's society is unique in the context of Western Europe in the intensity and the extent of its homophobic attitudes. In a huge research project into bigotry in Western countries conducted in 2007, out of the twenty-three countries surveyed including the United States, Northern Ireland was the most homophobic country surveyed, along with Greece.[36]

The 'Save Ulster from Sodomy!' campaign was started in the early 1970s by the DUP and headed by its political and religious leader, the late Reverend Ian Paisley, initially

Figure 1 Gay activist Tarlach MacNiallais wearing a 'Save Sodomy from Ulster' t-shirt outside Queen's University Belfast Students' Union in October 1983. Courtesy of the *Belfast News Letter*

based in County Down.[37] By this time, Paisley's breakaway denomination, The Free Presbyterians of Ulster, had adherents and churches across the rural areas east of the River Bann and in urban centres such as Belfast and Lisburn. This reach allowed for a concerted and persistent campaign, which promoted itself as a religious crusade, and lasted for over a decade. No one in Northern Ireland could be in any doubt whatsoever as to the position of the DUP on the matter of homosexuality and decriminalization. Material from a pamphlet by one of the campaign organizers, Alan Kane, a DUP local government councillor, stated explicitly the DUP's view on homosexuality:

> The opposition of the DUP to the legalisation of homosexuality in Northern Ireland is based on the grounds that such a detrimental move cannot be justified from any moral or Christian perspective and that it is contrary to the moral beliefs… of the overwhelming majority of people in Northern Ireland.[38]

Kane was of course far from incorrect in his assessment of the majority view, on both sides of the sectarian divide, and the religious basis of this view.

It is easy from outside of Northern Ireland to dismiss this religious rhetoric as that of the crank. But in Northern Ireland, the evangelical rhetoric of the DUP's campaign was no joke, and it was taken seriously by most people. It must be borne in mind the extent to which the Orange Order Lodges (of which there are 1,500 across the province) and unionist politics in general were at their core dominated by evangelically inspired politicians and ministers of religion, and this cannot be underestimated in this context. By the early 1980s, the leadership of the 'Save Ulster from Sodomy!' campaign was headed by Peter Robinson MP, recent First Minister of Northern Ireland.

'Save Ulster from Sodomy!' organized demonstrations, signed petitions in the hundreds of thousands and ran a continual campaign in the form of a crusade in the public space of the media and the streets. Significantly, the 'Save Ulster from Sodomy!' campaign also orchestrated waves of letter writing by the general public to the Secretary of State for Northern Ireland – the Northern Ireland Office files contain hundreds of these letters. It is remarkable that, at the height of the Troubles, with Northern Ireland riven by sectarian violence and hatred, people in Northern Ireland were confronted also with the lurid imagery evoked by the tone of the 'Save Ulster from Sodomy!' campaign. Its insistence on the use of the word 'sodomy' in all campaign materials meant that, at the least, the general populace could do little other than associate LGBTQ people with acts of anal sex between men. In Britain, anti-homosexuality had been characterized historically by silence and a lack of nomenclature, for fear of advertising the existence of the phenomena.[39] The campaign in Northern Ireland was unique, certainly in this period, for its unequivocal and strident use of the word 'sodomy'. The term was targeted primarily at gay men. In a highly masculinist society, the social and cultural ramifications of male homosexuality and the challenge to the traditional patriarchal family were perceived as all the greater. But the campaign also applied the concept of 'sodomy' in a much more traditional, pre-modern sense to attack and target what it regarded as unnatural, non-procreative sex and sexuality in general, including that between women.

LGBTQ lives and Northern Ireland's politics

The move to recall the Northern Ireland Assembly in 2019, in order to block or veto legislation that recognized LGBTQ equalities, was met with general incomprehension outside Northern Ireland. However, examination of evidence of LGBTQ lives in the 1970s and 1980s demonstrates the historicity of the intensely virulent and activist nature of anti-LGBTQ organizations in the province. The petition for recall in 2019 was led by Baroness O'Loan, a socially conservative and anti-abortion Roman Catholic and cross-bench peer, and signed by twenty-seven DUP Members of the Legislative Assembly of Northern Ireland (MLAs), plus the Ulster Unionist Party (UUP) leader at the time, Robin Swann, and two other UUP MLAs, along with the leader of the Traditional Unionist Voice, Jim McAllister. The main nationalist party, Sinn Fein, along with the Alliance Party, the Green Party, and the People before Profit party all refused to participate in the recall. Arlene Foster, the leader of the Democratic Unionist Party, even attempted to have the assembly's rules suspended to allow the bill to be introduced, in spite of the lack of cross-community representation present – a move which was blocked by the DUP speaker. In the end, the DUP-led stance in the assembly was widely condemned, not least within Northern Ireland. As Stephen Farry, at the time an Alliance Party MLA, stated, 'I am profoundly uncomfortable that the first time people are making an effort to have the assembly reconvened is to discuss how we can deny people rights.'[40] Dismissed as a DUP-led political stunt designed to appeal to that party's ultra-conservative and religious base, the assembly's recall lasted for no more than an hour and ended with the DUP staging a dramatic walkout when it could not get its way. The Westminster legislation to legalize same-sex marriage and abortion became law.

At the point of their dramatic walkout, the DUP appeared reactionary and ultra-socially conservative in their stance on marriage equality and women's reproductive rights. Other unionist parties in the assembly barely appeared less so, given they had supported the petition for recall on these grounds. Conversely, Sinn Fein, which had first attempted to achieve marriage equality in the Northern Ireland Assembly at Stormont in 2015, appeared socially progressive on the issues of marriage equality and abortion in 2019 and applied the party whip on both issues. Other parties, such as the UUP, the Social Democratic and Labour Partly (SDLP) and Alliance, remained ambivalent on these major social issues in Northern Ireland; the parties adopted a 'conscience clause' and did not whip elected representatives. Certainly, in comparison to mainstream political parties in Britain, all other unionist politicians in Northern Ireland appeared hostile or at best timid on the issues and therefore not contrasting greatly with the highly reactionary and deeply offensive backdrop of the DUP's hard-line stance, with its twenty-seven MLA members whipped to vote against any relaxation in Northern Ireland's near-total criminalization of abortion or the implementation of same-sex marriage. This was in spite of significant and very public campaigns within Northern Ireland to amend these laws within the province – the Love Equality campaign for marriage equality, and Alliance for Choice, Amnesty International UK and the Family Planning Association in regard to women's reproductive rights. The campaigns in Northern Ireland reflected a rapid and convincing swing in public opinion in the province today in favour of implementation of same-sex marriage and liberalization of the abortion laws.

Hostility in regard to these issues has been a persistent feature of nationalist politics and political parties too. Of course, Sinn Fein's stance in this milieu has shifted rapidly and beyond recognition in a handful of years. This was due to the referenda in the Republic of Ireland that voted for marriage equality in 2015 and also in 2018 the repeal of Clause 8 of the Irish constitution, which introduced decriminalized abortion for the first time in the Republic. Sinn Fein had been far from in the vanguard for action or progressivism in either of these areas, reflecting the religiously orientated social conservatism of most of its voters and members. The SDLP, which had been the majority nationalist party before the Belfast Peace Agreement in 1998, also had an abysmal track record in regard to its support of LGBTQ rights and women's reproductive rights in the province. Indeed, in the 1970s and 1980s, the Belfast Gay Liberation Society and the Northern Ireland Gay Rights Association (NIGRA) had had long running battles with the SDLP to persuade them to take any notice of LGBTQ rights and homosexual law reform at all. At their party conference in 1977, the SDLP 'overwhelmingly' opposed any changes in the abortion laws in Northern Ireland, but declared that to oppose bringing the law with regard to male homosexuality in line with England and Wales would be to 'align the party with Ian Paisley's "Save Ulster from Sodomy!" campaign and the party had to maintain its tradition of supporting civil rights'.[41] The SDLP's decision not to oppose homosexual law reform in the 1970s and early 1980s was sectarian, rather than a reflection of the liberalization of attitudes in its ranks towards gay men. Indeed, the sectarian division on 'civil rights' between the SDLP and the DUP is to this day a spurious one, as both parties have appeared as 'united' on the issue of keeping abortion criminal in Northern Ireland, and many SDLP members of the Northern Ireland Legislative Assembly had either voted to veto or abstained from voting, in the numerous marriage equality bills in the assembly up to the collapse of power sharing in 2017. In October 2019, the SDLP still declared itself a 'pro-life' anti-abortion party. Colum Eastwood, the SDLP leader, criticized the petition for recall; nonetheless, SDLP MLAs attended the recalled assembly and likewise staged a dramatic walkout after their refusal to participate in the election of a new speaker.

Northern Ireland, including urban centres such as Belfast and Derry/Londonderry, has proven to be one of the most hostile locales for LGBTQ people in the developed world. Indeed, within the UK, Northern Ireland's sectarianized, religiously conservative society and devolution in areas such as family law has more or less guaranteed that the assembly at Stormont would resist progressive legislation. This places Northern Ireland in sharp contrast and opposition to the other nations of the UK in regard to LGBTQ rights and reproductive rights. In a society riven by male-dominated violence and religiously orientated political and social antagonism, LGBTQ people at the very least have been wary about exploring their sexuality, and certainly emotions of guilt shaped and directed their lives, freedom of action and sense of agency. For many LGBTQ people, the only way to lead 'out' normal lives has been to leave Northern Ireland.[42] In terms of gender and masculinities, the 'Save Ulster from Sodomy!' campaign ensured that the Christian, heteronormative family and patriarchal values were most stridently promoted as the only acceptable expression of sexuality in the province. Indeed, the DUP's persistent vetoing of the marriage equality bill in recent years, and the ambivalence on the question of LGBTQ equalities among unionist politicians in general, as well as within the SDLP, is evidence of their persistent legacy among Northern Ireland's politicians to this day, whether those politicians be men or women. This all reminds us of the need to regionalize and localize queer lives in Northern Ireland in order to trace their distinctive historical trajectories within particular contexts of politics, religions and sectarianism.

Notes

1 Claire Mitchell, *Religion, Identity and Politics in Northern Ireland: Boundaries of Belonging and Belief* (Aldershot: Ashgate, 2006), 3. Mitchell adapts Philippe Bourdieu's concept of 'habitus', or culturally specific ways of thinking about the world and acting within it. Pierre Bourdieu, *The Logic of Practice* (Cambridge: Cambridge University Press, 1990).

2 See Mitchell, *Religion, Identity and Politics*, especially chapters 6 and 7, 'Religious ideology and politics', and 'Theology and politics'; also Patrick Mitchel, *Evangelicalism and National Identity in Ulster 1921–1998* (Oxford: Oxford University Press, 2003).

3 See Sean Brady, 'Why examine men, masculinities and religion in Northern Ireland?', in *Men, Masculinities and Religious Change in Twentieth-Century Britain*, ed. Lucy Delap and Sue Morgan (Basingstoke: Palgrave Macmillan, 2013), 218–51. Steve Bruce, *God Save Ulster! The Religion and Politics of Paisleyism* (Oxford: Clarendon Press, 1986), 151; and Mitchell, *Religion, Identity and Politics*, 28. Protestant evangelizing in Ulster receives significant funding from Fundamentalist Christian organizations in the United States. But politicized religious groups in Ulster, such as the Free Presbyterians, differ sharply from their American counterparts in that they will not work with conservative Catholics or conservative Jews in pursuit of their political objectives.

4 Thomas Hennesey, *A History of Northern Ireland 1920–1996* (Dublin: Gill & Macmillan, 1997); Diane Urquhart, *Women in Ulster Politics 1890–1940* (Newbridge: Irish Academic Press, 2000); Patrick Buckland, *Irish Unionism: Two: Ulster Unionism and the Origins of Northern Ireland 1886–1922* (New York: Harper & Row, 1973).

5 See Brady, 'Why examine men, masculinities and religion in Northern Ireland?', 218–51.

6 Ibid., 245.

7 Ibid., 219.

8 Fidelma Ashe, 'Gendering war and peace: Militarized masculinities in Northern Ireland', *Men and Masculinities*, 15, no. 3 (2012): 231–2.

9 See Louise Pawley, 'Brighton beach: Pleasures and politics of queer community, 1950–1994', chapter 8; and Alan Butler, 'Taking pride in Plymouth's Past', chapter 9 in this volume.

10 Public Record Office of Northern Ireland (PRONI), HSS/13/32/16, Cara Friend first Annual Report 1974–1975, 4–5. I am very appreciative of the special access given to me by archivists at PRONI to the Cara Friend archive, which is closed.

11 PRONI, HSS/13/32/16, Cara Friend second Annual Report 1975–1976, 1.

12 Ibid., 8.
13 Ibid., 8.
14 Ibid., 8–9.
15 'Police deny hounding Ulster homosexuals', *Belfast Telegraph*, 14 May 1976; 'Students plan gay rights action week', *The Guardian,* 10 May 1976. PRONI, D3762/1/10/1.
16 PRONI, D/3762/1/3/3, *NIGRA News*, September/October 1976, 3.
17 PRONI, D/3762/1/3/3, *NIGRA News*, March/April 1978, 2.
18 PRONI, Cara Friend archive, D4437/2/1-6, 6 August 1975.
19 PRONI, Cara Friend archive (befriending report files), D4437/2/11, 3 January 1975.
20 PRONI, D4437/2/12, 8 January 1975.
21 PRONI, D4437/2/7, 27 February 1977.
22 PRONI, D4437/2/7, 17 June 1981.
23 PRONI, D4437/2/12, 1 May 1975.
24 PRONI, D4437/7/4, 25 January 1989.
25 PRONI, D4437/7/4, 21 October 1988.
26 PRONI, D4437/7/4, 26 July 1988.
27 PRONI, D4437/7/1, 24 September 1979.
28 PRONI, D4437/7/1, 12 April 1978.
29 PRONI, HSS/13/32/16, Cara Friend second Annual Report 1975–1976, 3.
30 PRONI, D4437/2/18, 26 March 1983. Underlining in correspondent's letter.
31 PRONI, D4437/2/18, 17 February 1983.
32 PRONI, D4437/2/18, 24 January 1980. Underlining in report entry.
33 PRONI, D4437/2/1, 25 May 1975, with reply from Cara Friend on 13 September 1975.
34 PRONI, D4437/2/7, 19 June 1978.
35 See Mitchell, *Religion, Identity and Politics.*
36 Marian Duggan, *Queering Conflict: Examining Lesbian and Gay Experiences of Homophobia in Northern Ireland* (London: Routledge, 2012), 27. A European Union Equality Commission report in 2009 bears out the findings of the 2007 research cited by Duggan.
37 See Richard Jordan, *The Second Coming of Paisley: Militant Fundamentalism and Ulster Politics* (Syracuse: Syracuse University Press, 2013).
38 Public Record Office of Northern Ireland (PRONI), D/3762/1/11/5.
39 See Sean Brady, *Masculinity and Male Homosexuality in Britain 1861–1913* (Basingstoke: Palgrave Macmillan, 2005).
40 'DUP to return to Stormont to protest against abortion rights', Rory Carroll, *The Guardian 21 Oct 2019.*
41 PRONI, D/3762/1/3/3, *NIGRA News*, December 1977, 2.
42 Daryl Leeworthy, 'Rainbow crossings. Gay Irish migrants and LGBT politics in 1980s' London', *Studi Irlandesi: A Journal of Irish Studies* 10 (2020): 79–99.

4

Queer transplanting from the Himalayas to Yorkshire: Reginald Farrer's loves for men and alpine plants (1880–1920)

Dominic Janes

The death at the age of forty of the prominent writer and plant hunter Reginald Farrer in 1920 was not simply of concern to his own family and the botanical community.[1] Gardening was a passion shared by huge numbers of British people ensuring that books such as Farrer's *My Rock-Garden* (1908) were widely read and admired. Plant hunters were also popular celebrities whose exploits were celebrated as evidence of British scientific endeavour and physical endurance. He is remembered today for having done much to popularize the cultivation of alpine plants, but his life and work had a wider cultural significance than was apprehended even in the days of his fame.

Farrer was not intent on simply studying and collecting botanical specimens from the Alps and the Himalayas. He was also in love with the plants whom he termed 'the perverse little people of the hills'.[2] As indicated by the title of another of his books, *Among the Hills: A Book of Joy in High Places* (1911), it was only among such 'children of the hills' that he felt emotionally fulfilled.[3] Farrer regularly anthropomorphized the objects of his passion. Talking as other imperial Englishmen might have done of an admired human tribe, he labelled saxifrages as a 'glorious race'. Of *Saxifraga lilacina* (lilac alpine saxifrage), to give just one example, Farrer recorded that 'this year he bloomed in character, and I have never in all my life seen a more exquisite creature'.[4] That he thought of these plants as children on the cusp of puberty can be deduced from his remark on male and female flowers that a floral Romeo 'can fertilize Juliet and cause her to conceive'.[5] Such adolescent loveliness could bring on a state of ecstasy which implicitly had sexual overtones, as when Farrer confides in his readers that 'I grow stark drunk on the scent of the Cluster-Narcissus. It gives me a pleasure so sharp and deep as almost to be wicked, and an agony'.[6]

The nearest Farrer came to publicly declaring his love was for the plants that he anthropomorphized and addressed as male. One such was an elusive plant called *Eritrichium nanum* (alpine forget-me-not). Will he find him again, Farrer wondered, among the mist and scree? 'Ah, *Eritrichium* is near! Down, beating heart!… How the minutes pulse agonizingly by, growing into a sort of abscess of suspense, to break in a moment into the full rapture of relief…' as the two were reunited.[7] The bright blue 'eyes' of this flower were widely admired by connoisseurs but *The Times's* reviewer of Farrer's *In a Yorkshire Garden* (1909) warned the 'fanatical lover' to be wary of 'that beauty that tempts some gardeners like the sirens' song'.[8] This suggests that it was the plant hunter, rather than the objects of his passion, that was eccentric and perverse.

Farrer's life story ranges across Britain from London and Oxford to Yorkshire and Scotland. His travels took him widely across Europe and Asia. In the process he popularized the notion that people across rural, suburban and urban Britain could create exotic landscapes in miniature in their own back gardens. His work implied that the limitations of place – topographic, climatic, cultural and perhaps even sexual –

Figure 2 Reginald Farrer (*c.* 1910). Farrer Papers, RJF/2/1/2/3, Royal Botanic Garden Edinburgh Library and Archives. Reproduced with permission of the Trustees of the Royal Botanic Garden Edinburgh.

could be transcended by passion and devotion. This chapter will follow Farrer across the UK and on his journeys around the world. It will explore the ways in which his sexuality became entangled with the practice of transplanting alpine plants from foreign countries to Britain. In the process boundaries between human and plant were transgressed, and opportunities created through gardening to queer localities in the mother country.

Gilded youth from Oxford to Asia

Britain has hills and mountains, albeit ones of fairly modest proportions. Patriotic pride in these landscapes aligned with belief in the peoples of Britain as being marked by modesty and sobriety. The fertility of the lowlands supported an abundant and ordered population intent, it was widely assumed, on its own heterosexual reproduction. Reginald Farrer had other ideas. From a young age he looked beyond these parochial horizons towards erotic lands filled with exotic possibilities both botanical and human. He was born in London in 1880 and was the eldest son of James Anson Farrer, a barrister whose country residence was Ingleborough Hall at Clapham in the Yorkshire Dales. The Farrers were farmers who used their growing wealth to buy properties including most of the houses in the village which they sought, paternalistically, to improve. While other male members of the family focused on the work of investment and estate management, Farrer, from his early years, was fascinated by the untamed landscape of the high fells. The limestone cliffs that were a notable feature of the land behind the house were the inspiration for his early interest in rock plants.

The young boy had a harelip and was subjected to a series of unsuccessful medical operations. He was educated mostly at home and spent much time exploring the local fells. His passion for rock gardening originated at this time, but it was at Balliol College, Oxford, which he attended from 1898 to 1902, that he fell into the cultivation of aesthetic cultural tastes. He rejected the respectable evangelical pieties of his family and turned to orientalist literary expression, which he fostered through a visit in 1903 to Peking (Beijing), Korea and Japan. In so doing, he was following in the footsteps of a number of sexual fellow travellers, notably Edward Carpenter, but he then went further by converting to Buddhism.[9] All this costly self-cultivation was enabled by his access to financial support from his family. For the rest of his life Farrer took off on regular expeditions, first to the Alps and latterly to China. In the course of the First World War he joined the Ministry of Information and worked there under the novelist John Buchan, who had been his contemporary at university. He died of an infection when on a plant-hunting expedition to Burma.

Reginald Farrer was Osbert Sitwell's second cousin and the latter observed of his relation that 'I believe he was designed to shine in the world of talk and manners. With this purpose in view, he had been obliged to become highly stylized, almost affected, in his manner of conversation, since it would have been of no use to him to pretend to be ordinary'[10] The literary result was almost a stereotype of Wildean aestheticism and was pastiched as such in the pages of *Punch*.[11] In 1908 Farrer could be found opining that it was folly to say that 'plain faces can hide lovely souls. If the soul be lovely, the face must have its beauty too... nothing beautiful can ever be altogether evil'. Thus, there was hope for 'any beautiful man or woman who has ever followed desire through selfishness and treachery. For in the very fact of outward beauty lies the promise of inner good'.[12] Such attitudes stayed with him to the end, according to Sitwell, who quoted a letter sent from Burma during the 'last months' in which Farrer argued that 'there is nothing in the whole world worthwhile except the creation of beauty'.[13] He had, thus, imbibed the doctrine of art for art's sake and rigorously applied it to gardening. Growing vegetables was a utilitarian pursuit and, therefore, to him 'immoral'. By contrast 'the cultivation of a flower, that gives you no earthly reward but the solely spiritual one of completing loveliness', was essential.[14]

Farrer's fascination with Eastern mysticism was intense and sincere even though it was derived from a peculiarly Protestant British viewpoint. Roman Catholicism held a strong allure for a number of men with unorthodox sexual tastes in later nineteenth-century Britain, partly because of the freedom from the imperative to marry offered by its requirement for clerical celibacy, but also because of its aesthetic exoticism.[15] Farrer was notable for blending associations of Catholicism with Eastern religions. He was, thereby, transferring his cultural imagination from one place to another. Thus in *The Garden of Asia: Impressions from Japan* (1904) he wrote of viewing priests performing their duties in the 'chancel' of a Japanese temple in which 'their copes form, in the faint light, the effect of the east widow of Chârtres – a dim mist of kaleidoscopic splendours'.[16] His explanation for the similarity was that Catholicism had borrowed its liturgy from the East, an idea that was widespread in British Protestant circles, albeit as a slur on their Catholic opponents.[17] There are photographs of Farrer in Eastern dress, which he showed every indication of pleasure in donning (Figure 2).[18]

Four years after his time in Japan, Farrer discussed the temples of Ceylon (Sri Lanka) in much the same terms. The tooth relic of the Buddha was, we hear, kept at Kandy in a 'monstrance' and was displayed in a similar manner to the Roman Catholic Elevation of the Host. At the vital moment he observed that 'the Abbot is in ecstasy. An eager, fumbling movement, so emotional as to fail at first of its purpose, and the Holy Thing is revealed'.[19] This seems to echo, if with less textual self-assurance, the sensuous fascination of Dorian Gray, who 'loved to kneel down on the cold marble pavement, and watch the priest, in his stiff flowered vestment, slowly, and with white hands, moving aside the veil of the tabernacle'.[20] But Farrer, unlike Wilde's *homme fatal*, was uninterested in aestheticizing Christianity as can be seen from the jibe he inserted into his presentation of the *Cruciferae* family of plants (brassicas, mustards and cabbages) as uniformly ugly: 'the vast Natural Order of the Cross-bearers evidently thinks that in providing us with all our important vegetables it has done quite enough for humanity. For few other Natural Orders are horticulturally so barren of charm'.[21]

That Farrer did, however, share certain (homo)sexual tastes with Dorian Gray and, of course, with Wilde himself was made clear in what is his most substantial biography, Nicola Shulman's *A Rage for Rock Gardening: The Story of Reginald Farrer, Gardener, Writer and Plant Collector* (2001). It was, she argued, no accident that when at Oxford he set up a debating society named after Ganymede, the boy lover of Zeus.[22] Earlier garden historians had already alluded to the matter with remarks to the effect that

Farrer always idolized 'golden young men'.[23] These tastes were rarely made explicit in Farrer's own published writings but they did surface from time to time, as for instance on the occasion recounted in *On the Eaves of the World* (1917) when he took emotional leave of a favourite 'coolie'. This man, the reader is informed, was 'a rose-cheeked Adonis in the flush of sapid youth' whose person recalled the '*jeunesse dorée* of Balliol'.[24] In such passages Farrer linked the homoerotic delights of Oxford with those of the Himalayas. Because he anthropomorphized the plants he desired, his practices of transplanting to Britain brought the bloom of exotic youth to places such as his family's garden in Yorkshire. Farrer thus transformed suburban, metropolitan and domestic spaces into locales of queer desire.

While I argue that Farrer's ecstatic engagements with the botanical world were evidence of frustrated, or at least sublimated, desire, direct evidence for Farrer's same-sex love resides not in his published works but substantially in a series of letters now held at the Somerset Heritage Centre in Taunton. He wrote these to his sometime university friend Aubrey Herbert, who accompanied him to Ceylon on the RMA *Ophir* in 1907, but, perhaps with symbolic appropriateness, declined to disembark with him. Herbert was the elder son from the second marriage of the fourth Earl of Carnarvon, who had been Secretary of State for the Colonies under Lord Derby and Benjamin Disraeli, and Lord Lieutenant of Ireland under Lord Salisbury. Herbert worked in the diplomatic service, first in Tokyo and then in Constantinople, where his exploits inspired John Buchan to romanticize him as the eponymous hero of his novel *Greenmantle* (1916). Herbert married in 1910 and from the following year sat as an MP in the House of Commons. Farrer it may be noted, by contrast, never married and failed to get himself elected to Parliament on his one attempt in 1910. As a champion of Albanian nationalism Herbert was twice offered the throne of that country and he continued to interest himself in diplomacy and espionage in Turkey and the Balkans until his death from blood poisoning after a dental operation in 1923.

Many of the letters are incomplete and it seems likely that some of the more intense material has been intentionally mislaid, but what remains still evidences not simply an intense friendship but a sustained, if unrequited, love affair.[25] In one undated letter Farrer says that he has been emotionally unburdening himself to women. But, he complains, 'it is not the <u>real</u> self one gives them… one's real self always belongs to the men who <u>are closest to one</u> – To you I should sometimes like to make my wails'.[26] Another letter, dated 12 November (and assigned to 1909 in a later hand), is addressed to that 'curious and strange one' with whom Farrer says he has 'absolutely nothing in common'. Perhaps, Farrer asks Herbert, 'you have only a faint conception of how enormously I value you and revel in you and take refuge in you?'[27] And he also wrote the following:

> you are the only person that makes me at all human… I like being with you so much. I enjoy coming to life and feeling warm. But as a rule I am so chilly… But how silly to cry for moons: one is, I suppose, what one is; with no real hope of alteration: no man, by taking thought can add a cubit to his nature's nature, or put another inch or so around his heart. I wish I could fall in love again, though, with some more profitable person![28]

Literature and orientalism

The emotional landscape of Britain proved unrewarding to Farrer. His feelings for Herbert, as for other British men, went unrequited. He, therefore, developed an internal world of fantasy in which travel enabled connections with cultural, botanical and, if implicitly, sexual diversity. He succeeded in channelling his emotional energies into writing both plays and novels, but he was, of course, hampered by the dangers associated with open discussion of same-sex passion. After a youthful period of (bad) Wildean melodrama he developed a style that he might have compared optimistically to that of his literary heroine Jane Austen. A series of novels appeared that attempted to combine family romance with topical issues, as in *The House of Shadows* (1906), which laboured to explore suicide and euthanasia. The reader was asked to ponder the question of whether it was right for a person to kill himself if he had a malignant heritable disease. One possible reference of this was to sexual degeneracy since that was sometimes regarded as being passed down from generation to generation.

The Sundered Streams: The History of a Memory that Had No Full Stops (1907) was one of Farrer's livelier novelistic efforts. The central character, Kingston Darnley, was clearly based on Farrer himself. Darnley had less money than his peers at Oxford University and was much more inhibited. 'His friends', we learn, 'held the free, frank language only possible to the perfectly cleanly mind, naked and unashamed; he, for his part, was always uneasy in his nudity'.[29] Darnley, we learn, was a spiritual young man who was handsome albeit with 'an excessive personal daintiness'.[30] He was apparently very well informed on women's need for a man so as 'to feel the thrill of his virility in the deep fibres of their consciousness'. He was also well aware of his failings in relation to such matters. The only females drawn to him seem perverse in their tastes since he believes that 'it is only to the depraved woman that the saint is of personal interest and, even then, her interest is as depraved as her nature'.[31]

In due course Darnley does move on from the homosocial world of Oxford and get married, but his greatest epiphany occurs not in the marital bed but in contemplation of (masculine) nature experienced during the glorious sunrise of a morning when one yearns to be 'naked in the naked embrace of the world':

> The world stands out pure and glorious in its nudity – vivid, stainless, triumphant as the white flawlessness of the young Apollo newly risen out of the dark, formless void. The upsurging day is our emblem of youth fresh from slumber – beautiful, ardent, splendid in the clear glory of his build – before he makes haste to hide himself in the sombre trappings of convention.[32]

The visual effect of such a beautiful young man walking naked into one's bedroom can be appreciated from Leonard Raven-Hill's 'Wake Up, England!' (1916). It is an amusing coincidence that the man in bed in this cartoon, which was ostensibly all about the promotion of daylight saving, resembles Farrer (Figure 3).[33] Subsequent to this homoerotic encounter with the dawn, Darnley receives spiritual aid from a Buddhist 'bishop' before, in due time, falling into the fascinating company of a beautiful

PUNCH, OR THE LONDON CHARIVARI.—May 10, 1916.

WAKE UP, ENGLAND!

The Sun (*to Householder*). "NOW, THEN, WHY WASTE YOUR DAYLIGHT? SAVE IT AND GIVE IT TO THE COUNTRY."

[If only for the sake of economy in artificial light during War-time, the Daylight-saving scheme should have the support of all patriots.]

Figure 3 Leonard Raven-Hill, 'Wake Up, England!' *Punch* 150 (1916): 307. Reproduced courtesy of Keele University Library.

youth called Ivor Restormel.[34] An excuse for this same-sex passion is furnished by the convenient notion that Restormel possesses the reincarnated soul of a woman whom Darnley's migrant spirit had loved in a previous life.[35] On this basis, and to the understandable dismay of Darnley's wife, the youth is invited to move into the family household, where he duly becomes the best chum of their charming son Jim. All ends in tragedy when the two boys drown together.

If all this represents an inventive, if far-fetched, attempt to disguise a narrative of same-sex passion, the subsequent novel *The Ways of Rebellion* (1908) veers off into high camp. Here Farrer, in effect, turns up in glamour drag as 'Her Imperial Resplendence the Princess Anne Komnena'. This unlikely woman and Byzantine royal personage alternated between fads including a brief passion for 'Pan-Islamism...

but this enthusiasm soon waned before the attraction of botany, and in a little while Princess Anne was perlustrating the bogs and precipices of the Highlands in pursuit of rarities, while her long-suffering followers agonized behind, and wished that *Saxifraga cernua* and *Gentiana nivalis* has never been heard of'.[36] Anne's face is described as but a mask for her true feelings and she exhibits many of the other tropes of decadence.

If *The Sundered Streams* (1907) reworks Farrer's experience of Oxford, *The Ways of Rebellion* (1908) re-presents the geographies of his travels after leaving university. The novel moves between Scotland and Italy while paying due service to the 'golden splendour, the long agony and gorgeous death of the Byzantine Empire'.[37] Farrer proudly assembled over forty laudatory press-clippings for his travelogue *The Garden of Asia* (1904) from across the popular press, but the smaller collection of cuttings related to his fictional works provides eloquent testimony to the comparative public indifference to his novels.[38] It seems that his histrionic style was found incongruous when applied in British novelistic settings but was regarded as appropriate for travel narratives of the 'Orient'. It was thus only by combining his passion for exotic plants, travel and for writing that he was able to achieve popular success.

A parallel for Reginald Farrer's oriental, botanical and sexual interests is provided by the horticultural pursuits and literary legacy of Maurice Maria, self-styled Comte de Mauny-Talvande. De Mauny first came to public attention for having set up a school in France which – the presence of his English (and only subsequently estranged) wife notwithstanding – swiftly became associated with rumours of immorality.[39] The couple had a son who served in the First World War, and it was this experience that appears to have inspired De Mauny's first book, *The Suffering of Youth, 1914–1918* (1919). Such suffering was, apparently, what brought forth mature (and exquisite) manhood just as 'the gentian, of such striking and beautiful blue, from which it borrows its name, grows in hard, clayish soil, almost in the snow... [and the] rarest of lilies, black with golden tassels, is only to be found in the poisonous marshes of the Chinese frontier. Yet they are amongst the most beautiful and rarest flowers'.[40] Aesthetic forging in the military would not, however, benefit all sons. Pity one who had a 'father who would not study your nature and temperament... and crushed you as he would a flower in the bud, because you were a "Hybrid", different from the common everyday type'.[41] But the boy who enjoys parental understanding may seek and find a special friend older than himself who is modelled on his father.[42]

De Mauny's erotic fantasies seem, thus, to have blurred the boundaries between the generations and even between parents and lovers. It is hardly surprising, therefore, that, as he explains in *Gardening in Ceylon* (1921), the East was also a source of queer delight: of the 1100 'coolies' on a tea estate 'we are bound to find a treasure'.[43] 'I love this race of children', he wrote in *The Gardens of Taprobane* (1937); 'I love their innate, almost feminine distinction... The honey-colour of their skin, the bright colours of their clothes, harmonize with their surroundings; the greens of the tropical vegetation, the gold of the sands, the blue of sky and sea'.[44] In this account of his own island garden just off the coast of Ceylon, de Mauny explains that his gardener, Raman, and 'the garden are two in one; I cannot think of one without thinking of the other, and to-day, after eight years, they are both in the prime of youth'.[45]

There is much to abhor in these texts, redolent as they are with imperialism, racism, orientalism and paedophile eroticism, but they are significant as a comparator for Farrer's own works because of the way in which de Mauny's erotic gaze shifts back and forth between boys and flowers seen as natives and as transplants. The local plants, like their human proxies, served as objects of the admiring gaze of the colonial masters.[46] Supposedly primitive peoples could be understood as being at one and the same time close to their own erotic urges and teasingly childlike in their lack of adult inhibition.[47] When our attention shifts from Farrer's fictional writings to his series of books about plant-hunting in Asia, we can see his fascination in the exotic delights of the lands that he is describing, even if his passion for men is sublimated into his hunt for plants. This aspect of Farrer's work can be situated in relation to the ways in which erotic experiences and same-sex desires were layered into various aspects of the colonial experience.[48] Jill Dildur, however, has argued for a more positive appreciation of his legacy on the grounds that he was not an imperial supremacist but a man who employed forms of orientalist romanticization which did not rely on the crudest levels of stereotyping. It is notable that Farrer's own time in Ceylon does not seem to have produced much erotic or floral enthusiasm.[49] His particular mission was to transplant finds from cool high-altitude locations such as the Himalayas to a country (Great Britain) that was cool because of its high latitude. Farrer's geographical Other was, to some degree, more like an equal partner to Britain because it was climatically similar to it and thus coded as more masculine than the tropical lowlands. Furthermore, he critiqued the British homeland and sought to improve it by importing foreign plants, an act which Dildur identified as positive 'transculturation'. This resulted in what might be termed a queering – though she does not use this term – which promoted 'a general unsettling of the edges of colonial and national attitudes toward alterity'.[50]

De Mauny's writings are much more clearly decadent than those of Farrer. While the Anglophone Frenchman remained an obscure figure, Farrer rose to popular fame in Britain. Their erotic interests seem to have been related, but it seems that only the latter was able to speak to a wider constituency of readers. A possible explanation for why that was emerges from consideration of what Anne Helmreich has referred to as the 'conundrum of the aesthetic garden'.[51] She argues that popular gardening in early-twentieth-century Britain was torn between the desire of the middle classes for fashionable living and their concern not to appear self-indulgent or immoral. To that end the pursuit of beauty had to be combined with the effortful labour of planning and maintaining the garden in association with scientific interest in plants and the technicalities of their origins and cultivation. The diverse plantings of the Edwardian garden could thus appear as the evidences not of decadent accumulation but of British mastery over the imperatives of distance and climate. Through strenuous treks in hazardous conditions Reginald Farrer brought home seeds that, when germinated, furthered domestic fantasies of imperialist mastery by enabling his readers to behold the floral wonders of the Alps and the Himalayas in their backyards. But in the process the modest and sober landscapes of his native land were queerly aestheticized by the transplanted exotics that he brought home.

Hunting men and plants in the Himalayas

While de Mauny admired his tropical plants and boys, Farrer sought manly companions with whom to experience mountain highs. Of course, the avowed intention of plant-hunting expeditions was scientific, as he wrote in 1915 to excuse his absence, at that point, from war service.[52] Farrer, therefore, aimed to secure a botanically trained British companion for his Himalayan expeditions, but his personal motivations were tangled up with his erotic and emotional sensibility. For his 1914 journey he sought out William Purdom for the expertise on China that he had acquired as a plant hunter in the region after spending time at the Royal Botanic Gardens, Kew. He was the same age as Farrer and also – and perhaps not co-incidentally – 'tall and lean of magnificent Nordic physique.'[53] It was to be another case of unrequited love. Farrer's account of this time, published posthumously as *The Rainbow Bridge* (1921), was quirkily assigned thus:

Still
To Bill
It is my will
This Book is dedicated.

Although
I know
The Press will go
And say it's overstated.[54]

The dedication, of which he says his publishers disapproved, was to 'my beloved companion, Purdom, whom we will henceforth allow ourselves the freedom of knowing as Bill.'[55] And it was in Bill's company, if not with his direct participation, that Farrer experienced what he recorded as his most sublime ecstasies. His very prose begins to fall apart as he describes an ascent in the Tibetan borderlands as a state of 'agonizing with height and ecstasy... delirious in the vista of marvellous peaks all round me, swimming with silvery vapours, and blinding in the unmitigated glory of virgin snow.'[56] Farrer's vision slides in and out of focus between his companion, the sherpas and the 'fantastic pinnacles of dolomite jetting up from the slopes in phallic towers with streaming flanks of wetness in the sunshine.'[57] He would not find a wife or children to take his name, but in such places he found and proudly depicted new species of plant that would do so. He thus painted *Primula farreri* upright, blooming and beautiful among the phallic thrusting of mountain pinnacles.[58] A few years later Purdom's sister wrote to Farrer of their shared admiration for William, saying that she had repeatedly urged her brother to answer his many letters. Occasionally he did so, joking about the old days when Farrer was wont to call him Seductive Bill because of his charm.[59]

Purdom elected to stay in China and Farrer looked elsewhere for scientific advice and companionship. Euan H. M. Cox, who was seventeen years younger than Farrer, came with him on his final expedition in 1919–20. Scion of a jute-manufacturing family from Dundee, Cox went to Rugby School and then to Cambridge University before serving in the First World War. Invalided out of the army, he became John Buchan's secretary and duly met Farrer. The Cox/Farrer collaboration was neither as botanically successful nor as emotionally enjoyable as the Purdom/Farrer one. It seems that Farrer was sometimes depressed and often drunk. However, this picture of unhappiness is complicated by a set of letters that turned up at auction in 2008 and which are now housed in the Farrer Archive at the Royal Botanic Garden Edinburgh, where they are stored along with the main set of Farrer family papers. But while the latter are substantially composed of discreet letters of Reginald to this mother, these additional materials, dated 1919–20, are quite different in tone. Their recipient is not identified, but on internal evidence the most likely candidate appears to be Ernest Frederick Gye, who was one year older than Farrer.

Gye's father was a theatrical impresario and his mother, Dame Emma Albani, was an opera singer. Gye entered the British Foreign Office in 1903 and made his way slowly, and obscurely, up the ranks. He was a man of literary and musical interests who never married and, assuming that he has been correctly identified as the recipient of these letters, seems to have been a flamboyantly camp homosexual. He is addressed as 'poison', or 'venom', presumably because he exudes unhealthy vice, by Farrer who signs himself 'poppet'. The camp banter which composes these letters gives a decidedly queer complexion to Farrer's last months. It was, evidently, not only through plant-hunting and literature that Farrer attempted to displace some of his sexual frustrations at this final stage of his life.

On 8 June 1920 Farrer wrote to Herbert and his wife to ask their assistance in helping him to find a 'fair one': '"It is not good for man to live alone:" as I get along in the vale of years, I do feel the needs, the duty, the <u>rightness</u> of marriage closing in on me.'[60] Taken on its own terms, this might suggest the weariness of someone who had thought himself a confirmed bachelor even if it hardly reads like a ringing endorsement of heterosexual love. But almost a year earlier he had written to Gye to say that he had found himself yearning for a wife, but after a drink had decided this really was not what he wanted. 'Send me out Cleopatra herself in a carpet', he reported, 'and I would send her packing'.[61] Cox features in these letters under the nickname 'Jumps'. Farrer had alluded to the possible homosocial/homoerotic ambiguities of their relations in a letter to the younger man which argued that they were not sufficiently in sympathy to sustain a fellowship of the 'Achilles and Patrokles' kind.[62] To Gye he complained that, in the case of Cox, the gulf of age and social class was too great. This could be read two ways: either that these were genuine reasons for the failure of same-sex relations or that Farrer had been fantasizing that the return of his desires was possible. Whichever was the case these letters depict Cox as being in on the patter of smutty jokes and camp innuendo that Farrer was sharing with Gye. 'Jumps is at my shoulder', he wrote, at one point, 'plying me with loves for you'.[63] Furthermore they were both in the habit of referring to Cox's intended replacement in the role of Farrer's plant-hunting partner, Derek Milner, as 'Beautiful Boy' or simply 'BB'.[64]

Sadly, 'BB' never arrived due to a death in the family and Farrer looked elsewhere for at least casual companionship: 'BB has slain a sister to avoid my company, but I got off with a soldier man this morning who seems like coming with me and like being a pleasure if he does.'[65] Cox returned home where he wrote an account of his time with Farrer which he dedicated to Ernest Gye, who had given permission for (decorous) quotes from some of the plant hunter's correspondence with him.[66] Moreover, and tantalizingly, Cox was duly painted in brooding and intense mode by the homosexual painter Glyn Philpot.[67] All this notwithstanding Cox went on to marry. By contrast the comment of [Elizabeth] Bettina Varè, the wife of an Italian diplomat in Peking, that 'I remember your reason for liking China was no women and no music' suggests that Farrer's interests were both fixed and widely known.[68]

The Gye letters bring to the last months of Farrer's life a flavour of that aspect of Ronald Hyam's *Empire and Sexuality: The British Experience* (1990), which explored the diversity of ways in which the British Empire operated as a field of sexual opportunity.[69] Farrer, however, was not having a terribly gay time in either sense of the word. He continued to cruise the streets, but with mostly unsatisfactory results: 'I felt quite sad and solitary; nor have my street walkings here proved either persevering or productive, though the flesh has been most willing. A little man in the soldier's band has smiled at me, and that is the limit of my successes.'[70] In some ways he was – and seems to have felt himself to be – a failure. And yet that cannot have been a surprise to him since he had written in *In a Yorkshire Garden* (1909) that

> monstrosities, such as double daffodils, and geniuses, and militant suffragettes, are usually brief and evanescent phenomena, aborted variations from the race, that soon die out, of mingled weakness and sterility.
>
> That is the price that Nature imposes on genius and all such abnormalities, while a comfortable and perennial continuance is the consolation with which she rewards the normal, the typical, the conventional.[71]

Farrer's impact in Britain

Life in remote areas was a risky business. Many of Farrer's fellow plant hunters failed to pass middle age. He appears to have suffered an acute infection, perhaps diphtheria, which was aggravated by excessive drinking. When news of his demise in 1920 on the border of Burma and China reached the mother country, it provoked a mixed reaction. While his contributions to horticulture were widely acknowledged, his literary style came in for considerable criticism. The plant hunter Frank Kingdon-Ward found him 'guilty of hyperbole and extravagant language'.[72] *The Gardeners' Chronicle* identified him as the most 'picturesque' plant hunter who irritated those who looked towards botanical science rather than aesthetic appreciation.[73] And it was noted elsewhere that 'he wrote, as a rule, from a peculiar angle of his own, giving queer human attributes to his plants'.[74] He was, it seems, too much the amateur dilettante who might climb a mountain complete with 'a thunderstorm, hail, *Geranium argenteum*, and Asti Spumante at the top'.[75]

Nevertheless, his physical accomplishments were understood as, to some extent, making up for his personal effeminacy and sexual deviance. He was admired for that 'grit which brought a man of such comparatively frail physique through such difficulties and dangers'.[76] His service during the war, even though it had been brief and had not involved active military duty, was mentioned with appreciation. This redeemed even his Buddhism once 'his sense of patriotism awoke and swamped every political and ethical theory he ever had'.[77] Seen at a century's remove the life and work of Reginald Farrer continue to be of importance in the history of plant collecting and horticulture, but they also can tell us about some of the ways in which same-sex desire was displaced not merely onto homosocial friendships but also onto relations with the natural world. Farrer's obsession with beautiful little plants reminds us of the accumulation of bibelots and dandified attention to recondite particularities of detail and aesthetic effect.[78] His masculinity was, however, buttressed by his reputation as a mountaineer and active hunter – as opposed to a passive collector – of plants.

Writing was also part of his life's work, and he regarded his literary creativity as being, by implication, associated not just with frustrated desire in general but with same-sex desire in particular: 'Every man still left alive is crammed down to bursting-point with emotions of which he must relieve himself or go mad. And if feathered females do not happen to be his chosen outlet, he gets his utterance achieved somehow else, in a book or a poem'.[79] He admired Jane Austen above all other writers, referred to her as the 'Divine' and compared himself to various of her female characters.[80] Only Sappho and 'Divine Jane' stood as women among the top ranks of art, 'both of them expressers gone astray into a woman's body, and neither of them female in their mentality at all'.[81] By saying this Farrer was giving voice to the view that they were inverts, which is to say people physically of one sex but with the mentality of the other.

It was with such individuals who, like many plants, queerly mingled male and female attributes that he felt he had most in common. He also knew that his society at large was no more tolerant of sexual eccentrics than that of the times of Jane Austen, who, as he wrote in an influential piece of literary criticism in the *Quarterly Review,* 'behind the official biographies, and the pleasant little empty letters… we feel always… lived remote in a great reserve'.[82] This was pretty much the judgement of E. H. M. Cox on Farrer: his 'was a happiness only gained by dint of great self-control' and 'he had a peculiar power of living within himself'.[83] The result of this was that 'his was not an easy character to read… [but that] when he was engaged on anything to do with plants, he was like a being transformed. Then he was direct in his emotions… But remove him from his plants, and everything was clothed'.[84] Cox was writing long before popular understanding of closeted homosexuality but he intuited the prominence of secrecy and discretion in Farrer's life and personality.

Yet some queer men did see in the veiled Farrer a sexual compatriot. One example of this was the writer Robert Gathorne-Hardy and his partner Kyrle Leng, who shared a home at Stanford Dingley in Berkshire.[85] The queerness of their gardening and plant-hunting emerges from Gathorne-Hardy's *Three Acres and a Mill* (1939), which, he declared, was 'a record of over a period of twelve years of the home and garden that I share with a friend. Many of our flowers have been collected by us abroad'.[86] The importance of rock gardening to Gathorne-Hardy is clear from the fact that one of the main changes he made after moving into his country residence was to install a giant rockery. His photograph in the volume shows him 'in the rock garden' wearing a tight t-shirt.[87] Gathorne-Hardy also highlighted, albeit in code, that Farrer had been a flamboyant homosexual: 'The debt of rock gardeners to Reginald Farrer is, of course, unlimited', we read, 'but new readers of Farrer should be given one warning. He was, we are apt to forget, a product of the aesthetic nineties'.[88]

In 1952 the wit, playwright and musician Noël Coward released one of his most famous songs: 'There Are Bad Times just around the Corner'. His lyrics parodied a range of patriotic clichés including that of England as a garden. It needed, he quipped, manuring. Coward could be seen as exemplary of a certain kind of twentieth-century homosexual man whose life was centred on the urban and the urbane. Yet he, like many of his class, maintained homes both in the city and in the country. The garden, whether in its rural or suburban incarnations, was not necessarily an adjunct only to heteronormative family life. Those who assembled collections of exquisite plants, particularly miniature ones, could be compared to men such as Lord Ronald Gower. The art historian John Potvin, in his book on the visual culture of queer unmarried men, classed this artist as a 'bachelor of a different sort' whose 'alternative masculinity' centred on the collection of art objects, trinkets and *bric-à-brac*.[89]

Michael Camille has argued for the importance of such queer material practices: 'it is not just that the unmentionable nature of same-sex desire has often meant that the subject had to communicate the "secret" in a coded language, but the fact that this language was a system of objects. What could not be said could be spoken through things'.[90] Transgressive desire was often encoded through the collection of exotics because orientalism constructed Asia as feminine and effeminate. Eastern lands offered the promise of opportunities to queer men that ranged from homosocial bonding to homosexual passion.[91] High in the Himalayas, in pursuit of narcissi as 'white and delicate as sawn ivory', the queer plant hunter could combine the manly pursuit of mountain climbing with an obsession with nature's rarest and most precious art objects.[92] Moreover, the plant hunter himself would come to be seen as a glamorous and heroic figure.

Reginald Farrer spent much of this time travelling but he repeatedly returned to the garden in Yorkshire, where he transplanted many of his exotic finds. Derek Jarman's house in Dungeness is a famous example of the purposive queering of marginal space through gardening.[93] Because Farrer was, of necessity, secretive about his sexuality, his Yorkshire garden was not constructed as an openly queer space in quite the same way. Nevertheless, the heteronormative landscape of his family's estate, centred as it was on property investment and the perpetuation of the family line, was rejected by Farrer. Parts of the rock gardens survive, albeit in a deteriorating condition, as if providing eloquent testimony to his assertion that 'genius and all such abnormalities' were doomed to die out.[94] Yet Farrer's garden was not built to last for generations but was, like Jarman's, partly a personal meditation on happiness and the transient nature of beauty. His Yorkshire rock garden was not, for Farrer, as to some extent we might see it, a place of imperialist appropriation:

> Prosperity is a physical matter, a question of comfort and Dreadnoughts [i.e. battleships] and well-padded chairs, and an untaxed breakfast-table; happiness is entirely a soul-state, quite beyond all connection with comfort; and is found, by the wise nation or the wise individual, in quiet, secret places.[95]

The magnolias that bloom in the surrounding woodland gardens each spring are a testament to a queer passion for exotic mountain plants and the men who helped him find them. But Farrer did not only queer his family's country estate, he also contributed to the queering of gardens across Britain. His example suggested that people the length of the country could find an escape from the limitations of their class origins, geographical location and repressive culture. Since, as he put it, 'in a ten-yard strip at Brixton or Balham [i.e. ordinary London suburbs] you can triumphantly enjoy a thing of beauty'.[96] Farrer did not invent the practice of making rockeries but, through books such as *The English Rock Garden* (1919), he popularized it such that it became widespread in suburbia.[97] Such interests brought with them the possibility of queer fellowship based on the shared hobby of alpine gardening and the dreams that it sustained. Whether in the town or the country, in the north or in the south, a person could build and rule his or her own miniature Shangri-La, where queer pleasures were not criminalized but embraced. Gardeners meeting fellow enthusiasts at alpine plant shows might find they had other tastes in common. As Farrer put it in the coded language of his best-selling books, if 'it be a vain fancy to find personalities in flowers, then many gardeners, I believe, staid and respectable people, are guilty, in their secret hearts, of vain, delightful fancies'.[98]

Notes

1   I thank the editors for organizing the conference at which I gave quite a different paper and for their appreciation for my subsequent enthusiasm for queer gardening. I also thank the Trustees of the Royal Botanic Garden Edinburgh for permission to include extracts from the Farrer Papers and the South West Heritage Trust in relation to the Herbert Papers.

2   Reginald Farrer, *My Rock-Garden* (London: Edward Arnold, 1908), 2.

3   Reginald Farrer, *Among the Hills: A Book of Joy in High Places* (London: Headley, 1911), 33.

4   Farrer, *My Rock-Garden*, 132.

5   Farrer, *Among the Hills*, 33.

6   Reginald Farrer, *In a Yorkshire Garden* (London: Edward Arnold, 1909), 65.

7   Farrer, *My Rock-Garden*, 257.

8   *The Times*, 'Difficult Plants', 20 November 1909, 6.

9   Anthony Copley, *A Spiritual Bloomsbury: Hinduism and Homosexuality in the Lives and Writings of Edward Carpenter, E. M. Forster, and Christopher Isherwood* (Lanham,

MD: Lexington Books, 2006), 9–105; Christopher Reed, *Bachelor Japanists: Japanese Aesthetics and Western Masculinities* (New York: Columbia University Press, 2017), 5.

10 Osbert Sitwell, *Noble Essences or Courteous Revelations: Being a Book of Characters and the Fifth and Last Volume of Left Hand, Right Hand!: An Autobiography* (London: Macmillan, 1950), 16.

11 *Punch* 127, 'Our Booking Office' (1904): 162.

12 Reginald Farrer, *Alpines and Bog Plants* (London: Edward Arnold, 1908), 75.

13 Quoted in Sitwell, *Noble Essences*, 21.

14 Farrer, *In a Yorkshire Garden*, 180.

15 Dominic Janes, *Visions of Queer Martyrdom from John Henry Newman to Derek Jarman* (Chicago: University of Chicago Press, 2015).

16 Reginald Farrer, *The Garden of Asia: Impressions from Japan* (London: Methuen, 1904), 121.

17 Farrer, *The Garden of Asia*, 122; Dominic Janes, *Victorian Reformation: The Fight over Idolatry in the Church of England, 1840–1860* (Oxford: Oxford University Press, 2009), 93–110.

18 Royal Botanic Garden Edinburgh Library and Archives, Farrer Papers, RJF/2/1/2/3, in folder of materials relating to 1910, *Reginald Farrer*, undated photograph.

19 Farrer, *My Rock-Garden*, 76.

20 Oscar Wilde, *The Picture of Dorian Gray*, ed. Camille Cauti (New York: Barnes and Noble, [1890–1891] 2003), 128.

21 Farrer, *Alpines and Bog Plants*, 61.

22 Nicola Shulman, *A Rage for Rock Gardening: The Story of Reginald Farrer, Gardener, Writer and Plant Collector* (London: Short Books, 2003), 20.

23 John L. Illingworth, 'The Correspondence of Reginald Farrer', in *Reginald Farrer: Dalesman, Planthunter, Gardener*, ed. John L. Illingworth and Jane Routh, Centre for North-West Regional Studies, Occasional Paper 19 (Lancaster: Lancaster University, 1991), 72.

24 Reginald Farrer, *On the Eaves of the World*, Vol. 2 (London: Edward Arnold, 1917b), 301. Compare Christopher Lane, *The Ruling Passion: British Colonial Allegory and the Paradox of Homosexual Desire* (Durham, NC: Duke University Press, 1995), 63.

25 Margaret Fitzherbert, *The Man Who Was Greenmantle: A Biography of Aubrey Herbert* (London: John Murray, 1983), 20.

26 Somerset Heritage Centre (SHC), Taunton, SRO DD/Her/38, Letter, Reginald Farrer to Aubrey Herbert, emphasis in original. It should be noted that many of these letters are incomplete and it appears that the assemblage was redacted at some point.

27 SHC, SRO DD/Her/38, Letter, Reginald Farrer to Aubrey Herbert. Discussed in Fitzherbert, *The Man Who was Greenmantle*, 88–9.

28 SHC, SRO DD/Her/38/2, Letter, Reginald Farrer to Aubrey Herbert.

29 Reginald Farrer, *The Sundered Streams: The History of a Memory That Had No Full Stops* (London: Edward Arnold, 1907), 44.

30 Farrer, *The Sundered Streams*, 44.

31 Ibid., 47.

32 Ibid., 89.

33 Leonard Raven Hill, 'Wake Up, England!', *Punch* 150 (1916): 307.

34 Farrer, *The Sundered Streams*, 273.

35 Ibid., 325.

36 Reginald Farrer, *The Ways of Rebellion* (London: Edward Arnold, 1908), 184.

37 Farrer, *The Ways of Rebellion*, 299.
38 Royal Botanic Garden Edinburgh Library and Archives (RBGE), RJF/2/1/6/8, Reginald Farrer, personal book of press notices.
39 Robert Aldrich, *Colonialism and Homosexuality* (London: Routledge, 2003), 66–79.
40 Maurice Maria De Mauny Talvande, *The Suffering of Youth, 1914–1918* (London: Grant Richards, 1919), 28.
41 De Mauny Talvande, *The Suffering of Youth*, 27.
42 Ibid., 26.
43 Maurice Maria De Mauny Talvande, *Gardening in Ceylon* (Colombo: H. W. Cave, 1921), 17.
44 Maurice Maria De Mauny Talvande, *The Gardens of Taprobane*, ed. Bernard Niall (London: Williams and Norgate, 1937), 23–4.
45 De Mauny Talvande, *The Gardens of Taprobane*, 68.
46 Craig Smith, 'Every man must kill the thing he loves: Empire, homoerotics, and nationalism in John Buchan's *Prester John*', *Novel: A Forum on Fiction* 28, no. 2 (1995): 187; Ruth Livesey, 'Morris, Carpenter, Wilde, and the political aesthetics of labor', *Victorian Literature and Culture* 32, no. 2 (2004): 610.
47 Neville Hoad, 'Arrested development or the queerness of savages: Resisting evolutionary narratives of difference', *Postcolonial Studies* 3, no. 2 (2000): 140.
48 Christopher Lane, *The Ruling Passion: British Colonial Allegory and the Paradox of Homosexual Desire* (Durham, NC: Duke University Press, 1995).
49 Aldrich, *Colonialism and Homosexuality*, 41–3.
50 Jill Didur, '"The perverse little people of the hills": Unearthing ecology and transculturation in Reginald Farrer's alpine plant hunting', in *Global Ecologies and the Environmental Humanities: Postcolonial Approaches*, ed. Elizabeth DeLoughrey, Jill Didur and Anthony Carrigan (New York: Routledge, 2015), 69.
51 Anne Helmreich, 'Body and soul: The conundrum of the aesthetic garden', *Garden History* 36, no. 2 (2008): 273–88.
52 Bodleian Library, University of Oxford, MS Bonham Carter 171, folio 78, Letter, Reginald Farrer to Violet Bonham Carter, 9 August 1915, 78.
53 Alice Coats quoted in William T. Stearn, 'An introductory tribute to Reginald Farrer', in *Reginald Farrer: Dalesman, Planthunter, Gardener*, 6.
54 Reginald Farrer, *The Rainbow Bridge* (London: Edward Arnold, 1921), v.
55 Farrer, *The Rainbow Bridge*, 1.
56 Ibid., 81.
57 Ibid., 82.
58 Ibid., 274.
59 RGBE/2/1/6/5, Letter, William Purdom to Reginald Farrer, 11 April [no year].
60 SHC, SRO DD/Her/38, Letter, Reginald Farrer to Aubrey Herbert, emphasis in original.
61 RBGE, RJF/4/2, folio 2, Letter, Reginald Farrer to Ernest Gye, 26 July 1919.
62 RGBE, RJF/2/1/5/13, Letter, Reginald Farrer to Euan Cox, 10 February 1920.
63 RGBE, RJF/4/3.2, Letter, Reginald Farrer to Ernest Gye, 24 September 1919.
64 Shulman, *A Rage for Rock Gardening*, 111.
65 RGBE, RJF/4/12.1, Letter, Reginald Farrer to Ernest Gye, 23 December 1919.
66 Euan H. M. Cox, *Farrer's Last Journey: Upper Burma, 1919–20* (London: Dulau, 1926), v and vii.

67   Glyn Philpot, *Euan H. M. Cox* (*c.*1930), oil on canvas, 76.2 × 64.8 cm, Scottish
      National Portrait Gallery, Edinburgh (PG 3277); J. G. P. Delaney, *Glyn Philpot: His
      Life and Work* (Aldershot: Ashgate, 1999), 90 and 100–1.

68   Letter Elizabeth Varè to Reginald Farrer, 1 November 1916, RGBE RJF/2/1/4/1; see
      Shirley Ann Smith, *Imperial Designs: Italians in China, 1900–1947* (Lanham, MD:
      Fairleigh Dickinson University Press, 2012), 100–9.

69   Ronald Hyam, *Empire and Sexuality: The British Experience* (Manchester:
      Manchester University Press, 1990), 88–114. See also Philip Holden, 'Rethinking
      colonial discourse analysis and queer studies', in *Imperial Desire: Dissident Sexualities
      and Colonial Literature*, ed. Philip Holden and Richard J. Ruppel (Minneapolis,
      MN: University of Minnesota Press, 2003), 295–321; Aldrich, *Colonialism and
      Homosexuality*, 3; Joseph Allen Boone, *The Homoerotics of Orientalism* (New York:
      Columbia University Press, 2014), 54–98.

70   RGBE RJF/4/13.2, Letter, Reginald Farrer to Ernest Gye, 26 February 1920.

71   Farrer, *In a Yorkshire Garden*, 6.

72   Frank Kingdon-Ward, 'Obituary: Reginald Farrer', *Geographical Journal* 57, no. 1
      (1921): 69. Much the same accusation was made prior to Farrer's death in *Nature* 104,
      no. 19, 'Alpine plants for rock gardens', February 1920, 664.

73   *Gardeners' Chronicle*, 'Reginald Farrer', 20 November 1920, 247.

74   Clarence Elliott, 'The late Reginald Farrer: An appreciation', *Gardeners' Chronicle*,
      January 1921, 31.

75   Elliott, 'The late Reginald Farrer', 31.

76   *The Times*, 'Mr. Reginald Farrer', 19 November 1920, 13.

77   *The Times*, 'Reginald Farrer: Traveler, botanist, and writer', 13 December 1920, 16.

78   Janell Watson, *Literature and Material Culture from Balzac to Proust: The Collection
      and Consumption of Curiosities* (Cambridge: Cambridge University Press, 2004), 20.

79   Reginald Farrer, *The Void of War: Letters from Three Fronts* (London: Constable,
      1918), 169.

80   Jeff Mather, 'Camping in China with the divine Jane: The travel writing of Reginald
      Farrer', *Journeys* 10, no. 2 (2009): 53.

81   Farrer, *The Void of War*, 169.

82   Reginald Farrer, 'Jane Austen', *Quarterly Review* 228, no. 452 (1917): 2.

83   Cox, *Farrer's Last Journey*, xvi.

84   Cox, *Farrer's Last Journey*, 211.

85   Jonathan Gathorne-Hardy, *Half an Arch: A Memoir* (London: Timewell, 2004), 183.

86   Robert Gathorne-Hardy, *Three Acres and a Mill* (London: J. M. Dent, 1939), xi.

87   Gathorne-Hardy, *Three Acres and a Mill*, opposite 12.

88   Gathorne-Hardy, *Three Acres and a Mill*, 113.

89   John Potvin, *Bachelors of a Different Sort: Queer Aesthetics, Material Culture and the
      Modern Interior in Britain* (Manchester: Manchester University Press, 2014), 44.

90   Michael Camille, 'Editor's introduction', *Art History* 24, no. 2 (April 2001): 164.

91   Ronald Hyam, *Empire and Sexuality*, 32–8.

92   For an example of mountaineering and same-sex desire, see Alan Hankinson,
      Geoffrey Winthrop Young: Poet, Mountaineer, Educator (London: Hodder and
      Stoughton, 1995). For the desire for botanical rarities, see Niamh Downing,
      '"Fritillary fever": Cultivating the self and gardening the world in the writing of Clara
      Coltman Vyvyan', in *Women in Transit through Literary Liminal Spaces*, ed. Teresa
      Gómez Reus and Terry Gifford (Basingstoke: Palgrave Macmillan, 2013), 176.

93 Chris Steyaert, 'Queering SPACE: Heterotopic life in Derek Jarman's garden', *Gender, Work and Organization* 17, no. 1 (2010): 55; Dominic Janes, *Picturing the Closet: Male Secrecy and Homosexual Visibility in Britain* (Oxford: Oxford University Press, 2015), 179–92.

94 Farrer, *In a Yorkshire Garden*, 6; Rebecca Pullen, *Reginald Farrer's Rock Garden, Clapham, North Yorkshire: Analytical Survey and Assessment*, Research Report Series no. 7–2016 (Portsmouth: Historic England, 2016).

95 Farrer, *In a Yorkshire Garden*, 7.

96 Farrer, *Alpines and Bog Plants*, 3.

97 Reginald Farrer, *The English Rock-Garden* (London: T. E. and E. C. Jack, 1919). For a history of alpine gardening see Graham Stuart Thomas, *The Rock Garden and Its Plants: From Grotto to Alpine House* (London: Frances Lincoln, 2004), 59–84.

98 Farrer, *Alpines and Bog Plants*, 205.

5

A queer history of Parson's Pleasure, Oxford

George Townsend

A story well known among older generations in Oxford recalls three professors (or 'dons') of Oxford University sunbathing naked at a place called Parson's Pleasure. Suddenly a boat comes into sight along the stream occupied by a group of their students. Two of the dons cover their privates; the third covers his face and, in the aftermath, comments, 'I don't know about you fellows, but in Oxford I am known by my face – not my genitals'. With its odd mix of seaside postcard humour and insight into the esoteric world of academia, this story became a lasting part of local mythology. Alongside the likes of Walter Pater, Oscar Wilde and Evelyn Waugh, the sunbathing dons seemed to epitomize Oxford's reputation as a long-standing haven for (largely male) eccentrics, figures whose behaviour, within the semi-private enclaves of the university, stretched the bounds of social and sexual convention.[1] The third don has been identified as the classicist Maurice Bowra though, as Bowra's biographer argues, little evidence exists to back this up. Such stories are 'oral myths' intended to 'define what a great academic might have done'. Bowra was a great academic, and 'therefore became the focal point for traditional stories'.[2] Whether this 'oral myth' is apocryphal or not, its peculiar backdrop is, or was, real. A relatively small city with a population today of just over 150,000, Oxford is built around the confluence of two rivers: the Cherwell and the Thames. Parson's Pleasure is less than a mile from the city centre, centred on a cusp of land between two divisions in the Cherwell on the south-east corner of the University Parks. It was used for bathing from perhaps as early as 1607 until its closure, demolition and redevelopment into an area of park in 1992, and was well known by the twentieth century as a site where bathing and sunbathing were commonly practised in the nude, by men and boys only.[3]

By 1992, Parson's Pleasure was regarded as anachronistic, not least because it had withstood the rise of swimming costumes for over a century.[4] And it is this idea of anachronism – of a place being out of step with its era – that provides a basis here for thinking about Parson's Pleasure as a site of queer history. Rictor Norton suggests that the charge of anachronism has often been made as a means of suppressing gay history (not to mention many other marginalized histories), and particularly through an emphasis on the impermanent relationship between identity and language.[5] Simultaneously, 'strategic anachronism', to borrow Claire Hayward's phrase, has been

Figure 4 William Roberts, *Parson's Pleasure* (aka *On the Lawn*), *c.* 1944. Estate of John David Roberts. Reproduced with permission of the Treasury Solicitor.

a crucial tool for historians of gender and sexuality concerned with recovering such histories. In this context, a focus on 'queer' has been potent, illuminating spectrums of difference and making way for what Carolyn Dinshaw calls an affective 'touch' across time.[6] By focusing on Parson's Pleasure, a place hailed as anachronistic while it was in active use, I offer an alternative angle on this debate. I begin by considering the idea of anachronism in relation to various origin stories, before narrating the social and spatial development of Parson's Pleasure on the basis of newly recovered materials. I then identify some key examples of queer uses and representations of Parson's Pleasure and make a case for the queerness of the bathing place on a more fundamental level. It was not only the scene of queer acts and relationships, I argue, but was structurally queer by virtue of its closeting of certain practices of homosocial intimacy. This closeting took on a physical form: between 1865 and 1992 Parson's Pleasure was surrounded by wooden screens, shielding bathers from passers-by. Yet the erection of the screens also had the striking cultural effect of conserving certain ways of being in nature that were at odds with contemporary gender norms. The social make-up of bathers varied over the years but Parson's Pleasure retained the atmosphere of an alien time through the endurance of its bathing traditions. Its queerness and its anachronism were two sides of the same coin.

Origin stories

When Parson's Pleasure closed, newspaper reports emphasized its identity as the relic of an old-fashioned, male-dominated university culture. 'For more than a century', wrote Reg Little in the *Oxford Times*, 'dons and students have been baring all on the riverside, forcing modest women punters to avert their eyes… many people [regard] Parson's Pleasure as an anachronism'.[7] The *Daily Telegraph* offered a touch more historical background: 'Parson's Pleasure… was originally known as Patten's Pleasure and became popular with undergraduates and dons more than 300 years ago… Early records show a Mr Oliver Craven of Trinity College drowned there in 1666'.[8] While differing in tone and detail, these reports both link Parson's Pleasure to the university, with the end of the bathing place featuring as a belated sign of modernization. Despite this consensus about establishment ties, however, Parson's Pleasure seemed to lack any authoritative history and even today little has been written about it from an official perspective. The eight volumes of the *History of the University of Oxford*, with its formidable 7,330 pages, include no reference to Parson's Pleasure.[9] Until recently, its past has instead been kept alive through oral, and occasionally transcribed, anecdotes and theories, a number of which revolve around the name. Before piecing together the place's material history and queer representations, it is worth surveying some of these to get a sense of how a quasi-official account of Parson's Pleasure emerged over time.

With its singsong air of double entendre, the name has provoked many attempts to interpret and define. 'We never could trace that anyone of the name of Parsons had it', the attendant Charles Cox told an historian in the early 1900s, 'and we believe it is called "Parsons Pleasure" because so many of the University men who came here intended to be parsons'.[10] An 'Oxford Veteran' writing for the *Sydney Herald* took up the theme in a more romantic mode in 1913: 'Parson's Pleasure gets its queer name', the Veteran claimed, 'from the fact that all the members of the party of undergraduates who set the fashion of bathing there nearly a century ago took Holy Orders'.[11] Speculations with a different emphasis can also be found from before the modernization of the university gathered pace in 1871, the year students and teaching staff were freed from tests of religious belief.[12] In 1868, the name was understood to be a corruption of 'Parisian's Pleasure'.[13] The place had apparently been the resort of 'French students', who 'a century or two ago… selected that rather confined station on the river for their *baignoire*'.[14] Another theory reaches back further still, linking Parson's Pleasure with the English Civil War.[15] For as long as the bathing place has appeared in print, its name has been a subject of speculation, in one way or another figuring Parson's Pleasure as out of place in modern conditions.

This tendency came to a head in the early 1990s, by which time the Cherwell was viewed as a public thoroughfare that should be open to men and women equally. The bathing place had, according to a report from the university itself, brushed off the Sex Discrimination Act of 1975 with 'no more than a ripple', but such moves in wider society towards opening up male-only spaces inevitably caused friction; in 1982, the writer John Wain described visiting Parson's Pleasure and finding on its external wall a piece of graffiti reading, 'SEXIST POSEURS'.[16] 'Until recently', Reg Little explained in the *Oxford Times*, 'it was customary for ladies to disembark from their punts before reaching Parson's Pleasure and to walk round to pick up the punt again'.[17] With women no longer submitting to this inconvenience, the use of Parson's Pleasure for naked bathing and sunbathing and, more controversially, cruising and exhibitionism received greater public scrutiny. 'It was felt that some people were using Parson's Pleasure to display themselves', one student was quoted as saying in *The Times*; 'I have heard of people punting late in the evening... when the site was operative shall we say, who have been quite frightened'.[18] Nonetheless, though it may have been more acutely felt at this time, the idea of Parson's Pleasure as a hangover from the past was nothing new, and several sources suggest that the place's archaic quality had in fact been part of its appeal, aiding its longevity as well as its ultimate stigmatization – 'a kind of anachronism', as one former bather puts it, 'and wonderful for that'.[19]

In this regard, Parson's Pleasure resonates with what Terence Ranger and Eric Hobsbawm famously termed 'invented tradition': 'a set of practices normally governed by overtly or tacitly accepted rules and of a ritual or symbolic nature, which seeks to inculcate certain values and norms of behaviour by repetition, [automatically implying] continuity with the past'.[20] The practices of nude bathing and sunbathing at Parson's Pleasure were certainly accepted and enforced. 'Unaware of this usage', wrote the physicist Anatole Abragam, reflecting on a visit in 1948, 'I came the first time wearing bathing trunks, which I hastened to remove under reproving looks'.[21] Moreover, these practices were not explicitly ritualistic but were highly repetitive, and in some ways linked to the rituals of the city and university. Marked by a choir singing from Magdalen Tower at dawn, the first of May is traditionally regarded as the first day of summer in Oxford – and was therefore the first day of the bathing season. Lewis Tuckwell, a chorister at Magdalen College School in the 1840s and 1850s, recalled that, after singing the sunrise in, 'those of us who were able to swim... rowed up the Cherwell to Parson's Pleasure, where we disported ourselves in various ways until the time appointed for dinner'.[22] These ties between the bathing place and a calendar of public tradition recurred across generations. 'I believe there are those who... make a point of going [to Parson's Pleasure] on Christmas Day', commented the Precentor of Christ Church Cathedral in 1972, 'if only to drink champagne and eat Christmas pudding'.[23] The bathing place occupied an ambiguous position in the city's imagination. As well as causing greater friction with prevailing norms as time went on, it inculcated a sense of community and continuity that was embodied in a very literal sense.

At the same time, the invented tradition of the place sits oddly alongside Ranger and Hobsbawm's classic examples, such as the traditions of Scottish clans and the English royal family. These emphasize power and regalia, chiming more obviously with the university than the bathing place. As much as it seemed part of a waning culture of homosociality, Parson's Pleasure reversed many of the university's most iconic elements. Ubiquitous nudity offset a hierarchy of gowns and headgear. Grand facades, halls and quadrangles were replaced by a cluster of sheds and an unfiltered river. And – greatest blasphemy of all – visitors not only walked but sunbathed naked on the grass. Parson's Pleasure represented an inventive *inversion* of tradition, though this inversion was by no means subversive of university power. Frequently it was instead associated with a classical world the university had long revered and, particularly in the

Victorian period, sought to imitate.[24] 'The whole idea of wandering around in the buff discussing philosophy was felt to be essentially Greek', wrote historian Peter France. The 'ambience' of Parson's Pleasure recalled Plato's Academy, the original 'sacred grove with a wall around it'.[25] Like the 'heterotopia' theorized by Michel Foucault, Parson's Pleasure was simultaneously mythic and real in its combination of the classical and the everyday.[26]

This notion of the place embodying an idealized past also served to suppress alternative narratives. 'It's very old, very English', explained a bather named Peter Holmes in 1986. 'There's nothing homosexual about it, you understand, just eccentricity and perhaps a touch of "little boys showing off"'.[27] The past the place represented was, in this view, a time of pre-sexual innocence. Wain addressed issues of gender and sexuality at greater length: 'No sixties girl', he wrote,

> was going to get out of a punt just because [men were bathing in the] river... your Sixties girl had to sit bolt upright like a Victorian governess... From that moment, the atmosphere at Parson's Pleasure changed. Bathing together in the nude was one of those unselfconscious things that Victorian and Edwardian males were good at; not because they were a lot of homosexuals, but precisely *because* they had not been conditioned to see a sexual aspect in everything.[28]

For Wain, Parson's Pleasure was spoiled by an overreaching sexual revolution and haunted by a confusion of Victorian spectres – the governess, all prudery and repression – but also the unselfconscious youth not yet conditioned by feminism or Freud. One of the few sources from the period to unsettle such narratives appeared in the letters section of *Gay Times* in April 1992. Drawing attention to the 'centuries of tradition' that had been brought to an end with the closure of Parson's Pleasure, the letter resembles other accounts in its emphasis on the past, yet its characterization of the bathers themselves sticks out from the crowd: 'This unique place used mainly by gay men has been taken away from us.'[29] Invoking a group, an 'us', of 'mainly gay men', the letter raises crucial questions about who had access to and a sense of ownership over the place over the course of its history. If we go beyond the fanciful origin stories, establishing a fresh perspective on the site's evolution, what do we find?

Bathers in space

The drowning of Oliver Craven was one of a series that took place at Parson's Pleasure (then known as 'Patin's Pleasure' or 'Patten's Pleasure') in the seventeenth century.[30] However, the antiquarian Anthony Wood, on whom we rely for these early references, suggests the bathing place was not known exclusively by university men at this time. As well as three student drownings, Wood records the death in 1692 of Elizabeth Simons, a 'bed-maker at Wadham College', who 'drown'd herself at Patten's pleasure... She was got with child by [Samson Vallack], M.A. and commoner of Wadham College, who now lives at Plymouth... The maid was searched and found to be with child; and therefore being turned away and knew not what to doe, drowned her selfe'.[31] Though Wood mentions river bathing elsewhere, he makes no explicit reference to Parson's Pleasure as a bathing place, and it is unclear, too, what physical form the place took in this period.[32] Nonetheless, as well as being a bitter document of contemporary double standards, Wood's account of the death of Simons and her unborn child shows that Parson's Pleasure was familiar, or at least accessible, to women as well as men, and to people of mixed social backgrounds.

Further insights emerge from the early nineteenth century, when the bathing place was often called by another alternative name. 'We, the... proprietors of the ground called Loggerhead', announced an item in the *Oxford Chronicle* in 1827, '*hereby give Notice*, that all persons trespassing on the above grounds... will be prosecuted... with the utmost rigour of the law'. This hostility, directed explicitly against the 'number of persons who frequent that place for the purpose of bathing', persisted for some time.[33] In 1831, two 'lads' were severely injured by some broken glass bottles, which had been thrown into the Cherwell 'at a place called Loggerhead', apparently as a deterrent. Notably, the journalist reporting on the incident viewed this intolerance as relatively novel, lamenting that 'there is not now, as there was a few years ago, an open bathing place, with seats and ladders'.[34] In any case, the intolerance declined in the later 1830s. By 1837, the 'considerable damage' of the 1820s had been transformed into 'considerable revenue'.[35] Parson's Pleasure had been commercialized for the first time.

To what extent does the Parson's Pleasure of the 1830s and 1840s match up with accounts from the late twentieth century? To begin with, Parson's Pleasure – later thought to be quintessentially donnish – was contrasted with university bathing places at Iffley lock and Long Bridges. '[T]here is another at the Loggerhead near Holywell', reported the *Herald*, 'open to all parties for a trifling charge'.[36] The clergyman and journalist Thomas Pearce similarly disassociated the place from the university during this phase. "'Parson's Pleasure!'" he writes, 'Why, I wonder? Because the bachelor parsons of that celebrated and classic land are, or were, so fond of water?... in my time they weren't, nor, indeed, were the Dons'. Parson's Pleasure instead epitomized Oxford as a 'swimming town' and was frequented by a variety of the city's inhabitants, from 'charities' ('very small boys' who perhaps entered for free) to a respectable local doctor.[37] Further indication of the clientele appears in 1844, when Frederick Irwin stood as a witness against the bathing place's then-proprietor, John Cox. Irwin had seen Cox strike William Luff over the head with a punt pole at Parson's Pleasure.[38] Luff was a local chemist and Irwin a 'hair-cutter', who for fifty years made it his 'daily custom to take, summer and winter, his morning bath in the Cherwell'.[39] Parson's Pleasure was open to all parties, including members of the university and its associated institutions – but it was not yet a university enclave.

In the 1980s and 1990s the notoriety of Parson's Pleasure was inextricable from its exposure to the Cherwell, a popular summer route for pleasure boaters. Up until the late nineteenth century, however, the site was noted for its seclusion. The Cherwell was an 'almost unknown river' and the architect Phillip Webb recalled bathing at Parson's Pleasure in the 1850s with a young William Morris, having accessed the place down an obscure 'little path'.[40] Pearce describes the approach in greater detail. After passing a holy well, an old cock-fighting pit and cottage gardens, you would cross a 'picturesque wooden bridge'. Then, a 'quarter of a mile of charming short-fed grass brought us to where the river bent at a right angle, through meadow fields flat as a bowling green… The water, until you turned the angle, was "hard bottom"… Round the corner all was mystery and depth'.[41] Parson's Pleasure was semi-rural, situated on the boundary of the city's jurisdiction, and the area used for bathing loosely defined. It was commercialized to some extent and privately owned – the land by Merton College, the 'fishery' by a local surgeon – but nonetheless retained some sense of the 'open bathing place'.[42] Perhaps the only reminder of the city and modern civility was a clutch of changing sheds introduced in 1845 – much to the irritation of poet Arthur Hugh Clough, who described the buildings as an 'unsightly erection', vowing to find a new place to bathe.[43]

The form of Parson's Pleasure then changed significantly in the 1860s. The university was steadily consolidating its ownership of land and water in the area through the newly assembled University Parks Curators. In addition, the university established what became known as Mesopotamia Walk, a footpath surrounded by two branches of river, linking neighbourhoods to the east with North Oxford via Parson's Pleasure and the University Parks.[44] Having previously been a secluded resort, Parson's Pleasure was incorporated much more closely into the city as Mesopotamia became a well-used route for work and pleasure. It went without saying that the bathing place had to be screened off. In a meeting with the vice-chancellor, Mr Eaglestone of the city council asked whether 'with regard to "Parsons' Pleasure"… the University intended to put any screen up that it might be retained?' The vice-chancellor's reply was prickly. 'He did not think the University would pledge themselves to retain the bathing place to the City for ever', related the *Herald*, 'but they did not intend to do away with it now, [having] sent for an estimate for the erection of a screen'.[45] Parson's Pleasure came close to disappearing and, like Mesopotamia and the newly improved Parks, remained open on the university's terms.

A little over twenty years later, American journalist Robert Barr wrote an account that illuminates several post-enclosure changes. Having been informed about Parson's Pleasure by an Oxford 'man' (an undergraduate), Barr approaches Mesopotamia and finds a 'gate in the thick hedge', encountering en route 'hosts of earlier men… each with a damp towel over his shoulder'. On entering, he is met with a number of 'small boxes' made up of the 'divisions of a shed that formed a sort of wall on two sides of the grounds… There is a green lawn in the V-like enclosure, and flowing past the lawn is the clear Cherwell'. Up in a tree Barr notices a 'sort of rookery [hanging] over the water'. The 'men' clamber up to this rookery 'and drop down unexpectedly here and there… you have to be continually on the lookout for men of high educational attainments… plunging in around you in all directions'.[46] Compared to Pearce, who emphasizes a mixed clientele and spatial openness, Barr stresses the closeness of Parson's Pleasure and its role in exclusive undergraduate routines. Barr's own presence indicates that non-university members were able to enter, but this seems to be the exception rather than the rule. The character of the space at Parson's Pleasure had changed. Before 1865 a visit entailed a movement outwards – out to the edge of Oxford past various markers of urban liminality. Barr's account, on the other hand, describes a move inwards, into a discrete, albeit in some ways still unofficial, outpost of the university. Parson's Pleasure represented not only privatized public space but an interiorized outdoors, a closet that, like C. S. Lewis' famous wardrobe, opened onto nature.

Further changes were made in the 1930s, when the enclosure was doubled in size and redecorated.[47] Encouraged perhaps by the new fashion for tanning and nudism, this expansion enhanced the social aspect of the space, as can be seen in Stanley Roy Badmin's contemporary watercolour, *Parson's Pleasure* (1938). The painting focuses almost entirely on the open green space of the riverbank – populated by nude figures sunbathing, chatting, reading and playing games – and the lofty trees beyond. The river with its swimmers and divers occupies only a sliver of the picture's right hand side.[48] In 1934, a bathing place for women and children, later known as Dame's Delight, was added nearby – a subject for rejoicing among women bathers. 'Here you may wear beach pyjamas to your heart's content', wrote one excited student.[49] Yet with Dame's Delight being overseen by a male attendant and the wearing of bathing suits enforced, its character was quite different to that of its male counterpart. 'The swimming pool was opened last Thursday, to everyone's joy', noted a student journalist, '[but] we cannot help wishing… that swimming as a sport need not be taken quite so seriously. It should belong to the pleasant, drifting life of the river, where all cares may be forgotten.'[50] Even as similar facilities were opened to women, the particular micro-culture of Parson's Pleasure remained distinctive, conserving elements of a traditional bathing culture in a socially exclusive form. Simultaneously, entrance requirements seem to have relaxed somewhat in this period. In 1940, the Curators permitted soldiers stationed in the city to use the bathing place in their spare time.[51]

This story of physical and social change also raises questions about the people who ran Parson's Pleasure. Renting the site from 1841 onwards, John Cox and his wife Ann founded a minor dynasty of bathing place attendants, with their son, Charles, becoming the most famous among them.[52] Charles occupied his post for three quarters of a century, first under his father and then as head attendant, and looms large in official documents and newspaper reports, as well as literary representations.[53] The family's lease ended with Charles' retirement in 1914 and the place was then managed by a series of attendants appointed by the Curators – though remarkably the guardianship of Parson's Pleasure passed back to the family's descendants in later years. Alfred Cooper, who was the attendant by 1966 and kept the role until 1973, was John Cox's great grandson. When Cooper retired, having 'worked, for the love of it, long hours, seven days a week', he proved expensive to replace. The Curators decided that Parson's Pleasure would remain open without charge and without anyone to act as a lifeguard – or to police bathers' behaviour.[54] The family had played a central role in shaping and maintaining the place over the course of more than a century. As well as lifeguarding and running swimming lessons, they opened and closed Parson's Pleasure each day, took payments for entry and the rental of towels, and kept the towels and cubicles clean, the grass mown and foliage under control. In short, their work facilitated bathers' leisure and mediated bathers' relationship to nature and to the local past. When Cooper retired, Parson's Pleasure was untethered from this side of its lineage; but in a peculiar sense this made it all the more anachronistic, the space echoing in its newly unattended state a pre-enclosure wildness and disinhibition.

Queer space

Parson's Pleasure was enclosed by the university in 1865 and culturally dominated by university members between the 1860s and the interwar period at least. Its practices can be traced back to a tradition of more open and mixed public bathing, however, and in some respects it reverted to this tradition in the mid-twentieth century – particularly from the early 1970s onwards. The claim of later writers that 'distinguished and witty classicists' were the 'inspiration' for Parson's Pleasure therefore tells us more about the wealth of mythology that grew up around it than any historical reality.[55] How do claims about the place's relation to sexuality and gender fare by comparison – Peter Holmes's assertion that there was 'nothing homosexual' about Parson's Pleasure or Wain's protestation that the bathers of its heyday were anything but a 'lot of homosexuals'? Having carved out a space beyond the quasi-official narrative, what forms of queer use and representation come into relief?

Male friendship is a recurring feature in the sources covered above. A series of pairs emerges: two lads injured by broken glass, Irwin and Luff (who lived in the same building in 1841), Webb and Morris, Clough and his close friend Matthew Arnold.[56] Then, in a collection of verse from 1898 by little-known poet Edmund St Gascoigne Mackie, friendship overflows into something resembling romantic love. Mackie grew up and was educated in Oxford and only later, in various locations across the world, wrote *Charmides, or 'Oxford Twenty Years Ago'*, a series of elegies about a dead childhood friend.[57] On several levels, the collection signals its own participation in what Linda Dowling terms the 'homosexual counterdiscourse', a new wave of writing in the late nineteenth century that endorsed male love through a reappraisal of ancient Greek culture.[58] Mackie acknowledged a direct debt to John Addington Symonds, a classicist and writer on homosexuality who himself celebrated the spectacle of bathers at the Serpentine in London.[59] In addition, the collection's title draws on a dialogue by Plato, in which Socrates debates with a beautiful youth, Charmides, about the value of *sophrosyne*, or temperance. It was this dialogue that famously caught the ire of one of Symonds' critics. 'The emotions of Socrates at the sight of the beauty of young Charmides', wrote Richard St John Tyrwhitt in 1877, 'are not natural: and it is well known that Greek love of nature and beauty went frequently against nature'.[60] Within the collection, 'Charmides' is the pseudonym of Mackie's deceased friend, and the poems explore memories of spaces and occasions the young pair once shared. Many are situated along the Cherwell (usually pronounced 'Char-well', suggesting a further element of play in the collection's title), including a poem called 'Parson's Pleasure'. 'Do you remember that straight gravel-walk[?]' the poem begins, 'At dawn in June, / When we passed down to bathe, what scented showers / Of pink and crimson petals strewed our path'.[61] Playing with the metaphor of a couple emerging from church after their wedding (a motif made clearer in the second edition, in which 'showers of pink and crimson petals' becomes 'showers of may-bloom like confetti'), the opening celebrates same-sex love.[62] The approach to Parson's Pleasure is aligned with an imagined transition into a world where such love can be publicly celebrated and, contrary to the likes of Tyrwhitt, it is precisely 'nature' that enacts the celebration.

The lines that follow undercut this celebratory tone, however. 'Do you remember the old willow stump?' Mackie continues, 'And how you swam (although I warned you not) / Far out and swimming, gathered water-lilies?' The bathing place becomes a place of foreboding, with the narrowly averted trauma of Charmides being pulled under prefiguring some graver misstep to come. Then, finally, a funereal atmosphere takes hold, as Mackie closes with a parallel between lily-gathering and his own one-handed practice of writing: 'And I, too, swim far out to gather flowers: / And with one hand I toil, that I may hold / These buds of song above the stream of Death'.[63] The romantic setting hardens, nostalgia becoming kitsch, like florid decorations on a tomb. On the one hand, the poem expresses what historians have termed 'romantic friendship', its imagery of marriage between friends recalling the alternative history of texts and memorials explored by Alan Bray.[64] On the other, the removed temporality of the poem figures Parson's Pleasure as the site of a love remembered but never realized – love ultimately shrouded in regret.

In *L'Aube Ardente*, first published in serial form in 1915, Abel Hermant draws on a similar range of references. The novel's protagonist, Philippe, is a wealthy and bored Parisian who visits Oxford in pursuit of philosophical guidance. On route he reads the famous opening of Plato's *Phaedrus*, in which Phaedrus and Socrates settle down for a conversation beside the Ilisus, just outside Athens. After arriving in Oxford and acquainting himself with the city, Philippe goes to a bookshop and finds a locally printed book of verse by a mysterious American named Ashley Bell. He then makes his way to Parson's Pleasure, where his daydreams come to life. 'At that moment', writes Hermant, 'there entered a tall young man… his face… of a beauty so perfect, of a brilliance so extraordinary, that an amateur of Hellenism could hardly defend himself from comparing [the swimmer] to the immortal gods'.[65] Before long, Philippe encounters the Whitmanesque Ashley Bell in person at the bathing place, recognizing him from a portrait in the poetry book. Philippe determines to enter the poet's inner circle and succeeds through the introduction of a student named Rex Tintagel. He then passes the summer as one of Bell's acolytes, and he and Tintagel enter into an intimate friendship. Saturating the place with romantic overtones, Hermant reimagines Oxford as a kind of Platonic utopia with Parson's Pleasure at its heart.

As well as being implicitly celebrated in these texts, queer behaviours provoked tension in some bathers' accounts of Parson's Pleasure. The publisher Grant Richards recalls being taught to swim by Charles Cox in the 1880s and, at a later, unspecified date, seeing the writer Frederick Rolfe 'sitting under the Parson's Pleasure willows… surveying the yellow flesh tints of youth with unbecoming satisfaction'.[66] Grant Richards was formerly Rolfe's publisher and their relationship was often far from amicable.[67] The veracity of this anecdote is therefore uncertain – though Rolfe does mention bathing at Parson's Pleasure each morning during a spell in Oxford in 1900.[68] From a less obviously partial standpoint, sailor and travel writer Eric Hiscock recalls similar behaviour during his childhood in the 1910s. 'Chief among [the voyeurs]', Hiscock writes, 'was a tall, pot-bellied, bearded sprig of the Lewis Carroll family tree… he sat and fastened his eyes… on any swimmer under the age of consent… the nude majority found The Dodder… one of Parson's minor displeasures'.[69] C. S. Lewis, a regular at Parson's Pleasure for several decades, experienced displeasure of another kind when he went to bathe one afternoon in 1922. 'Some pups there', he writes in his diary, 'who, even naked, I divined to be either Sandhurst cadets or very young officers... You can see them looking out of the corners of their eyes to see whether you're admiring them'.[70] In the literary Parson's Pleasure of Hermant and Mackie, the bathing place represents a *locus amoenus*, a kind of idealized place familiar from a wider queer iconography of bathing. A comparable aesthetic appears in the paintings of Henry Scott Tuke and Thomas Eakins, for example, and in the photographs of Wilhelm von Gloeden.[71] In practice, however, the scene was not always so lovely. Parson's Pleasure could be a site of unwanted attention and display from outsiders, distinguishable by their ignorance of local etiquette – but also from insiders like 'the Dodder', to whom others negligently turned a blind eye.

In earlier years, when the 'neo-pagan' habit of naked river bathing was considered a widespread nuisance in Oxford, the idea of homoeroticism on the riverbank being in any way picturesque was ridiculed in local newspapers.[72] 'In these days of hyper-aestheticism', wrote *Oxford Times* editor George Rippon in 1881, 'we are often startled to hear naked ugliness eulogised as being intrinsically beautiful but I doubt if... Mr. Oscar Wilde... would admire nudity as exhibited on the banks of the Thames'.[73] Yet it was precisely Wilde whom writer Frank Harris later depicted 'on a bench under some trees in Oxford' with Walter Pater by his side – Wilde so enraptured by the sight of students bathing that he produced a speech extempore, advocating a 'new paganism'. When the speech came to a close, Pater apparently 'slipped from his seat and knelt down by [Wilde] and kissed [his] hand'. 'You must not, you really must not', was Wilde's response:

> '"What would people think if they saw you?'
> "[Pater] got up with a white strained face.
> "'I had to," he muttered, glancing about him fearfully, "I had to – once...."'[74]

Stripping this anecdote of its many speech marks in his biography of Wilde, the French writer Philippe Jullian placed Wilde and Pater not on a 'bench under some trees in Oxford' but 'reclined on a seat at Parson's Pleasure'.[75] For some writers, the queer potential of Parson's Pleasure was irresistible, regardless of the facts. Its appeal lay in the grey area between myth and materiality.

This ambiguity also affected visual representations, as in an oil painting from 1944 by the former British War Artist and associate of the Vorticists, William Roberts. Roberts moved with his wife and son to nearby Marston for the duration of the Second World War and painted a series of Cherwell scenes during this period, including one of Parson's Pleasure (see Figure 4). The painting features a group of hulking nudes talking and sunbathing on the bank, presented in his signature 'English Cubist' style. As art historian Andrew Gibbon Williams notes, however, the subject is an unusual one for Roberts inasmuch as it mixes his habitual championing of everyday life with nudity and classical allusion. Only the 'pipe-smoking river god, towel draped over head, anchors the subject in the present', with screens, sheds and attendants absent from the frame.[76] While the frank social nudity of the figures seems to set the painting apart from earlier, more sentimentalized representations, Roberts draws on a similar palette of references to Mackie and Hermant (albeit with a little more irony). Echoing in its content the scene with Socrates and Phaedrus beside the Ilisus, and in its form recalling the Ilisus statue from the Parthenon, the painting at once implies and masks Parson's Pleasure as queer space. Social nudity becomes a form of dressing up, just as the historical place itself blurs into an idealized Arcadia.

Many of the sources that are most frank not only about queer desire and aesthetics at Parson's Pleasure but queer community emerge after the place's demise. A few months after the closure, artist and interior designer Andrew Protheroe made a pastiche of Roberts' painting which Elton John hung above the pool of his London home until 2003.[77] This suggestive domestication of the bathing place marked the beginning of a process that is still ongoing, of Parson's Pleasure being incorporated into queer heritage, even as it remains alive in the memories of many, queer and straight, who bathed there. In fiction, Parson's Pleasure has emerged more explicitly than before as a site of flirtation. 'One unusually warm Sunday afternoon', writes Arthur Motyer, 'we went… across the Parks to Parson's Pleasure, where we swam in the nude and lay together afterwards in the sun, although I had to roll over onto my stomach so Clifford wouldn't see what was happening. After a little while, I noticed that he rolled over, too'.[78] Motyer went to Oxford as a Rhodes scholar in 1945 and after retiring from a career as an academic made his sexuality public in 2004 through the publication of the semi-autobiographical *What's Remembered*.[79] Parson's Pleasure features several times across the text.

Local and public history projects have also highlighted Parson's Pleasure as a site of queer heritage. Pride of Place, an Historic England initiative led by academic historians, established a crowdsourced online map of England, to which contributors have added many places of LGBTQ significance. 'I would not use the word "gay" of Parson's Pleasure when I knew it in the early 1970s', one contributor says, 'though a lot of the students who used it were affected by or involved in gay lib… It was homosocial rather than frankly erotic… I spent sunny afternoons there, studying and staring, taking a swim, sometimes chatting with friends'.[80] The Oxford-oriented 'Tales of Our City' project has similarly tapped into living memory in pursuit of a re-connection with place. When the Tales team organized an exhibition, entitled 'Queering Spires', in collaboration with the Museum of Oxford, Parson's Pleasure was represented alongside pubs, nightclubs and other places through pictures, maps, cartoons and text. The historian Ross Brooks has also sought to uncover and reappraise local history through academic research, as well as the encyclopaedic website Queer Oxford. His recent article on the male homoerotics of 1930s Oxford features analysis of several sources relating to Parson's Pleasure, including photographs of a bather from the 1930s by Cyril Arapoff. 'The young man is pictured apparently perusing – cruising – other naked men at the enclosed facility', Brooks writes, '[making these images] a rare photographic record of gay cruising in twentieth-century Britain, possibly the earliest such document that exists for any country'.[81] Parson's Pleasure has both become part of a growing and increasingly accessible queer history movement and emerged, as Brooks's findings suggest, as a potential landmark for queer history per se.[82]

If the bathing place is coming out, then, what does an out Parson's Pleasure look like? As the above-quoted Pride of Place contributor signals, Parson's Pleasure was an anachronism not only in its ties to university and public bathing culture but in relation to the insurgent gay liberation movement of the 1970s. The term 'gay' – then highly contemporary and politically charged – seems to him an odd fit with its archaic homosociality. One former habitué I interviewed recalls some connections between the bathing place and local political movements. 'I belonged to... the Campaign for Homosexual Equality', he says, 'and we took a punt from the Cherwell boathouse to Parson's Pleasure and then we had a picnic... Most of us without any clothes on'. But Parson's Pleasure was also attended by many people beyond this activist network. 'Straight people went there', he explains, 'Gays and straights got on quite well, [only] one or two were a bit antagonistic'. He also describes how differences of class and sexuality were both felt and transgressed: 'there were university men, dons and that, that went there', he recalls. 'And obviously they were... different from me... they were *dons* and I was just a servant at the college'. At the same time, Parson's Pleasure was a space of commonality:

> everybody goes and strips off in front of each other... And it was like no problem about it, it was something they wished to express. And the dons – I don't think they were the ones that were actually you know being sort of like – they just went there for the health reasons really [laughter] – put it that way.

In this late period, Parson's Pleasure played host to multiple masculinities, including those of working-class gay men and older straight academics. Tensions were occasionally felt but on the whole bathers were unified by an unusual way of being together in nature: 'Everybody that takes their clothes off in public is slightly, well not, eccentric – they are normal, but you know you're not quite the same are you?'[83]

Any final definition of Parson's Pleasure as a queer space presents certain problems. A balance is still being negotiated between the quasi-official narrative, which crystallized in the 1980s and 1990s and has influenced perceptions of the bathing place ever since, and the potential results of historical research and a wider attentiveness to lived experience. There is also a recurring ambivalence about the place's character both between and within available sources. 'Slugs in the dressing hutches, no life in the water... the chill of a morgue over the whole place on all but the most fervent dog days', wrote journalist C. E. Montague in the 1920s, 'And yet a grave part of death's menace is that under the mould we may forget Parson's Pleasure'.[84] This ambivalence also features in queer interpretations. In Yves Navarre's 1975 novel *Killer*, one character describes Parson's Pleasure as a 'paradise of naked men', while for the young gay protagonist it is a 'nice little ghetto', a theme to which he later returns: 'I was born soiled, and the more I accept myself the more I purify myself, the more I give myself, the more I possess and realise myself. I am not made for the devious paths, the shames and the ghettos'.[85] With historical commercialization, enclosure and institutional gender segregation shaping its character well into the twentieth century, the queerness of Parson's Pleasure dovetailed with a deep social conservatism. As the site of a range of intimacies between men, and between men and nature, Parson's Pleasure was to some a ghetto – a 'cyst within the social organism', as Symonds might have called it – to others a paradise, a fruitful source of nourishment, community and aesthetic inspiration.[86]

Notes

1 For discussion of Wilde and Pater as the subject of gossip, see 121–2. For an account of Waugh's association with the 'queer chic' of interwar Oxford, see Ross Brooks, 'Beyond brideshead: The male homoerotics of 1930s Oxford', *Journal of British Studies* 59 (October 2020): 821–56.

2 Leslie Mitchell, *Maurice Bowra: A Life* (Oxford: Oxford University Press, 2009), 178.

3 Andrew Clark (ed.), *Register of the University of Oxford*, Vol. 2, *1571–1622*, Part 3, *Degrees* (Oxford: Clarendon Press, 1888), 220.

4 Ronald Hyam, *Empire and Sexuality: The British Experience* (Manchester: Manchester University Press, 1990), 70.

5 Claire Hayward, 'Queer terminology: LGBTQ histories and the semantics of sexuality', *Notches: (re)marks on the history of sexuality*, 9 June 2016, accessed 29 September 2019: https://notchesblog.com/2016/06/09/queer-terminology-lgbtq-histories-and-the-semantics-of-sexuality/.

6 Hayward, 'Queer terminology'; Carolyn Dinshaw et al, 'Theorizing queer temporalities: A roundtable discussion', *GLQ: A Journal of Lesbian and Gay Studies* 13, nos. 2–3 (2007): 177–95.

7 Reg Little, 'Shows over for nude bathers', *Oxford Times*, 31 January 1992, 1.

8 Michael Fleet, 'Unashamed pleasures of Parson's come to an end', *Daily Telegraph*, 31 January 1992, 3.

9 Trevor Henry Aston (ed.), *History of the University of Oxford* (Oxford: Oxford University Press, 1984–1994).

10 Ralph Thomas, *Swimming* (London: Sampson Low, Marston & Company, 1904), 352.

11 'An Oxford Veteran', *Sydney Morning Herald*, 1 November 1913, 4.

12 Michael J. Turner, '"Maintain the old institutions in their quiet old way": Beresford Hope and the religious and political dimensions of university reform in Victorian Britain', in *History of Universities*, Vol. 31, ed. Mordechai Feingold (Oxford: Oxford University Press 2018), 168.

13 Bookworm [pseud.], 'Local Antiquarian Gleanings', *Oxford Journal*, 18 January 1868, 6.

14 Francis Gledstanes Waugh, '"Parson's Pleasure" at Oxford', *The Field*, 16 May 1868, 387.

15 M. E. Grant Duff, *Notes from a Diary, 1889–1891* (London: John Murray, 1901), 15–16.

16 'Curators of the University Parks: Report for the year 1975–6', *Oxford University Gazette*, July 28 1976, 984; John Wain, 'Parson's Displeasure', *Spectator*, 16 October 1982, 14–15.

17 Little, 'Show's over'.

18 Roberts, 'Nude dons'.

19 'Parson's Pleasure', open-source map entry, the website of Pride of Place, accessed 25 February 2020: http://www.oxfordhistory.org.uk/cornmarket/east/24_25.html

20 Eric Hobsbawm and Terence Ranger, *The Invention of Tradition* (Cambridge: Cambridge University Press, 1992). First published 1983 by Cambridge University Press.

21 Anatole Abragam, *De la physique avant toute chose?* (Paris: Éditions Odile Jacob, 2000), 132–3. First published 1987 by Odile Jacob (Paris). My translation.

22 Lewis Tuckwell, *Old Magdalen Days, 1847–1877* (Oxford: Blackwell, 1913), 12.

23 *About the University*, BBC Radio Oxford, broadcast 28 December 1972.

24 Linda Dowling, *Hellenism and Homosexuality in Victorian Oxford* (London: Cornell, 1994).

25 Peter France, *Greek as a Treat: An Introduction to the Classics* (London: Penguin, 1993), 1–3.

26 Michel Foucault, 'Of other spaces', trans. Jay Miskowiec, *Diacritics* 16, no. 1 (1986): 22–7.

27 Peter Holmes, 'Oxford Blue', *The Times*, 26 May 1986, 14.

28 Wain, 'Parson's Displeasure'.

29 'Parson's Pleasure', *Gay Times*, April 1992, 24.

30 *Clark, Register, 220; Life and Times of Anthony Wood, Antiquary of Oxford, 1632–1695*, Vol. 2, 1664–1681, ed. Andrew Clark (Oxford: Clarendon Press, 1892), 80; *Life and Times of Anthony Wood, Antiquary of Oxford, 1632–1695*, Vol. 3, 1682–1695, ed. Andrew Clark (Oxford: Clarendon Press, 1894), 306, 399.

31 *Life and Times*, Vol. 3, 399.

32 Ibid., 156.

33 John Pinfold, Thomas Cripps and John Coles, 'Notice', *Oxford Chronicle*, 4 May 1827, 4.

34 'City and county intelligence', *Oxford University and City Herald*, 11 June 1831, 3.

35 'Deaths', *Oxford Chronicle*, 10 June 1837, 2.

36 'University Intelligence', *Oxford University and City Herald*, 5 June 1847, 3.

37 Idstone [Thomas Pearce], 'Swimming and bathing', *The Field*, 9 May 1868, 362.

38 'City Police Court', *Oxford Journal*, 4 May 1844, 3.

39 'Deaths', *Oxford Journal*, 18 August 1888, 5.

40 William Warde Fowler, *Kingham: Old and New* (Oxford: Blackwell, 1913), 111; William Lethaby, *Phillip Webb and His Work* (Oxford: Oxford University Press, 1935), 15.

41 Idstone, 'Swimming and bathing', 1868.

42 John Steane, 'The Oxford University parks: The first fifty years', *Garden History* 32, no. 1 (Spring 2004): 87–100; 'City and county intelligence', *Herald*, 1831.

43 *Prose Remains of Arthur Hugh Clough*, Vol. 1, *Life: Letters: Prose Remains*, ed. Blanche Smith (London: Macmillan, 1888), 98.

44 Steane, 'University Parks', 88.

45 'Street commissioners meeting: The improvement of the parks', *Oxford University Herald*, 18 February 1865, 10.

46 Luke Sharp [Robert Barr], '"Parson's Pleasure": The place where "Oxford", The place where the "men" of Oxford take a plunge', *Detroit Free Press*, 21 August 1887, 3.

47 ['Over the vacation … '], *Isis*, 26 April 1933, 3.

48 Annebella Pollen, 'Utopian bodies and anti-fashion futures: The dress theories and practices of English interwar nudists', *Utopian Studies* 28, no. 3 (2017): 451–81; David Wootton, *Chris Beetles Summer Show 2016* (London: Chris Beetles, 2016), 48.

49 'Swimming', *Isis*, 25 April 1934, 17.

50 'From the river' (1934), *Isis*, 9 May, 17.

51 'Curators of the Parks. Minutes of meetings. 1940–80', WPβ/20/5b, minutes book, Bodleian Library, Oxford, 3.

52 John Cox, 'Loggerhead, or Parson's Pleasure', *Oxford Chronicle*, 11 November 1865, 5.

53 'Death of Mr. Charles Cox', *Oxford Journal Illustrated*, 31 March 1920, 2.

54 Draft report for 1973–4, Parks Correspondence from 19 June 1972 to 12 December 1976, UR6/PCU/1, file 6, Bodleian Library, Oxford.

55   France, *Greek as a Treat*, 1.

56   '24–25 Cornmarket Street: Burger King' (2016), page on Oxford History website, accessed 20 March 2020, shorturl.at/glvNQ.

57   Edmund St Gascoigne Mackie, *Charmides and Other Poems Chiefly Relating to Oxford* (Oxford: Blackwell, 1912), [ix].

58   Linda Dowling, *Hellenism and Homosexuality*, xiii.

59   Matt Cook, *London and the Culture of Homosexuality, 1885–1914* (Cambridge: Cambridge University Press, 2003), 36–7; Mackie, *Charmides* (1912), [viii].

60   Richard St John Tyrwhitt, 'The Greek spirit in modern literature', *Contemporary Review*, 29 (March 1877): 552–602.

61   Edmund St Gascoigne Mackie, *Charmides, or Oxford Twenty Years Ago* (Oxford: B.H. Blackwell, 1898), 38.

62   Mackie, *Charmides* (1912), 47.

63   Mackie, *Charmides* (1898), 38.

64   E. Anthony Rotundo, 'Romantic friendship: Male intimacy and middle-class youth in the northern united states, 1800–1900', *Journal of Social History* 23, no. 1 (1989): 1–25; Alan Bray, *The Friend* (London: University of Chicago Press, 2003).

65   Abel Hermant, *L'Aube Ardente* (Paris: Librairie Alphonse Lemerre, 1919), 77. My translation.

66   Franklin Thomas Grant Richards, *Memories of a Misspent Youth* (London: Heinemann, 1932), 26.

67   A. J. A. Symons, *Quest for Corvo: An Experiment in Biography* (Harmondsworth: Penguin, 1966), 136. First published 1934 by Cassell & Co (London).

68   Frederick William Rolfe, *Without Prejudice* (London: Allen Lane, 1963), 51–2.

69   Eric Hiscock, *Last Boat to Folly Bridge* (London: Cassell, 1970), 3–4.

70   C. S. Lewis, *All My Road before Me: The Diary of C.S. Lewis, 1922–1927*, ed. W. Hooper (London: Harcourt Brace Jovanovich, 1991), 41–2.

71   For discussion of von Gloeden's 'choreographed scenes of classical homoeroticism' among '*faux*-antique props', see Richard Meyer et al, 'Queer photography?', *Aperture*, no. 218 (Spring 2015): 25–31. For an influential account of homoeroticism in Eakins and Tuke, see Emmanuel Cooper, *The Sexual Perspective: Homosexuality and Art in the Last 100 Years in the West* (London: Routledge, 1994) and for a more recent examination of Eakins, see Christopher Looby, 'See/Eakins/Swimming', 3 May 2020, *LA Review of Books*, accessed 29 September 2021: https://lareviewofbooks.org/article/see-eakins-swimming/.

72   Jack O'Lantern [George Rippon], 'Notes from Oxford', *Oxfordshire Weekly News*, 30 June 1880, 6.

73   Jack O'Lantern [George Rippon], 'Our local notebook', *Oxford Times*, 20 August 1881, 8.

74   Frank Harris, *Oscar Wilde: His Life and Confessions* (New York City: Frank Harris, 1916, 47–9).

75   Philippe Jullian, *Oscar Wilde* (Paris: Librairie Académique Perrin, 1967), 51. My translation.

76   Andrew Gibbon Williams, *William Roberts: An English Cubist* (Aldershot: Lund Humphries, 2004), 94–105.

77   *Elton John & His London Lifestyle* [auction sale catalogue] (London: Sotheby's, 2003), 144.

78   Arthur Motyer, *What's Remembered: A Novel* (Toronto: Cormorant, 2004), 48.

79   Noreen Shanahan, 'Professor Arthur Motyer had a profound impact on his students', 31 July 2011, *The Globe and Mail*, accessed online, 29 September 2021: https://www. theglobeandmail.com/news/national/professor-arthur-motyer-had-a-profound-impact-on-his-students/article589520/.

80   'Parson's Pleasure', Pride of Place map, 2016. The project was led by Alison Oram at Leeds Beckett University, with Justin Bengry and Claire Hayward as principal researchers.

81   Ross Brooks, 'Beyond brideshead'.

82   Since this chapter was written, Parson's Pleasure also featured as the subject of Charles Parker Prize–winning radio documentary, *The Bathing Place*, which aired on BBC Radio 4 in July 2021. Produced by Hunter Charlton and researched, written and presented by myself, the programme includes archival sounds and interviews, a reading of Mackie's 'Parson's Pleasure' and an interview with Samson Dittrich, a young gay and trans historian who over the summer of 2020 regularly swam and spent time with friends at Dame's Delight.

83   Anonymous, interview by George Townsend, audio recording, 12 September 2016, Oxford.

84   Christopher Morley, *Ex Libris Carissimis* (Philadelphia: Philadelphia University Press, 1932), 83–4.

85   Yves Navarre, 'The Oxford Notebook', in trans. Stephen Adams, *New Writing and Writers 17* (London: John Calder, 1980), 167, 169, 181. Adams's translation represents an extract from Yves Navarre, *Killer* (Paris: Flammarion, 1975).

86   *John Addington Symonds (1840–1893) and Homosexuality: A Critical Edition of Sources*, ed. Sean Brady (London: Palgrave Macmillan, 2012), 18.

6

Tracing queer Black spaces in interwar Britain

Caroline Bressey and Gemma Romain

Among the pages of one of Barbara Ker-Seymer's photograph albums held in the Tate archive is a loose black-and-white print, cut square and mounted on card. In the photograph five women sit in and around what seems to be an open top car (see Figure 5). The women are a close group, framed tightly by the photograph and the space of the car.[1] The image is not dated, but the women's clothes, hats and hairstyles reflect the images of young flappers which appeared in advertisements of cars in interwar Britain and America, selling the new technology's association with modernity and sexual liberation.[2] One individual challenges the usual depictions of the flapper which appeared in fashion magazines.

On the far left of the group as we view them, a young Black woman meets our gaze directly. With her Eton crop, she appears both modern and confident. She also seems to be sitting outside of the car, perhaps balancing on a wheel arch, but despite her perch, she looks comfortable, part of the group.

Who makes up that group is not entirely known; two of the women, including the young Black woman are, as yet, unnamed. Written on the back of the image are the names of two of those in the photograph, one the American-born Ruth Baldwin, the other (probably) Dorothy Wilde, niece of Oscar, known as Dolly. Both were part of the crowd of Bright Young Things, whose circle of queer life and love was established in the creative and bohemian spaces of interwar London.[3] In the foreground of the image, and sitting in what would be the driver's seat, is the photographer Barbara Ker-Seymer. In 1928 Ker-Seymer had begun working as an assistant for the aristocratic photographer Olivia Wyndham. They quickly started a relationship and Barbara moved into Olivia's Chelsea home at 19 King's Road, where they were neighbours of Ruth and her partner Joe Carstairs, an heiress who became a well-known and successful powerboat racer.[4]

As part of her photographic practice Barbara Ker-Seymer began taking snapshots of her circle of queer friends and the albums reflect a multi-ethnic friendship network. The images and their handwritten labels (where they appear) capture their visits to the English countryside, stays at 'Diamond Cottage' in Winchester, meals at cafes in Paris and trips across France (where both Dolly and Joe had served as ambulance drivers during the First World War). It is among these papers that the print of the five women has been preserved. The young Black woman with them is not the only Black

Figure 5 Photograph of Barbara Ker-Seymer (2nd from right) seated in car with four other people. © The estate of Barbara Ker-Seymer. Photo: Tate.

person who appears in these albums. These Black people who were a part of Ker-Seymer's social group helped create the cosmopolitan spaces in which they thrived. The friendship networks revealed through the production of personal and professional images highlight the presence of Black queer life in interwar London, of white queer artists involved in Black life and of Black entertainers of diverse sexualities involved in friendships or connections with elite white queer people.

The places where Black individuals became part of queer friendship networks, were employed, admired and desired included public spaces like the British Museum, art galleries, theatres, clubs, and parties on steam boats. These were spaces that sat in-between the public and the private, like photographers' and artists' studios, and entertaining rooms in residential homes. But there are also intimate archival spaces created through personal photographic albums, diaries and letters like those produced by Barbara Ker-Seymer. In this chapter, we draw on archives which, read with and against the grain, give some insight into the experiences of Black queer people living in interwar Britain, whose lives intersected with white artists, musicians and writers including Edward Burra, Ker-Seymer, John Banting and Nancy Cunard, who were drawing inspiration from the 'Harlem Renaissance'.

Here we focus particularly on three individuals who appear in Key-Seymer's private albums: Jimmie Daniels, Edna Lloyd Thomas and the unnamed woman in the group photograph. Through these three people, we map queer Black spaces around Britain and beyond, tracing out a presence in public spaces and private places including sitting rooms, clubs, studios, country cottages and the psychiatrist's chair. These Black geographies encompass transatlantic migrations, municipal town tours and local geographies of friendship groups. These mappings locate Black *and* queer lives in and around Britain and challenge assumptions that Black queer people were to be found only in the clubs of Soho. Certainly they were here, both Jimmie Daniels and Edna Thomas performed in London, but queer Black spaces were also found in small towns and rural Britain, and through the archives we explore how comfortably (or not) these people were able to make and live parts of their lives in Britain's urban and rural queerscapes.

Though still limited in comparison to the breadth of studies on British life in the early twentieth century, we know increasing amounts about the spaces of cultural and ethnic diversity in interwar Britain, a time when individuals from the British Empire and wider African and Asian diasporas lived and worked across the country. The diversity of the Black presence in the early twentieth century reflected the geographies of imperial networks and changing political contexts. Black communities in Britain were made up of individuals from the Caribbean, the wider African diaspora and the United States. They included Black working-class women working as nurses and cooks and men who worked and lived in British port towns, connected to seaport trades that employed them on- and off-shore. Some were recently arrived migrants, others grandchildren born into long-established families. Many would be scarred by the racialized violence that erupted across Britain in 1919. That June, in Liverpool, Charles Wotton, a 24-year-old Bermudian man, drowned after being chased by a mob and pushed into the waters of Queen's Dock. His death marked a shocking moment in days of anti-Black terror in Liverpool, and African, South Asian, Chinese, Caribbean and Arab communities in Glasgow, Hull, London, Liverpool, Newport, South Shields, Salford, Cardiff and Barry all found themselves under attack, on the streets and in the press, throughout the year.[5]

During the 1920s racism, most obviously in the form of the 'colour bar' in everyday experiences such as finding housing or entering places of entertainment, was painfully and angrily recorded by Black activists.[6] Open discrimination in employment continued into the 1930s and was one of the concerns regularly highlighted by the League of Coloured Peoples when it was established in 1931. The second Pan-African congress held sessions in London in the summer of 1921, hosting over 100 delegates, and by the late 1920s West African students were part of a number of active organizations that were drawing attention to and challenging everyday acts of racism in Britain.[7] They included members of the African Progress Union, founded in December 1918 and chaired by Britain's first Black mayor John Archer, and the West African Students Union (WASU), which was established in 1925.

Histories of Black *and* queer life in Britain are limited in published sources. Our own work is part of a small though growing body of research and both academic and creative writing which explores Black queer lives before the arrival of the Windrush in 1948.[8] In his work on London and the politics of twentieth-century decolonization, Marc Matera draws attention to the queer cosmopolitan spaces of Soho associated with the sounds of Black London. The range of clubs in Soho provided work and convivial spaces for Black musicians from Britain, the Caribbean and Africa. Through such spaces of performance some Black musicians, artists and writers socialized with the cosmopolitan groupings of London's avant-garde including the 'Bright Young Things' as they embraced, not without problems, certain elements of Black culture. As Matera documents, in 1935 British musicians managed to get a virtual ban on African American musicians touring and working in Britain and showed little interest in supporting Black British musicians.[9] This racialized hostility had affected Black performers in Britain, like the African American Florence Mills, over a decade earlier. As we outline below, Mills and her company's presence on stages in Britain during the 1920s were very popular, including among queer communities. For one young woman Mills' presence stirred a deep desire in her, causing her to fall in love with a woman seemingly for the first time.[10] For others, the popularity and success of Black culture represented a direct threat to white supremacy. In 1933, the choral master Sir Henry Coward stated in a public lecture on 'Musical Art' that he approved 'of Hitler's decision to banish from Germany night clubs and nigger music'. He added, 'We must ban jazz. It has already led to the lowering of the prestige of the white races.'[11]

How queer Black folk in interwar Britain came to know of, use and feel themselves within queer, cosmopolitan spaces they were able to access is hard to grasp, but there are sources that can reveal something of their inner lives. We know something of the African American performer Jimmie Daniels, who appears in Ker-Seymer's albums; the young woman in the car is both a real and reimagined individual in the narrative we present here. The piecing together of individual Black queer lives is a painstaking work, as Gemma Romain's biography of Patrick Nelson illustrates. Nelson's biography highlights the different ways a wide array of archival sources can be used to recreate a biography of an individual life, drawing on personal correspondence, newspapers, government and military records, paintings, poetry and photographs. Born in Jamaica to a working-class Catholic family in 1916, Nelson migrated to Britain in 1937 in order to take up the position of a valet in Wales.[12] Following a brief return to Jamaica, Nelson moved to Britain in 1938, and at one point became a law student. He also worked as an artist's model and posed for Edward Wolfe and Duncan Grant. He and Grant would become lovers for a short while, but maintained a friendship for twenty-five years until Nelson's death in 1963.

In the spring of 1937 Patrick Nelson arrived at the Penrhos estate to begin his new job as a valet. The estate at Holyhead, Anglesey, in north-west Wales was one of the residences of the Stanley of Alderley family, and from the early 1930s home to Lyulph Victor Henry Owen Stanley, who inherited it on his twenty-first birthday in late 1936. A photograph of the house in the Anglesey Archives depicts a large country house with two wings overlooking a pristine lawn. Wicker chairs are set up on the grass, grouped together, ready to be lounged upon, but not by Patrick Nelson. He had travelled from Jamaica, where he had worked as a hotel valet, not to visit this country residence but to join the domestic staff of the household. Like his employer, Nelson was twenty-one and both Nelson and Lyulph were queer men, but their class and racialized identities point to vastly different experiences of queer life. Lyulph had the opportunity to travel for pleasure, and it is likely he first met Nelson while in Jamaica and perhaps arranged for him to migrate to and work for him in Britain.

Nelson's role of valet entailed attending 'entirely to his master's personal needs'.[13] He could be expected to undertake numerous personal and intimate tasks from overseeing Lyulph's wardrobe and ensuring his suits were well pressed to attending to his master's bath.[14] It may well have been viewed as a privileged post but could also have been seen, as Lucy Lethbridge has argued, as a post that inhabited a 'particular loneliness', a role that could leave a young man 'stranded somewhere between the camaraderie of the servants' hall and that of the drawing room'.[15] Nelson may have had little opportunity to bridge the gap as he was expected to travel with Lyulph and likely spent time with him in London when Lyulph enrolled to study at the Royal College of Music in 1937. It is perhaps through queer spaces in London frequented by the city's bohemians, and to which he had access through Lyulph, that Nelson met members of Duncan Grant's Bloomsbury group.

Nelson stayed with the Stanleys for just a few months; by November 1937 he found himself sailing back to Jamaica. Reading with and between the lines of his letters (which survive in Duncan Grant's archive), it seems possible that the short period of employment in Wales may have been because Lady Stanley found out about an affair between her son and Nelson. The power dynamics of such a relationship would have placed Nelson in a very insecure position. As Matt Cook found, although for some servants positions of 'living in' could provide opportunities 'to find sex, relationships, some camaraderie', they faced a 'double insecurity: both job and home could be lost if they were found out'.[16] For Patrick Nelson, a Black and working-class migrant with few if any kinship networks in England, these insecurities would have been even greater.

Nelson did return to Britain the following year, initially living in Bristol and then in London. For a time in 1938 he lived at 24 Netherton Grove in Chelsea, but his day-to-day experiences of Chelsea and London are not remotely represented in the pictures of Ker-Seymer's album. For Nelson work was hard to come by and he felt the pressure of searching for employment, working in domestic service and as an artists' model. The arrival of war would change the relationship between Patrick and Duncan Grant as the latter visited London less often and it seems Patrick was never invited to the Bloomsbury group's country retreat at Charleston. In the early months of the war Nelson began serving with the Auxiliary Military Pioneer Corps and was posted to France with the British Expeditionary Force. His capture in 1940 and him being held as a POW had a profound effect on his mental health and the remainder of his life.

For Nelson, coming from a working-class family in Jamaica, life as a valet in Britain offered some freedoms, but as a Black queer man, there seems little to connect his social and economic experiences to those of the African American performer Jimmie Daniels or the young woman pictured in the car. The lives of queer Black people in early-twentieth-century Britain are still to be pieced together in a systematic way. When recovering Black histories during the interwar period, images including the photographic and painted portraits created by artists such as Grant of Black sitters such as Nelson provide a frame in which we can try to uncover the multi-ethnic history and experiences of interwar London. But often, the archive that remains to be explored is not that of the Black sitter but the white artist. The white artists' archives such as those of Duncan Grant and Barbara Ker-Seymer provide important though clearly limited sources.

The Black individuals in the album such as Daniels and the young woman in the car are presented and preserved in the archive through the lens of a white woman photographer, and though these individuals were part of Ker-Seymer's circles of friendship, letters written in the 1920s reveal the extent to which racism remained engrained within their primarily white spaces. Tracing out Black queerscapes through intersecting archives of images, letters and performance spaces of the primarily white archives can resurface Black queer identities. They also surface racism and exoticism and, in doing so, suggest how the intersections of class, colonial struggle and racism made living Black queer lives in Britain difficult. But within the sources are also representations of conviviality, mobility, 'freedom', friendship and love.

Within the pages of Ker-Seymer's photograph albums there are a number of portraits of queer Black individuals who were living and working in interwar Britain. They were friends with, or at least acquaintances of, Ker-Seymer's social group. Among them is Jimmie Daniels, who appears on a number of pages of Ker-Seymer's albums. In one print he holds the Black American singer Elisabeth Welch in his arms; on another page, five studio portraits of him taken in June 1934 picture him smiling and posing in and out of shadow.[17] Born in Texas in 1908, Daniels developed his career as a performer following a period of time working as a secretary in New York. He started working on Broadway and became a professional singer, opened the Bronze Studio club in New York and toured across Europe during the 1930s. In the mid-1930s he performed at Frisco's in Soho and the well-known and popular London branch of the dance club Ciro's.[18] It is possibly here that Daniels met the Scottish writer and film director Kenneth Macpherson. In another photograph preserved in Ker-Seymer's albums, Daniels and McPherson are pictured together in a domestic setting.

They sit close and comfortably, perhaps sharing an armchair.[19] Another pictures them, now 'Ken and Jimmie', presumably on holiday in France. They are pictured relaxing, eating, swimming and drinking together in and around a villa on the Côte d'Azur in the summer of 1938.[20]

These images form part of the everyday pictures Ker-Seymer took of her circle of queer friends alongside her studio practice. Ker-Seymer had studied at Chelsea Polytechnic becoming friends with fellow students including Edward Burra, Billy Chappell and Clover Pritchard. After art school they continued their friendships through socializing in London and the spaces that supported their shared loves of jazz music, cinema, theatre, art and through their prolific letter writing. As Jane Stevenson highlights, this friendship group, while artistic, was not restricted to painters. After leaving college Billy Chappell became a professional dancer and Ker-Seymer would become an influential modernist photographer.[21]

Like Ker-Seymer, McPherson played an important part in the development of modernist artistic practices in Britain. In 1930 he worked with Paul and Eslanda Robeson on the experimental silent film *Borderline*, which he wrote and directed. A film filled with scenes of queer desire, it is also an experimental modernist examination of racism and 'inter-racial' relationships. At the time of its production, Macpherson was married to lesbian writer Bryher (the British heiress Winifred Ellerman) and it was the small production group POOL (consisting of Bryher, Bryher's lover the American writer H.D. (Hilda Doolittle) and Macpherson) who produced

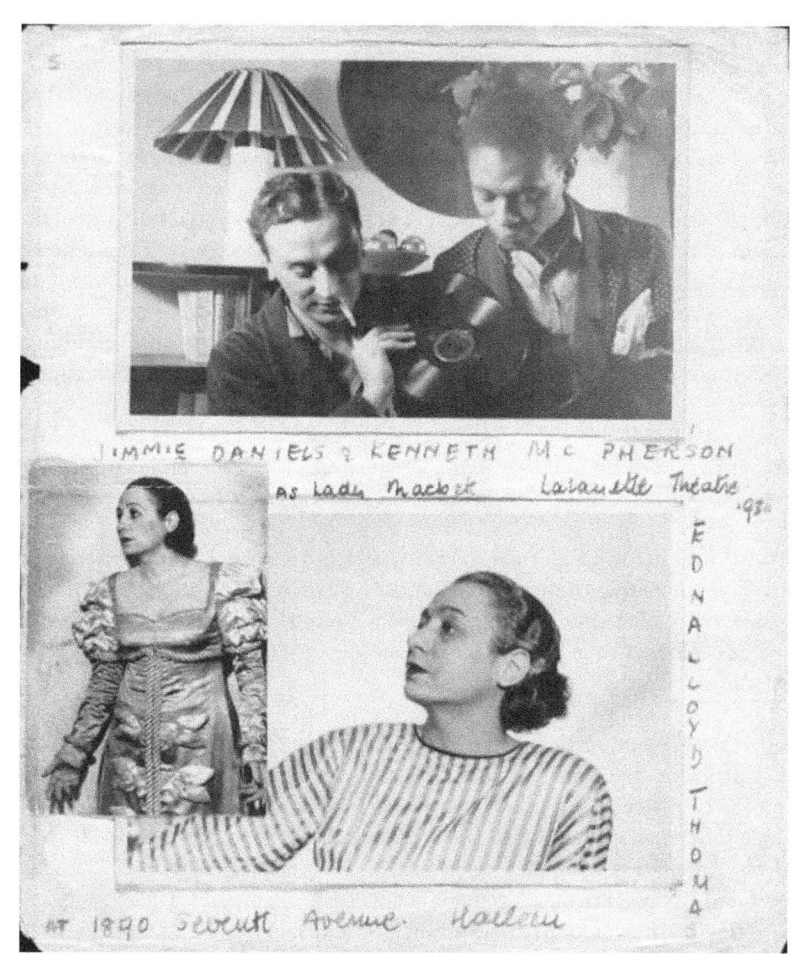

Figure 6 Three photographs of Kenneth Macpherson, Jimmie Daniels and Edna Lloyd Thomas. Photograph album, September 1935–8, page 3. TGA 974/5/5 © The estate of Barbara Ker-Seymer. Photo: Tate.

this film, which was shot in Switzerland.[22] But in the film these scenes exist within an imaginary framework of Black culture in relation to white co-producers ideas of nationalism, desire, anti-racism, modernism and the contradictory racialized logics of film narrative and production.[23] For Hazel Carby, the effect was 'to freeze Robeson into a modernist ideal of the Negro male, outside of history'.[24] Indeed, Eslanda recorded in her diary that 'Kenneth and H. D. used to make us so shriek with laughter with their naive ideas of Negroes that Paul and I often completely ruined our make-up with tears of laughter, and had to make up all over again', but also that 'We never once felt we were colored with them'.[25] It was a few years after the release of *Borderline* that Jimmie Daniels and McPherson met.

Ker-Seymer's photograph of Daniels and McPherson seemingly pictures them at home; a table lamp behind the chair they share is placed on the top shelf of a bookcase. Their focus is drawn down, away from the camera, the ash collecting on the end of McPherson's cigarette as they look through vinyl records.[26] It is not possible to see the labels on these records, but it is easy to imagine at least some of them were jazz recordings. Jazz was embraced by a range of people in interwar British society, including Britain's artistic and bohemian communities. This was a time when, despite the racialized prejudice Black performers could face, 'Harlem was in vogue' and Ker-Seymer's group of friends shared a love of jazz music and its association with modern identities.[27] Their letters show there was a (perhaps large) degree of 'performance' held both in the remaking of their white identities through consumptions and appropriations of Black popular culture and their personal relationships with Black people.

Members of Ker-Seymer's friendship group bought jazz and blues records, in shops such as Levy's of Aldgate, and they wrote to each passionately about the music they had purchased or wished to buy.[28] On 25 January 1927, she wrote to Edward Burra:

> Billy & I have got some glorious new nigger records. I've got Edith Wilsons song 'If you can't hold the man you love, Dont cry when he's gone' sung by a gorgeous negress, & the other side is divine it's called 'Mamma stayed out the whole night long, but mamma didn't do no wrong' sung by a glorious negro couple called Butterbeans & Susie.[29]

We see in this letter expressions of love for Black music and culture, but a consumption of these art forms that easily sat with deeply racist language; Black people had been clear on the offensiveness of use of the 'n' word since the nineteenth century.[30] Yet, in this circle individual claims of 'loves' for Black culture and people could sit with and be expressed alongside a complete ignorance of contemporary Black political action or debates on the use of racist terminology.

The letters written among this assembly of friends and acquaintances in the 1920s predate the rise in the 1930s of jazz bottle parties, cafes and small jazz clubs in Soho populated by Black and white Londoners.[31] However, as Judith Walkowitz has shown, in the 1920s 'shady nightclubs' like The 43 in Soho supported a diverse clientele, but these had limits. They were spaces where 'elite British metropolitan culture set the tone', where 'interracial couples were a rare sight... as were same-sex couples'.[32] For Ker-Seymer and her friendship group, their main interaction with the Black presence in the 1920s seems to have been through music and by attending hugely popular revues starring Black entertainers from America and people of the African diaspora living in Britain.

Both Edward Burra and Ker-Seymer adored the *Blackbirds* revue which took hold of popular British cultural life in the late 1920s. Opening before packed theatre audiences in September 1926, *Blackbirds* was important not only for white society *Vogue* readers keen to learn 'what the negro has made of jazz' but also for members of the Black diaspora in Britain.[33] Sold-out performances at the London Pavilion on Piccadilly Circus and 'Blackbird'-themed society parties confirmed the stardom of its lead performer, thirty-year-old African American Florence Mills.[34] James Wilson argues that Mills' performances can be seen to represent 'the modernist tension between savagery and civilisation', as seen in films like *Borderline*, but that she also collaborated with the white songwriters and producers to challenge stereotypical assumptions of Black womanhood.[35] The many ways her work could be read meant Mills was an inspiration to many British admirers. Her financial success from poor origins inspired working-class fans; her anti-racist politics made her a role model for Black women in Britain, while her beauty, flapper style and cross-dressing characters stirred lesbian desires.[36] The week before buying the Edith Wilson and the Butterbeans & Susie record, Ker-Seymer attended a *Blackbirds* performance, and wrote of her delight about the show to Burra in January 1927. She exclaimed:

> Oh Eddie, <u>BLACKBIRDS</u>!!!!!! I went to the 2nd edition last night…. Edith Wilson was the cabaret dancer in the most glorious frock of orange satin (<u>skin</u> tight) embroidered with diamonds, with a black velvet poppy on the hem and black cotton stockings with orange satin strap shoes, it really was a triumph in costumes.[37]

British elites socialized with *Blackbirds* stars and embraced Black culture in these environments of performance. However, Black performance was also exoticized and romanticized by white consumers, theatregoers and fans, who often objectified Black entertainers. This was the era of 'negrophilia', where Black culture was adopted as a way of embracing that which was perceived as modern and exciting by white artists.[38]

Yet, undoubtedly, friendships and long-lasting relationships survived these complex intersections of myth, desire and actuality within queer circles. By the late 1920s Ker-Seymer had become friends with bisexual Grenadian entertainer Leslie Hutchinson; in a letter to Edward Burra in February 1929, she told her friend about attending a party hosted by John Wells at his Hampstead Studio.[39] She went with a group which included Leslie and his brother; it was, she told Burra, one of the best parties she'd been to in years – before it was raided: '… never have I seen so many B's, every B in London was there without exception in the most glorious costumes you've ever seen, there were no women but us'.[40]

Another Black performer who became part of Ker-Seymer's circle was the African American actress and singer Edna Thomas. In the archive she appears in a series of photographs taken in the 1930s. In one she is pictured as Lady Macbeth, the character she played in the Federal Theatre Project's all-Black cast production of *Macbeth*, directed by Orson Welles in 1936.[41] Another depicts her leaning against a wall in a dress with wide billowing sleeves emphasizing a dramatic vertical print. These images were taken some time after Edna Thomas had begun a relationship with Olivia Wyndham, Ker-Seymer's former lover with whom she had lived in Chelsea during the early stages of her photographic career. In the late 1920s, at the age of age of forty-one, Edna had a revelation while dancing with a woman: 'something very terrific happened to me', she recalled, 'a very electric thing. It made me know I was homosexual'.[42] A few years later she met Wyndham, who pursued Thomas and moved to the United States to live with her in Harlem.

Edna Thomas' presence among Ker-Seymer's albums is a cutting intervention into the carefree prints laid out for the collection. Thomas' life was marked by the violent legacies of British colonialism, the institutionalization of slavery in the United States and its legacies in the labour of domestic service undertaken by Black people in settler colonial societies. Though for Patrick Nelson placement as a domestic worker in Britain may have offered some sexual and cultural freedoms, W E B DuBois saw domestic service as preserving 'the last vestiges of slavery and medievalism'.[43] Born in Virginia in 1886, Edna's great-grandmother was enslaved and Edna was the product of a rape upon her mother by the white man who employed her when she was twelve.[44] Following a difficult childhood, Edna Thomas did not find the alternative life she hoped for in either of her two marriages. Instead she found her freedoms on the stage, where, as Saidiya Hartman puts it, she 'became other selves'.[45]

Throughout the 1920s Thomas successfully performed across Britain, though it is not clear if she was acquainted with Ker-Seymer or her circle during her early tours. In 1923 she performed at the Wigmore Hall, and in 1924 she played at the Coliseum, where she was described in *The Observer* as 'gorgeously crinolined and gracefully art-conscious' while she 'sings the negro "spirituals" she has already made so popular'.[46] She developed a broad fan base; one man saw her nineteen times, and bell boys in hotels were excited to tell her their sisters had heard her perform more than once.[47] In *The Graphic*, a British critic demonstrated many racist assumptions as he wrote admiring of her 'wonderful grasp of negro *psychology*' both by 'her artistry and her intensive research in to the characteristics of negroes, who have for generations served her people in the South'.[48] Such critics, who acclaimed her successful 'interpretation' of the spirituals she sang, were seemingly unaware that she was 'a Negro'.[49]

In the winter of 1926 Thomas returned to Britain performing in spaces not usually associated with Black lives, nor thought of as queer Black spaces. She appeared on the bill as part of the Eastbourne Music Festival and the following autumn was back on British stages performing a 'delightful recital' at the Pleasure Gardens Theatre in Folkestone, Kent, for the Bouverie Society. During the same 1927 season the *Bath Chronicle* looked forward eagerly to her return performance at the Pump Room.[50]

It was some time during the months following these performances that Edna had the electrifying experience that changed her understanding of her sexuality. Thomas' recollections of her sexual awakening and relationship with Wyndham were collated by George W. Henry, who in 1937 published initial findings into a study of 'Psychogenic Factors in Overt Homosexuality' for the *American Journal of Psychiatry*.[51] The paper presented four case studies from an intended 100 'socially adjusted men and women' who were presented as individuals who had volunteered for the study to support 'a scientific investigation of a human relationship which they believe is unjustly frowned upon by society'.[52] In the paper Thomas was given the name Mary Jones and described as a 'successful Negro actress', now close to fifty years old.[53] It was during this account that Thomas recalled the electrifying dance she had experienced with a woman at the age of forty-one, an experience that had encouraged her to pursue relationships with a number of women before she met Olivia Wyndham. Although they reportedly met in New York, it seems likely that, given the importance of African American performers to the cultural experience of Ker-Seymer and her friends, Wyndham may have previously seen Thomas in one of her performances in Britain.[54] However they met, with Wyndham, Thomas found a relationship that 'affords a tenderness I have never known'.[55]

At the time Henry undertook his research, Thomas and Wyndham had been living together in Harlem for five years, and in that time, Edna explained, Wyndham had 'come to be very, very dear to me not just for sex alone – it's a very great love'.[56] Henry suggested this had come as some surprise to Edna, running against her expectations, as 'white women are reputed to be less faithful then [*sic*] the coloured'.[57] Kenneth McPherson also left Britain for New York to live with Jimmie Daniels. In the archives, the photograph of Jimmie and Kenneth looking through records is stuck onto the same album page of two images of Edna Thomas, with a note suggesting all three were taken at 1890 Seventh Avenue, Harlem.[58] This apartment block was the address of the home of Edna Thomas, Lloyd Thomas and Wyndham, and also for a while the home of Jimmie Daniels.[59] When Edward Burra visited New York in 1933 for a trip that was very important to his work, he too stayed there. Thomas and Wyndham took him to the cosmopolitan spaces of Harlem, including the Theatrical Grill, 'where Burra encountered Harlem's best-known drag queen, "Gloria Swanson"' and these experiences of the queer spaces of Harlem 'became the material for his artwork'.[60]

The images from inside 1890 Seventh Avenue in Ker-Seymer's work show queer lives lived in the United States, specifically New York, which perhaps offered a freedom for these mixed same-sex couples not available to them in Britain. Their migrations, along with those of Patrick Nelson, are a reminder that queer Black spaces are not fixed by city boundaries or national borders. Their unfixed place in Britain's queerscapes speaks to the many issues Nadia Ellis identifies in mapping queered belonging in the Black diaspora: 'identity, and black queer desire: the effect of migration on the construction of the self; the politics of competing localities; the conjunctions and disjunctions of nationalism and sexual identity'.[61] The Black women and the majority of the Black men identified within Ker-Seymer's albums are African Americans. Black British people do not seem to have really been part of her crowd, and with their absence, the complex intersections of queer desire with narratives of the British class system and colonial (non)belonging are avoided.[62]

The one possible challenge to this assumption is the young woman in the car. How the young Black woman in the car fits into the local and international networks of Ker-Seymer's friendship group is not easy to gauge. It is possible she was one of the women who made up the *Blackbirds* chorus. It is just as likely she would have been an audience member at any such performance; a woman from Britain, a Caribbean country, the United States; she may have been a member of the West African students Union, founded in London in 1925. It is possible the young woman was employed as a domestic labourer in a country house as Patrick Nelson was; it is possible, though her position within the group makes this feel unlikely. Perhaps there is some significance that the image in which she appears is a loose print and not in one of the albums. Perhaps not.

The geographical location of the group in the car, while unidentified, is striking in the context of Black history in Britain. As Tinkler and Warsh illustrate, automobile advertisements presented women with cars as an essential part of feminine modernity: cars facilitated independence, freedom and control.[63] The image of the women and the car is not taken in a club or a studio; it is an image taken beyond the spaces of urban cosmopolitanism and as such reflects a mobility of the Black presence in Britain rarely portrayed in the early twentieth century. In the background of the image is a whitewashed house; possibly it is Diamond Cottage, which appears in another of Ker-Seymer's albums, marking her visit there in 1941.[64]

Rabinovitch-Fox observes how, for the modern women epitomized by the flapper, the car became intertwined with other symbolisms of modern urban life, alongside skyscrapers and technological developments in print and photography. This was in addition to the possibilities of the car for 'providing a space to experience and experiment with… new courting customs and sexual practices'.[65] As such, Rabinovitch-Fox argues that car advertisements 'helped in the legitimization of certain ideas such as women's right to express their sexuality, their sense of mobility, and to exert their economic independence'.[66] Such a description could also certainly fit the confidence and joy expressed by the group of queer women in the print. The Black woman's position in this car strikes a contrast to Patrick Nelson's experience in the rural – where he perhaps also drove a car, but if so, it would have been as a chauffeur. During the 1930s, the chauffeur-valet was a not unlikely double role, and Nelson could drive.[67] In the qualifications for his military service it is noted that he was a driver in civilian life.[68] Alongside the modern, queer and gendered identities we can read onto the Black woman's body, the photograph also presents us with a depiction of a sense of belonging in rural Britain that is rarely portrayed between the wars.

To understand further the re-inscribing of Black bodies into rural spaces, we can draw on the work of the contemporary Black artist Ingrid Pollard. In her work, Ingrid Pollard seeks to challenge the symbolic access to British identities, particularly a sense of belonging to English landscapes. Through remapping and re-representing the Black presence in Britain, uniquely so in the context of the English countryside, Pollard re-inscribes Black identity on the English terrain. In her introduction to *Postcards Home*, one collection of her work, Pollard reflects on the importance of family photo albums and the stories that go with them. By the time she had left home, taking photographs had become part of her everyday activities. These included 'Reclaim the Night' demonstrations, the first conference of the Organisation of Women of African & Asian Descent (OWAAD), which was founded in 1978,[69] and a canoeing and walking holiday in Hereford with her Black Lesbian group.[70] Pollard's 1980s photo essay 'Pastoral Interludes' depicted how uncomfortable she and other Black bodies were in the rural spaces to which countless English people retreat.[71] The series of five tinted pictures, a project which began as holiday snaps, depicts individuals in a rural landscape alongside a text which, as Phil Kinsman surmises, 'speaks of a sense of dread in visiting the countryside, of not belonging, of a threat of violence, even death'.[72]

In their exploration of 'queer country', Bell and Valentine outline the many forms of 'rurality in the gay imagination' which present it as a safe space for same-sex desires.[73] But any such romanticization of the rural is one filtered through a white lens. For many Black people the English countryside was not (nor is it now) a place of joy, freedom or retreat. As the accompanying text to one of the images in Pollard's essay recalls: 'I wandered lonely as a Black face in a sea of white. A visit to the countryside is always accompanied by a feeling of unease; dread.'[74] During her trips to the Lake District, Pollard recalls 'searching the postcard-stand for the card that shows a sunny upland scene with a Black person standing, looking over the hills. Never finding it.'[75] The narrative for Pastoral Interlude speaks to way the history of slavery is made seemingly invisible, and the threat of violence that remains for Black bodies in rural spaces; the sense that: 'The owners of these fields, these trees and sheep want me off their GREEN AND PLEASANT LAND. No Trespass, they want me DEAD.'[76] Pollard's work challenges the absences around and gives sight to the histories of Black people in the rural. Though Pollard has argued that you do not have to dig very deep beneath the surface of rural landscapes to find new narratives of the past, the histories she and other artists and scholars uncover remain challenging.[77]

Francesco Cattani argues, in Pollard's work, by placing Black people in a rural setting, 'far from the city where they are supposed to live and stay... she displays something different.'[78] The Black woman in the print preserved by Ker-Seymer displays something different again. She does not seem to be out of place; there is no sense of unease or dread portrayed as she looks directly at us from the green and pleasant land around her. The directness of her gaze is captivating. It is possible to imagine her among the 'craggy rocks, rushing streams and lowly sheep' where Ingrid Pollard searched for a familiar face.[79] This lone Black women's trip does not seem to reflect a fleeting pastoral interlude but a shared, relaxed day out with friends. It is frustrating not to be able to understand where her boldness came from – or how it was lost to us. Although, since attention prompted by the bicentenary of the abolition of the slave trade in 2007, we now know more about journeys into rural England by Black people, the journey behind the presence of this woman is seemingly as unknowable now as in the 1980s.

The unknown woman in the car, Edna Thomas, Jimmie Daniels and Patrick Nelson are just four people who were a part of the Black queerscapes of interwar Britain. Their archival presence as represented here is held within the albums of one individual and one extended network of friends. Such histories of blackness and queerness in Britain rarely intersect. As the artist and archivist Ajamu has reflected, 'There was a big gap around the Black gay and lesbian experience in the UK. I can tell millions of stories about my family and the Black experience. I can tell a million stories about being gay. But in terms of Black *and* gay … … '.[80] This reflects the place of the Black British queer archive, one which, as Mary Stevens observes, has been 'doubly marginalized by the splintering of activist historiography into discrete categories of a heteronormative Black history and an exclusive monochromatic queer history'.[81] For Nadia Ellis this is an even more surprising and damaging division than it might initially seem given that 'this trade-off belies the shared subject positions of the homosexual and the black migrant: [who had] a strikingly similar relationship to the laws and discourses that governed their status in 1950s and 1960s England'.[82] Furthermore, she outlines, 'the logic of homophobia and anti-migrant racism relies on similar language. In the most prejudicial accounts of sexual and racial alarm, homosexuality and exponentially increased West Indian presence in Britain become indices of the nation's decline'.[83]

Yet, as historians have sought to uncover the histories of queer and Black lives as part of the challenge to legal discrimination and social oppression, in narratives of LGBTQ+ history and Black history, Black queer people have routinely been rendered 'just invisible'.[84]

Jimmie Daniels, Edna Thomas, Patrick Nelson and the unknown woman mark important archival interventions at this intersection, but they cannot begin to embody the breadth of experiences which Black people encountered in queer spaces in interwar Britain. Patrick Nelson attests that clearly not all Black queer men were able to enjoy the personal economic control or freedom of relationships experienced by Jimmie Daniels.[85] The young Black woman, who is part of Ker-Seymer's group expressing their 'modernity and freedom', speaks not just to a freedom of sexuality associated with the technology of the car and women's sexuality.[86] She speaks also to the potential mobility of Black individuals to inhabit spaces of the English countryside.

This chapter has not been able to reveal much about how these individuals, or Black people more generally, felt about their place, representation or experiences in these spaces. This is something we need to try and access. If we are really to interrogate how queer spaces were created and consumed, we need to know how Black and other people of colour 'performed', expressed or understood their cosmopolitan identities. Tracing out their place in Britain's queerscapes requires a mapping of personal geographies and transnational migrations and an examination of how opposition to racism and political awakenings intersected with performances of 'modernist cosmopolitanism' people could make use of or simply enjoy with their lovers, friends and partners in clubs, bars, country retreats, studios, their homes and their cars.

Notes

1   Photograph 'Barbara Ker-Seymer and others', Tate Archives, TGA974.6.25, Barbara Ker-Seymer.
2   Einav Rabinovitch-Fox, 'Baby, you can drive my car: Advertising women's freedom in 1920s America', *American Journalism* 33, no. 4 (2016): 372–400.
3   Also known as the Bright Young People, the National Portrait Gallery presented 'Cecil: Beaton's 'Bright Young Things' in 2020; digitized images of some members of the group can be viewed on the gallery's website: https://www.npg.org.uk/collections/search/group/1356/.
4   On Joe Carstairs see Kate Summerscale, *The Queen of Whale Cay: The Extraordinary Story of 'Joe' Carstairs, the Fastest Woman on Water* (London: Bloomsbury: 2012).
5   Peter Fryer, *Staying Power: The History of Black People in Britain* (London: Pluto Press, 1984); Jacqueline Jenkinson, *Black 1919: Riots, Racism and Resistance in Imperial Britain* (Liverpool: Liverpool University Press, 2009).
6   For example Claude McKay recalled the racism he faced in Britain in his memoir *A London Way From Home* (1937); see Gemma Romain and Caroline Bressey, 'Claude McKay: Queering spaces of black radicalism in interwar London', in *Sex, Time and Place: Queer Histories of London, c1850 to the Present*, ed. Simon Avery and Katherine M Graham (London: Bloomsbury Academic, 2016), 115–31.

7   Fryer, *Staying Power*; Hakim Adi, *West Africans in Britain, Nationalism, Pan-Africanism and Communism* (London: Lawrence and Wishart, 1998).

8   In addition to sources cited here, see for example the 2020 novel *Lote*, by Shola von Reinhold and Ronald Cummings, "On the (im) possibility of black British queer studies." In Garrido, F. E., Koegler, C., Nyangulu, D., & Stein, M. U. (Eds.). *Locating African European Studies: Interventions, Intersections, Conversations* (2019), 278–293.

9   Marc Matera, *Black London: The Imperial Metropolis and Decolonization in the Twentieth Century* (Oakland, CA: University of California Press, 2015).

10   Caroline Bressey and Gemma Romain, 'Staging race: Florence Mills, celebrity, identity and performance in 1920s Britain', *Women's History Review* 28, no. 3 (2019): 380–95.

11   Hull, *Daily Mail*, 22 May 1933, 4.

12   The material on Patrick Nelson is taken from Gemma Romain's biography, *Race, Sexuality and Identity in Britain and Jamaica: The Biography of Patrick Nelson* (London: Bloomsbury Academic, 2017).

13   Edith Waldemar-Leverton, *Servants and Their Duties: A Helpful Manual for Mistress and Servant* (London: C. Arthur Pearson, 1912), 36–7.

14   Waldemar-Leverton's, *Servants and Their Duties*.

15   Lucy Lethbridge, *Servants: A Downstairs View of Twentieth-Century Britain* (London: Bloomsbury, 2013), 83.

16   Matt Cook, *Queer Domesticities: Homosexuality and Home Life in Twentieth-Century London* (Basingstoke and New York: Palgrave Macmillan, 2014), 27.

17   Tate Archive TGA 974/5/1 (they also appeared photographed together in TGA 974/5/5); June 1934, Tate Archive TGA 974/5/4.

18   On his presence at Frisco's in *The Bystander*, 18 September 1935, 10.

19   Tate Archive TGA 974/5/5 (they also appear together with Zena Douglas and Rolando in a series of images in the same album taken in October 1936).

20   Tate Archive TGA 974/5/6.

21   Jane Stevenson, *Edward Burra: Twentieth-Century Eye* (London: Random House, 2007), 85.

22   Macpherson and Bryher were also editors of the modernist journal *Close Up*; for more on the group and the film, see Annette Debo, 'Interracial modernism in avant-garde film: Paul Robeson and H.D. in the 1930 Boderline', *Quarterly Review of Film and Video* 18, no. 4 (2001): 371–83.

23   Jean Walton, '"Nightmare of the uncoordinated white-folk": Race, psychoanalysis, and borderline', *Discourse* 19, no. 2 (1997): 88–109.

24   Hazel V. Carby, *Race men* (Cambridge, MA: Harvard University Press, 2009), 67–8.

25   Cited in Martin Duberman, *Paul Robeson: A Biography* (New York: Open Road Media, 2014), 131; see also Susan McCabe, 'Borderline modernism: Paul Robeson and the Femme Fatale', *Callaloo* 25, no. 2 (2002): 639–53.

26   Tate Archive TGA 974/5/5 (they also appear together with Zena Douglas and Rolando in a series of images in the same album taken in October 1936).

27   David Levering Lewis, *When Harlem Was in Vogue* (New York: Knopf, 1981).

28   Stevenson, *Edward Burra: Twentieth-Century Eye*.

29   Ker-Seymor to Edward Burra, 25th January 1927, Tate Archive TGA 974.2.1.12.

30   On the long-standing offense taken to the 'n' word dating back to the nineteenth century, see Bressey, *Empire, Race and the Politics of Anti-Caste*.

31   See Judith Walkowitz, *Nights Out: Life in Cosmopolitan London* (New Haven, CT: Yale University Press, 2012).

32   Ibid., 221.

33   *Vogue*, Late August, C. B. Cochran Scrapbooks V&A THM/97.

34   *Evening Telegraph*, 13 January 1927, 2; *Hull Daily Mail*, 18 January 1927, 6.

35   James F. Wilson, *Bulldaggers, Pansies and Chocolate Babies: Performance, Race and Sexuality in the Harlem Renaissance*, 2nd edition (Ann Arbor: University of Michigan Press 2013), 218.

36   On these different fan expressions, see Bressey and Romain, Staging Race, *Women's History Review*.

37   Tate Archives, 974.2.1.1-43 – Letters from Barbara Ker-Seymer to Edward Burra, 1925–1929, 974.2.1.11 – 14th January (about) 1927.

38   Not all those within the Bright Young People set embraced ideas of Black culture even in this romanticized form; for example Evelyn Waugh included racist caricatures of Black entertainers in his writings and mainly attended shows such as the *Blackbirds* revue because of his attraction to socialite Olivia Plunkett-Green. James Donald, *Some of These Days: Black Stars, Jazz Aesthetics, and Modernist Culture* (New York: Oxford University Press, 2015), 16–17. See also, Gemma Romain, '1926: Interwar London and race', in *The Royal Academy of Arts Summer Exhibition: A Chronicle, 1769–2018*, ed. Mark Hallett, Sarah Victoria Turner and Jessica Feather (London: Paul Mellon Centre for Studies in British Art, 2018): https://chronicle250.com/1926.

39   On Leslie Hutchinson and the British swing scene, see Andy Simons, 'Black British swing', *JAJRC Journal* 41, no. 3 (2008): 35; and 'Black British swing: Part 3', *IAJRC Journal* 42, no. 1 (2009): 55–66.

40   Ker-Seymer to Edward Burra, Tate Archives TGA974.2.1.39. The use of 'B' for Buggers was a contemporary slang.

41   Andy Piascik, 1936: Macbeth with an All-Black Cast Plays Bridgeport: https://bportlibrary.org/hc/african-american-heritage/1936-macbeth-with-an-all-black-cast-plays-bridgeport/; TGA 974/5/5.

42   George W. Henry, 'Psychogenic factors in overt homosexuality', *American Journal of Psychiatry* 93, no. 4 (1937): 889–908. See also Jonathan Ned Katz (who approximates the year to be 1928) and Edna Thomas ('Mary Jones'): 'a tenderness I have never known', outhistory.org/exhibits/show/edna-thomas–mary-jones.

43   DuBois cited in Hartman Saidiya, *Wayward Lives, Beautiful Experiments: Intimate Histories of Riotous Black Girls, Troublesome Women, and Queer Radicals* (London: Serpents Tale, 2019), 206.

44   Hartman, *Wayward Lives*, 205.

45   Ibid., 211.

46   *The Era*, 18 July 1923, 6. 'Lopokova at the colosseum', *The Observer*, 6 April 1924; *Westminster Gazette*, 10 July 1923, 12. Also see Ivan H. Browning, 'Across the pond', *The Chicago Defender*, 20 August 1927.

47   *The Era*, 16 April 1924, 11.

48   *The Graphic*, 19 April 1924, 4.

49   For example, see W. S. Meadmore's column in *The Sphere*, 21 June 1924, 24.

50   *Folkestone, Hythe, Sandgate & Cheriton Herald*, 15 October 1927, 7; *Bath Chronicle and Weekly Gazette*, 15 October 1927, 15.

51   On the broader context of the study, see Henry L. Minton, 'Community empowerment and the medicalization of homosexuality: Constructing sexual identities in the 1930s', *Journal of the History of Sexuality* 6, no. 3 (1996): 435–58. Thomas was given pseudonyms in the report(s), and Minton identifies Edna Thomas as the subject.

52 Henry, 'Psychogenic factors in overt homosexuality', 889, 90.

53 Minton, 'Community empowerment and the medicalization of homosexuality'.

54 On the possibilities of fan desire, see Bressey and Romain, 'Staging Race'.

55 Henry, 'Psychogenic factors in overt homosexuality', 889, 98; Hartman, *Wayward Lives*.

56 Ibid.

57 Ibid., 902.

58 TGA 974/5/5, 3. Daniels and Key-Seymer were still in touch in the 1940s when she photographed him in military uniform.

59 See James Daniels in the New York, United States, Arriving Passenger and Crew Lists (including Castle Garden and Ellis Island), November 1937, ancestry. co.uk record drawn from Microfilm Publication T715, 8892 rolls. NAI: 300346. Records of the Immigration and Naturalization Service; National Archives at Washington, D.C.

60 Reina Lewis and Andrew Stephenson, 'Introduction: Queer visual historiographies', *Visual Culture in Britain* 18, no. 1 (2017): 9.

61 See Nadia Ellis, *Territories of the Soul: Queered Belonging in the Black Diaspora* (Durham: Duke University Press, 2015), 104.

62 Ibid., 108.

63 Penny Tinkler and Cheryl Krasnick Warsh, 'Feminine modernity in interwar Britain and North America: Corsets, cars, and cigarettes', *Journal of Women's History* 20, no. 3 (2008): 113–43.

64 The location of the cottage is not apparent from the archive.

65 Rabinovitch-Fox 'Baby, you can drive my car', 372–400, 375.

66 Rabinovitch-Fox, 'Baby, you can drive my car', 399.

67 Lucy Lethbridge on valet chauffeur.

68 Romain, *Life of Patrick Nelson*.

69 For a reflection on the conferences, see Brixton Black Women's Group, 'Black women organizing', *Feminist Review* 17, no. 1 (1984): 84–9.

70 Ingrid Pollard, 'Looking back at ways of working', *Postcards Home* (2004): 8.

71 Phil Kinsman, 'Landscape, race and national identity: The photography of Ingrid Pollard', *Area* 27, no. 4 (1995): 300–10.

72 Ibid., 301–2.

73 They note the reality of contemporary lives is often 'tales of isolation, unsupportive social environments and a chronic lack of structural services and facilities'. David Bell and Gill Valentine, 'Queer country: Rural lesbian and gay lives', *Journal of Rural Studies* 11, no. 2 (1995): 113–22, 116.

74 Ingrid Pollard, Pastoral Interlude, 1988: http://www.ingridpollard.com/pastoral-interlude.html.

75 Ingrid Pollard, Postcards Home, 2004, Wordswoth Heritage, 58.

76 Ingrid Pollard, Pastoral Interlude, 1988, original emphasis http://www.ingridpollard.com/pastoral-interlude.html.

77 Caroline Bressey, 'Cultural archaeology and historical geographies of the black presence in rural England', *Journal of Rural Studies* 25, no. 4 (2009): 386–95.

78 Francesco Cattani, 'Swamping the country: Ingrid Pollard's cartography of Englishness', *Black Arts in Contemporary Britain* 15 (2010): 85–102.

79 Ingrid Pollard, *Postcards Home*, 58.

80 Ajamu X., Topher Campbell and Mary Stevens, 'Love and lubrication in the archives, or rukus!: A Black queer archive for the United Kingdom', *Archivaria* 68 (2010): 271–94, 281, original emphasis.

81   Ibid., 271–94, 272.

82   See Ellis, *Territories of the Soul*, 131; see Chapter 3 for a discussion of these intersections in British research undertaken in the 1950s and 1960s.

83   See ibid., 131.

84   Ajamu X., Campbell and Stevens, 'Love and lubrication in the archives, or rukus!' 271–94, 280.

85   For example, see Gemma Romain's biography of Patrick Nelson, Gemma Romain, *Race, Sexuality and Identity in Britain and Jamaica: The Biography of Patrick Nelson, 1916–1963* (London: Bloomsbury Publishing, 2017).

86   Rabinovitch-Fox, 'Baby, you can drive my car', 375.

7

London suburbs and the co-creation of LGBT+ Jewish identities

Searle Kochberg and Margaret Greenfields

LGBT+ London is typically associated with the 'Soho Scene' and gentrified parts of Islington, Hackney and Vauxhall. In contrast 'Jewish London' is often associated with a mythologized East End, first entry point for many Jewish immigrants in the nineteenth century, and with the north and north-west inner suburbs of Stamford Hill and Golders Green. In this chapter we set out to expand these geographically limited 'imagined spaces' and explore how people who are both LGBT+ and Jewish describe a hybridized presence in London's wider suburbs. We propose that suburban London itself may feature as a 'character' in the consolidation and constitution of LGBT+ Jewish identities in the capital and explore how co-creative methodologies of working with/in LGBT+ Jewish communities can broaden a sense of belonging – in particular through 'reconstructing' ritual in non-traditional settings. In these ways we engage with the rarely discussed interplay of LGBT+ and Jewish identities beyond central London but importantly not beyond London. While our methodology has broader reach, our substantive claims relate to the specificity of London's suburban spaces and we deliberately don't extend them to other places.

We present our exploration predominantly through the prism of two research projects which between them explored how a queer blending of particular spaces and Jewish commemorative ritual might aid the constitution of LGBT+ Jewish 'places' as experienced by groups or individuals. Here we are using the word 'place' to imply an active, experiential relation between space and identity.[1] The first project was the Arts and Humanities Research Council-funded *Ritual Reconstructed*,[2] an inter-disciplinary, mixed-methods study (2014–15). The second was Kochberg's doctoral research project, *My Jewish London: Performance and Identity in Co-Creative Documentary Practice*,[3] which used a co-creative 'walking film' research methodology to explore gay male Jewish experience in/of London. This thesis proposes the existence of queer ephemeral places of the mind and body and in so doing challenges conventional representations of 'Jewish London'. Both projects expose notions of mainstream religious and social exclusion, and contemplate an LGBT+ Jewish 'place' of religious praxis and ethnicized identities. They move beyond the heteronormative spaces of traditional faith rituals located in the home or synagogue, and the 'traditional' spaces of queer conviviality and connection in Soho, Islington, Hackney or Vauxhall. Our projects are imbued with the spirit of 'bricolage',[4] the process of tinkering with, breaking down and rebuilding ritual processes, to bring union to, and make meaningful connections between, previously discrete locales, activities and groups.

In this chapter we thus examine hitherto underexplored parts of suburban London, looking to reclaim them as specific spaces that have personal, and perhaps collective, LGBT+ Jewish meaning. These 'places' may be long-lasting or ephemeral, and help to articulate an LGBT+ identity as experiential rather than fixed and essentialized, as part of a process of becoming a 'whole human being'. This form of coalescence, which comes about through performative ritual incorporating both LGBT+ and Jewish identity elements, can be associated with the process of 'identity negotiation' in which 'identity consistency' is obtained through undertaking repeated cultural routines in a familiar cultural environment.[5] Conversely, 'identity change, chaos or turmoil'[6] can occur when there is a mismatch or requirement that someone seeks to locate or engage with, in an unfamiliar, new or hostile environment. Both were in play for project participants who showed in this process of bricolage how suburbia – as an idea and also a series of actual places – enables and supports identity negotiation and reconstruction.[7]

Our first section takes the reader through what is generally understood as Jewish London – identified as such by analysis of census data, by the Institute for Jewish Policy Research[8] and by Orthodox Judaism movements, and the adoption of self-defined *eruvs*,[9] or religious Jewish boundaries.[10] The chapter then proceeds to consider how certain suburban spaces in Greater London – some acknowledged Jewish areas, others not – become defining 'characters' in LGBT+ Jewish experience. We show how spontaneous, ephemeral LGBT+ Jewish 'places' are experienced through the creative wanderings and ritualistic tinkering of LGBT+ Jews in London's suburbia.

Setting the scene: London Jewish space

Nathan Abrams, an academic writer on Jewish film and commentator on UK Jewish cultural life, has referred to *Minhag Anglia*, a Hebrew term meaning both 'the tradition of England' and also an informal policy advocated by Modern Orthodox Jewish leaders in the UK to create a blend of Jewishness and Britishness.[11] In effect, this is about assimilation and is a world away from the high levels of visibility of ultra-Orthodox Haredi Jews who live clustered in tight-knit, high-residential density enclaves in Stamford Hill, Golders Green and increasingly in more distant north-west London suburbs such as Hendon or Hertsmere.[12] We use a migration model to analyse LGBT+ Jewish public space around the peripheries of London (Golders Green/Hendon/Hertsmere) to which first-generation Jewish immigrants moved after periods in the inner city.[13] This model is core to popular Jewish and non-Jewish conceptions about the 'authentic' places 'where Jews belong' in London. This migration model and these territories offer fixed, hegemonic notions of where Jews are and where they need to be. This doesn't necessarily serve the interests of Jewish groups who do not define themselves in those concrete terms, but who locate themselves instead in the more indefinite spaces which were the focus of *My Jewish London* and *Ritual Reconstructed*.

These projects looked to more flexible Jewish 'places' across Greater London 'where encounters and informal interaction can bring a sense of community and local identity'.[14] Here space becomes imbued with personal investment and experience, and vice versa; and these places became especially 'meaningful location[s]' for the Jewish LGBT+ individuals engaging with them.[15] We found that this queering of locality might be associated with mobility: moving away from established Jewish public enclaves and moving through public space (as part of the film-based project), and in the process 'moving' established Jewish narratives.

In both projects the rejection of the notion of 'inert' space[16] opened up the possibility of space becoming a meaningful 'character' – or 'place' – in any personal spatio-temporal narrative defined by geography or history on film (or captured in interview). Accordingly, our studies explore the extent to which these activities can construe new locales, new 'places'[17] and new Jewish social subjectivities. This micro-focus, which entwines the geographical and personal domains of identity and history, can be missed if there is too great a focus on an essentialized and 'authentic' Jewish life.[18] Such conceptions often draw upon a reification of historical settlement locations or specific and set urban narratives of migration, religious tradition and Ashkenazi ritual practice.[19] Online and face-to-face interaction are clearly evident across the LGBT+ Jewish community in London. Online links help reinforce cohesiveness among groups such as the Jewish LGBT+ Group (formerly the Jewish Gay and Lesbian Group – JGLG), Keshet UK,[20] Rainbow Jews[21] and Gay Jews in London (GJIL).[22] However, even in an age of virtual spaces, real London locales and the Jewish community's experience of them play a significant part in building a Jewish sense of place which is entwined with the geographies of LGBT+ identity and experience. Indeed, our contributors frequently mentioned their connection to particular places and the importance of other 'queer Jews' who were often there too.

It is worth noting that the increasing recognition of LGBT+ public participation has taken place alongside the decreasing visibility of overt 'Jewish-ness' in the public sphere. The circumspect attitude of much of UK Jewry and reluctance to be clearly identified as a member of the community is a well-documented phenomenon. It is seen to relate to many factors, including: the small size of the UK Jewish population (at 0.5 per cent of the UK population based on census returns[23]), the processes of assimilation into wider society,[24] perceived hostility and antisemitism in political and online spheres, and some highly publicized attacks on the 'visibly Jewish' (often Ultra-Orthodox) community in the UK.[25] In London the way Jewish people 'self identify' as 'other' in the public realm may be mitigated by the fact that about two-thirds of Britain's 300,000 Jews live within Greater London, with many of the major Jewish, including LGBT+ Jewish, organizations based there. The feeling of dis-ease, anxiety and a desire to blend in has nevertheless led even in the capital to what Brook has rather harshly called a 'self-effacement', leading to 'timidity, the bedfellow of mediocrity'.[26] This uncertainty is compounded for LGBT+ Jews, as they are faced with homophobic 'violence and harassment, frequently in public places'.[27] And yet, despite these anxieties, we found that gay Jewish men (at least) used the 'challenging' public realm to explore the diversity of their Jewish subjectivities. We discovered that the ways in which gay Jewish men experience their self-identified public 'Jewish London' environments may at times facilitate the performing of elements of experience in places where identities are potentially 'simultaneously asserted and "under threat"'.[28] As they cruise and wander through the suburbs, their shifting experiences captured on film of/in public spaces help characterize LGBT+ Jewish places as unfixed – part imagined, part abstracted, part remembered, part here and now.[29] On the other hand, some transgender and lesbian participants said that their experiences as Jewish women were often related to safe, distinctive, private spaces in the home, through online networks or in some smaller communal settings.[30]

The Greater London spaces explored in *Ritual Reconstructed* and in *My Jewish London* are best understood as sites of negotiation, contestation and reimagining, where 'there is always already a play of the multiplicity of racial and cultural voices'.[31] Both research projects identified suburban spaces that challenged the accepted mapping and psycho-geography of Jewish London. In one case study in *My Jewish London*, a Jewish Modern Orthodox enclave of Canons Park is fleetingly transformed into a place of LGBT+ Jewish meditation, through a contributor's re-enactment of his queer appropriation of an ancient Jewish 'cleansing' ritual in Stanmore Marsh. In the 1980s in a Unitarian Church Hall in Golders Green, a reworked traditional Purim Spiel created a temporary footprint to LGBT+ Jewish experience.[32] It was performed with camp Broadway songs, references to cruising in the local Hampstead Heath and shopping in Golders Green Road, all at a time when mainstream Jewish venues would not have accepted such references. Elsewhere, in Streatham, a south London suburb with no particular Jewish public profile, a local community of Progressive Jews appropriated their Synagogue space from 2012 to 2015 to mark London Pride in 'their way', in marked contrast to the 'official' Jewish Pride events occurring in the central London 'cathedral' synagogues.[33] In another case study in *My Jewish London*, a former synagogue site in Queens Park, now a Muslim community centre, becomes a temporary memorial site for LGBT+ Jewish experience and desire as a gay man reflects on early sexual experiences at the synagogue and coming out to his mother in the late 1980s. The bricolage involved in these three examples helps to break down, rebuild and bring into being new Jewish sites and new rituals incorporating both LGBT+ and Jewish memorializations and practices. In each case the individuals pursue a politicized 'mobility of thought', and transform themselves 'in the act of transforming their material surroundings'.[34] LGBT+ Jewish suburban places manifest in 'spatial environments in which Jewish things happen, where Jewish activities are performed, and which in turn are shaped and defined by those [particular] Jewish activities'.[35]

The community participants of both research projects are members of Progressive Judaism, which strives to broaden the spectrum of Jewishness by arguing for experience rather than essence, and identity/ies that represent a broader canvas than are found in more traditional 'Modern Orthodox' Judaism. Yet despite the variety of Judaisms and the greater acceptance of LGBT+ identities within some progressive strands of the faith, there remains a persistent and nagging perception among project participants that residence within Orthodox Jewish-dominated London enclaves is widely accepted as the normative model of Judaism. The challenge is thus to reject, break down and ultimately reconstruct LGBT+ Jewish experiences and places that can then be foregrounded and accepted as legitimate on their own terms.

Suburban London: A main character in hybridized LGBT+ Jewish identities

Mainstream historical tropes of the experiences of UK Jews tend to be organized around three subplots, all of which originate in the journey narratives of Hebrew Bible (the Old Testament, or Tanakh): Exodus, Wilderness and Exile. In our projects, these three themes – and indeed the sense of 'homecoming' articulated by many respondents, where opportunities were identified for blending identities and public recognition and acceptance of their Jewish and LGBT+ selves – emerged repeatedly in data we collected, or artefacts produced as part of the *Ritual Reconstructed* 'ritual bricolage' activities.[36]

The theme of Exodus draws precedent from the biblical book of the same name; Wilderness from both Exodus and Numbers; and Exile from the narratives in Genesis, Ezra, Esther and Daniel (also in the Old Testament). These key 'biblical' narratives are heavily deployed in historical writing by UK Jews and in many major TV documentaries on British Jewish history.[37] For instance, popularly in narrative and documentary film, Jewish London journeys verge on a prescribed teleology, 'progressing' from the inner city ghetto to the wealthier suburb enclaves.[38] We would argue, however, that this is an inadequate model; the Jewish metroscape is better understood as infinitely more nuanced, where 'the suburb [functions] as a continuum of the city's spatial-social complexity'.[39]

In terms of representation of Jewish migration across Greater London to suburban space, the dominating trope is thus Exodus. It looks back at the 'Yiddishkeit' (close-knit, often poverty-stricken, Orthodox Askenazi Jewish way of life) in the traditionally imagined post-migration 'heartlands' of East London,[40] while Exile informs narratives of (enforced) diaspora and international migration. For our participants, 'Exile' can also equate to rupture and separation from prior Jewish practice, often while negotiating a newly 'out' LGBT+ identity seen as being at odds with 'authentic' heteronormative Judaism.[41] In a focus group in *Ritual Reconstructed*, a transgender participant who was a member of a United Orthodox synagogue referred to the sense of being 'outcast' as they began the process of transitioning. In turn, a cisgender gay man who was formerly strictly Orthodox stressed that 'Coming out… it's something that doesn't exist in the [Haredi] world… so that is why I wouldn't let myself believe that I can go there'.

The concept of Wilderness and its accompanying theme of 'personal spiritual wanderings'[42] dominate the narratives of LGBT+ Jews in the two research projects. Both would suggest that for LGBT+ Jews living in the capital, a simple teleological conception of movement from inner to outer London Jewish place is inadequate.[43] Both projects locate their narratives in a diversity of experience and material spaces across London. As already indicated, these locations trigger a more abstracted autobiographical sense of place, or a series of arrested personal moments looking back then forward, then back again in time, rather than presenting the stories as univocal and 'progressive'.[44] In our projects, such personal moments are likely to originate in the suburbs, effecting a queering of space, such as experienced by one on-screen collaborator in his *My Jewish London* co-created film. In his feedback questionnaire the participant describes his filmed walk in Canons Park, north-west London, as 'allow[ing] me to think and explore [my subjectivity] at my own pace. Like a soliloquy'.[45] The filmed walk method of minimum intervention on the part of the filmmaker and long duration shots facilitate an uninterrupted autobiographical reflection. However, the locale is crucial too. The participant's response on camera and audio is geographically specific, grounded in personal history; this man grew up in Canons Park.

In an episode from another film for *My Jewish London*, the on-screen collaborator, a graphic artist and garden designer, wanders through Queen's Park and suburban Brent, to Edgware Road, just north of Marble Arch, in central London, in what was a largely spontaneous performative encounter with public spaces. The shifting tableau of the filmed walk helps characterize an autobiographical and geographic LGBT+ Jewish 'place' that is not fixed, that is explicitly part imagined, part abstracted, part remembered, part here and now. Again, this person spends most screen time in the suburban location of his choice: Queens Park, where he grew up. Here in moments of abstracted thought, he relives his migration from Colombia, the transcultural rupture of his relocation to the UK at the age of ten, and the painful relationship he had with his father as a closeted gay son growing up in the suburb. Even as a middle-aged gay Jewish man he still feels the sense of isolation and separation. As discussed earlier, he walks around Queens Park on film and encounters a synagogue-that-was, now a Muslim Community Centre. The building triggers complex feelings about his first teenage gay sexual encounter there, in what can be envisaged as a 'sacred space', and his later coming out to his mother, at the age of thirty-five, after attending the same synagogue. 'I felt comfortable... with quite a few memories that I had not visited since I was a young man... outside the Brondesbury Synagogue (as it was then)', he said.[46] Here, the act of walking through suburban, residential Queen's Park generated spontaneous feelings of the past: 'places' of the participant's gay and Jewish self, hidden, half forgotten, until he was placed in a situation that triggered his memory. Similarly, elsewhere in this film, Edgware Road is imaginatively re-envisaged as 'Jewish', even though the location and the recorded mise en scène would belie that fantasy. The on-screen collaborator emerges from a central London Middle Eastern grocery eating a pastry, and spontaneously addresses the camera. In his imagination he has refashioned London's 'Arab quarter' into a 'foreign' 'Jewish Israeli' place. Here, in the participant's mind, a public space is overwritten as an imaginative palimpsest. By engaging with place and religious identity, this Colombian-born gay Jewish artist (with many family members now in Israel) is able to show an 'extravagant ease to innovate'.[47]

This part of Edgware Road facilitates, for this individual, an experience and understanding of what LGBT+ Jewish visibility and identity feels like, illustrating a level of nuance and intersectional sensitivity absent in mainstream Jewish discourse in the UK. The formation, recreation and performance of such a hybridized identity would be impossible without the rupture and separation (Exodus and Exile) from 'authentic Judaism'.[48] It is envisaged in both geographical terms as a place peopled by a 'Jewish community' and as imagined space in which certain marginalized identities and behaviours are allowed to manifest. In other words, locality is conceptual as well as material, and always experiential. Any queering of locality and self is typically preceded by a period in the 'Wilderness' of spiritual wandering in resonant locales outside of the centre. Only after this wandering, in what is for many liminal 'Jewish' suburban space, can our protagonists reach their personal 'Promised Land', where they can be their LGBT+ Jewish selves without needing to reject or compromise two fundamental elements of their identity, with all that such suppression would entail.[49]

Synthesizing queer Jewish identities in the suburban context

One of the films produced for *Ritual Reconstructed* was *Pride Seder*,[50] a co-creative collaboration between South London Liberal Synagogue and the researchers/ filmmakers involved in the project. Although by 2015 (when the film was made) there were eve-of-Pride religious services held at the two central London 'cathedral' Progressive synagogues (in St Johns Wood and at Marble Arch),[51] the Pride Seder held in Streatham predates both and marks a personal initiative of (now Emeritus) Rabbi Janet Darnley. Her aim was to specifically memorialize and celebrate LGBT+ Jewish identities in suburban south London, not in the centre of mainstream Jewish activity. In the film, Rabbi Darley stressed the underpinning concept of the Pride ritual as one that used Jewish tradition and tropes to celebrate the freedom from oppression of LGBT+ people in London:

> The word Seder means 'order' [in Hebrew], so by using that word there means there is an order to our Pride service. And if you think about what the Seder service is usually used for, which is Passover,[52] Passover is the story of liberation. So it seemed that this was a perfect template for a service celebrating Pride as well.

The inner suburbs of Streatham and nearby Brixton have attracted large numbers of LGBT+ residents, including Jews, their families and friends during the post-1980s diversification and gentrification of these areas. In *Pride Seder*, the inclusive South London Liberal Synagogue community (comprising members who are straight, LGBT+ and those identifying as non-binary) marks Pride as a moment for them in celebration and in memoriam. Their local reaction to Pride manifests in the adaptation of the Passover Seder plate. It contains pink and black triangles of Nazi oppression; exotic fruits signifying the 'fruits' (a play on the pejorative term for gay); and a high-heeled shoe, symbolic of drag queens and transgender people during the defining Stonewall Riots of 1969. Elsewhere on the table, specially prepared rainbow-coloured foods celebrate Pride and the Rainbow flag. During the service, participants dip a finger into glasses and ritually drop wine onto their plates (mirroring the ritual naming of the Plagues in Egypt performed during a Passover Seder) to mark the plagues that have befallen LGBT+ people throughout history, and the loneliness felt by LGBT+ people who – exiled by their communities – wander in the Wilderness. It would seem that mobility and wandering are necessary preconditions of queer Jewish activity and change, based on the evidence of our research. Indeed, a number of politically progressive Jewish initiatives have often moved away from the central London headquarters of Jewish thinking and activity. In the social hall of their synagogue building, South London

Synagogue community members and friends transform themselves and 'their material surroundings'[53] in an act of queer co-creation of both ritual and filmed performance.

In circumstances where identities are 'simultaneously asserted and 'under threat', an imagined material space is created where 'subjects can come to cite themselves in recognized as well as unpredictable ways'.[54] This sense of the assertion of and threat to identity is a central theme in the accounts of LGBT+ Jewish London experience. In the traditional religious community 'hubs', LGBT+ Jewish identities were hidden or excluded, but in other rather mundane or obscure local suburban locales, we find the seeds of social change and the origins of LGBT+ Jewish activism and assertion.

South London bedsits as well as suburban north-west London Synagogue halls each played their part as queer meeting points for the original LGBT+ Jewish groups of the 1970s and 1980s. Being safe but also beginning to be visible were difficult factors to reconcile. A participant from the Heritage Lottery-funded project *Rainbow Jews* (2012–14) said,[55]

> I had already gone to, heard about the Jewish Gay Group circa 1974 (?)[56]... I had to go to some tiny bedsit in Clapham to meet someone who was from it ... I realized there was a tiny, tiny network of people that had coffee evenings and socials [which] had by the 1980s grown into a regular meeting for gay men at the Reform synagogue at Alyth Gardens, in north west London, Golders Green.[57]

The collective support afforded to gay men in the Jewish Gay Group by the early 1980s provided scope for the 'Queer Purim Spiel', which premiered at the Unitarian Church Hall, Hoop Lane, Golders Green, north-west London on 17 March 1984. For gay men in the 1980s at the margins of Jewish religious and cultural life, the Spiel was an ideal opportunity to explore and playfully celebrate their gay and Jewish identities. Recalling the occasion on film in 2015, the actor and Jewish scholar Barry Davis – who wrote and performed in the Spiel – was clear that the Jewish Gay Group was building on the mainstream Purim tradition of dressing up:

> It's lots of fun and it's dressing up... Purim is a time you can let go and you are allowed to do, at least from the religious point of view, what you can't do at other times of the year... [Despite] a law that religious Jews adhere to against transvestism... the rabbis... sanctioned dressing up, cross dressing for Purim. And enjoying yourself, and getting drunk even.[58]

The Spiel featured 'a mixture of specifically Jewish references, including suburban locales, which some people get and some people won't, and specifically gay references [relating to local haunts and experiences] which most people will get because they are drawn from that world'.[59] Our 're-construction' of the Spiel for *Ritual Reconstructed* used a transcription of the original audio recorded event to capture the original script and incorporated a significantly wider range of LGBT+ identifying performers (see Figure 7). This part of the project included a linked filmed discussion between the original gay male participants and the new performers (including the researchers). They reflected on the growing inclusion of trans and lesbian people in the years

Figure 7 A March 2015 restaging of the mid-1980s queer Purim Spiel at Liberal Judaism's West Central London Synagogue. Image from a film made by Searle Kochberg. Reproduced with permission of the University of Portsmouth

between the two events. In this way, we co-produced a new form of LGBT+ Jewish narrative that moved through 'time and space' and involved retrospective reflection on how both Jewish and LGBT+ identities, understandings and narratives have evolved over a thirty-year period.

Once again we see how the historic mapping of London LGBT+ Jewish activism and experience points to politically and temporally significant impulses emerging from geographic places outside of the centre. Importantly, the re-enacted performance made reference to both suburban iconic locales and middle-class 'performative, successful, arriviste' West End locations known to both audience and performers as places where Jewish family life would play out in the public arena. Here, the 1980s Spiel and its 2015 recreation artfully blend issues of place, temporality, LGBT+ and Jewish identities, carrying diverse historical socio-geographical meanings for performers and the audience.

The role of ritual in locating Jewish identity and 'place' in the suburban public space

The liturgy of traditional Orthodox Judaism includes a religiously mandated taboo against (male) homosexual acts (Leviticus, chapters 18 and 20) and the 'homo-secularism'[60] of much of LGBT+ society. For Jews who are LGBT+ and who have needed to either hide their sexual orientation to remain embedded within their community or who report facing misunderstanding or mockery from secular identifying LGBT+ peers, this journey in the spiritual 'Wilderness' has often been excruciatingly painful.[61] The theme of 'homecoming' to a place where an individual felt able to be comfortable with their hybridized identity as they located and negotiated a place or community where their identity as a religiously practising 'Queer Jew' was understood, respected and affirmatively valued emerged strongly within the research narratives in both studies. As a final example of how a particular place, ritual and performative LGBT+ Jewish identities can coalesce to recreate something new through the process of creative bricolage,[62] we revisit the Canons Park case study from *My Jewish London*.

Each year, on the first day of Rosh Hashanah (the Jewish New Year), after attending religious services in synagogue, observant Jews perform the ritual act of 'Tashlich',[63] a term which comes from the Hebrew word meaning 'to cast'. In this ritual, individuals symbolically shake out from the corners and pockets of their garments pieces of bread or another food, with the crumbs passing into running water (a stream, a river etc.). This ritual, usually performed collectively after a service, indicates the casting away of our sins in preparation for an especially important and reflective period in the Jewish religious calendar. For an LGBT+ Jew, in an environment where they are closeted, or for someone struggling with a conflict of identity between faith and sexual orientation, the casting off of 'sin' associated with being LGBT+ can be agonizing.

In the north-west London suburban case study filmed shortly before Rosh Hashanah, the gay Jewish onscreen collaborator makes his way from Canons Park tube to the nearby park, Stanmore Marsh. What began as a reflective talk to camera about his personal history – Jewish suburban locale, identity – turns into a spontaneous act of performative religious ritual as the participant recalls his teenage years. He stops at a footbridge above a stream, and in an unexpected re-enactment of Tashlich, he takes the remnants of a packet of crisps from his pocket. He then walks off the footbridge and crunches up the crisps and releases them into the stream below. In that filmic moment, his personal LGBT+ Tashlich New Year ceremony is enacted, and with it a confrontation of what Tashlich meant to him as a teenager:

> Thinking about situations I had been in, sometimes with other guys, and thinking 'does this make me a bad person, or is this just intrinsically part of who I am?' And I always struggled with that each Rosh Hashanah.

Reflecting subsequently on this filmed act, the onscreen collaborator said that 'it all came naturally – for example the 'Tashlich scene... This allowed me to deconstruct my youth'. What emerged on film was an act of reconstruction deeply rooted in a sense of place that had meaning for him as a gay Jew, as he reconfigured a Jewish New Year ritual known to him since childhood. This action, like others captured in *Ritual Reconstructed* and *My Jewish London*, enabled the participant to enter a place fostering assertive, urban suburban familiarity, and yet which was threateningly 'liminal' (he felt marginalized and alien 'coming home').[64] The liminal nature of the local park of his childhood allowed for reflection and distancing. The ritualistic 'scenes of play and experimentation'[65] in this way do not 'simply express [dominant] cultural values or enact symbolic scripts', but actually affect 'changes in people's perceptions and interpretations'.[66]

Conclusion

In this chapter we explored the complex, multi-factorial relationship between queer and Jewish place and identity. In writing up the findings of the research projects for this chapter, we experienced a sense of circularity, layering up detail and perspective as we went over the examples in each section. This non-linear narrative approach mimics the LGBT+ Jewish experiences that community members recounted within the projects. Unlike the mainstream, progressive narratives told in 'official' versions of Jewish London histories, ours tells personal stories as experienced by LGBT+ Jews – nuanced, located within a suburban/urban continuum, performative, part remembered past and part documentary present. The continued investment in activism at a local suburban level remains significant. If our research supports a view that positioning ourselves in particular locales 'places' us in personal, cultural and historical narratives that can enable a positive LGBT+ Jewish identity and experience, it also affirms that these places are *themselves* only a product of our own making, of our activity within them. In so doing, we posit that our collective practice, our understandings of, and relationships to, each other and the places we inhabited are profoundly changed through the act of such creative risk-taking. This surely lies at the heart of meaningful co-production and the practice of respectful inter- and intra-community identity negotiation.

Notes

1   Tim Cresswell, *Place: A Short Introduction* (Oxford: Blackwell Publishing Ltd., 2004).
2   See https://ritualreconstructed.com/the-project/ and https://gtr.ukri.org/projects?ref =AH%2FM006085%2F1.
3   Searle Kochberg, '*My Jewish London: Performance and Identity in Co-Creative Documentary Practice*' (PhD diss., University of Portsmouth, 2019).
4   Claude Lévi-Strauss, *The Savage Mind* (London: Weidenfeld and Nicolson, 1974).
5   Stella Ting-Toomey, 'Identity negotiation theory: Crossing cultural boundaries', in *Theorizing about Intercultural Communication*, ed. William B. Gudykunst (Thousand Oaks, CA: Sage, 2005), 211–33.
6   Ting-Toomey, 'Identity negotiation theory', 214.
7   Lévi-Strauss, *The Savage Mind*.
8   David Graham, *2011 Census: Initial Insights into Jewish Neighbourhoods* (London: Institute for Jewish Policy Research, 2013).
9   Eruv: Hebrew for 'intermingling', normally used to describe a ritual enclosure in a public area within which Orthodox Jews can carry or push objects (like prams) normally forbidden in public on the Sabbath.
10 Sophie Watson, 'Symbolic spaces of difference: Contesting the eruv in Barnet, London and Tenafly, New Jersey', *Environment and Planning D: Society and Space* 23 (2005): 597–613.
11 In terms of numbers, United Synagogue (Modern Orthodox) membership is the largest and most powerful in the UK, using canonized Ashenazi religious practices and liturgy brought to the UK from across Europe during the great nineteenth-century waves of migration to London. Thus, as a UK religious identity label,

'Modern Orthodox' is to a large degree synonymous with the ideological construct of the US-based brothers Boyarin and Boyarin identified as 'authentic Judaism' (Daniel Boyarin and Jonathan Boyarin, 'Diaspora: Generation and the ground of Jewish identity', *Critical Theory* 19, no. 4 (1993): 693–725). These authors critique such a Jewish identity blueprint, rejecting a singular 'authentic' Judaism, which they term the 'uni-vocal discourse' in (Diaspora) Jewish identity. They and others (e.g. Janet R. Jakobsen, 'Queers are like Jews, aren't they? Analogy and alliance politics', in *Queer Theory and the Jewish Question*, ed. Daniel Boyarin, Daniel Itzkovitz and Ann Pellegrini (New York: Columbia University Press, 2003, 64–86) see a self-conscious appropriation of subjectivity as the way forward, in which identity/ies are something we 'do' rather than something we essentially are, enabling a Jewish identity that can encompass continuity and change. This is also the position advocated by Progressive (i.e. Liberal and Reform) Judaism in the UK, denominations that have been at the forefront of most LGBT+ Jewish discourses and initiatives.

12   Donatella Casale Mashiah and Jonathan Boyd, *Synagogue Membership in the United Kingdom in 2016* (London: Institute for Jewish Policy Research, 2017).

13   Louis Wirth, *The Ghetto* (Chicago: Chicago University Press, 1928); Ben Gidley, 'Diasporic memory and the call to identity: Yiddish migrants in early twentieth century east London', *Journal of Intercultural Studies* 34, no. 6 (2013): 650–64; Gerry Black, *Jewish London: An Illustrated History* (Mansfield: Breedon Books Publishing Co Ltd., 2007).

14   Angela Piragauta, 'Sociability and ethnic identity', in *Suburban Urbanities*, ed. Laura Vaughan (London: UCL Press, 2015), 263–86.

15   Cresswell, *Place: A Short Introduction, 7.*

16   Jon Anderson, 'Talking whilst walking: A geographical archaeology of knowledge', *Area* 36, no. 3 (2004): 254–61.

17   Cresswell, *Place: A Short Introduction.*

18   Boyarin and Boyarin, 'Diaspora: Generation and the ground of Jewish identity'.

19   Stuart Charmé, 'Varieties of authenticity in contemporary Jewish identity', *Jewish Social Studies* 6, no. 2 (2000): 133–55.

20   KeshetUK is the British branch of an international Jewish LGBT+ organization that works to promote inclusion and diversity awareness for LGBT+ Jews and their families across all aspects of communal life. See https://www.keshetuk.org/.

21   Rainbow Jews was a landmark history and heritage project (2012–14), coordinated through Liberal Judaism, with original funding from the Heritage Lottery Fund. It charts the history of the LGBT+ Jewish community in Britain from the 1950s to the present day. It includes oral history films and TV shows made by Searle Kochberg with University of Portsmouth colleagues and students. See http://www.rainbowjews.com/.

22   Founded in 2009 to provide a welcoming space for gay Jewish men in London. See http://www.gayjewsinlondon.com/.

23   David Graham, Marlena Schmool and Stanley Waterman, *Jews in Britain: A Snapshot from the 2001 Census* (London: Institute for Jewish Policy Research, 2007).

24   Black, *Jewish London: An Illustrated History*; Graham et al, *Jews in Britain: A Snapshot from the 2001 Census.*

25   Keith Kahn-Harris and Ben Gidley, *Turbulent Times: The British Jewish Community Today* (London: A&C Black, 2010).

26   Stephen Brook, *The Club: The Jews of Modern Britain* (London: Constable and Company Limited, 1989).

27   European Union Agency for Fundamental Rights, *European Union Lesbian, Gay, Bisexual and Transgender Survey: Results at a Glance* (Vienna: FRA, 2013); Sam

Francis, 'Call for law change over increase in homophobic hate crimes in London' (2020). Available at: https://www.bbc.co.uk/news/uk-england-london-51049336 (accessed 8 April 2020).

28   Valerie Hey, 'The politics of performative resignification', *British Journal of Sociology of Education* 27, no. 4 (2006): 439–57.

29   Walter Benjamin, *Illuminations* (London: Fontana Press, 1992); Walter Benjamin, *One Way Street and Other Writings* (London: Penguin Classics, 2009); W.G. Sebald, *The Rings of Saturn* (London: Vintage Books, 2002).

30   This was particularly so for a number of older lesbians, who reported that they found themselves with less voice or visibility in both LGBT+ and broader Jewish realms in recent years since the decline in overtly public-facing feminist movements and identity narratives. In the 1970s, it was often closely linked to Jewish feminist discourse around gendered patriarchal religious practices. See further Elli Tikvah Sarah, *Trouble-Making Judaism* (London: David Paul, 2012); and Elli Tikvah Sarah, 'Talking my way in', *European Judaism* 49, no. 2 (2016): 14–21.

31   Benjamin, *Illuminations*, 137.

32   Alan Day, 'Purim Spiel is smash hit musical at Golders Green' (1984).

33   So called, because these synagogues are large, impressive buildings, and located at the heart of the Progressive Jewish movement in London, geographically and ideologically.

34   Jessica Dubow, 'The mobility of thought: Reflections on Blanchot and Benjamin', *Interventions: International Journal of Postcolonial Studies* 6, no. 2 (2004): 216–28. Terry Eagleton, *Why Marx Was Right* (London: Yale University Press, 2011).

35   Lipphardt Anna, Julia Brauch, Alexandra Nocke and Shelley Hornstein, 'Exploring Jewish space: An approach', in *Jewish Topographies: Visions of Space, Traditions of Place*, ed. Julia Brauch, Anna Lipphardt and Alexandra Nocke (Aldershot: Ashgate Publishing Limited, 2008), 1–23.

36   Illustrations of 'Ritual Bricolage' objects explored in *Ritual Reconstructed* can be accessed at https://connected-communities.org/index.php/project_resources/bricolage-items/.

37   The early Channel 4 TV series by Paul Morrison, *A Sense of Belonging* (London: Channel 4, 1991), and the book on which it is based (Howard Cooper and Paul A. Morrison, *A Sense of Belonging: Dilemmas of British Jewish Identity* (London: Weidenfeld and Nicholson, 1991)) are key examples of this approach. Similarly, Simon Schama's three-volume text is magisterial history: *The Story of the Jews (Bodley Head 2013-ongoing)* and five-part BBC television series mirrors these familiar terms by using phrases such as 'Exile', 'Transit' and 'Homecoming' for specific sections of the books and series.

38   See Kochberg, *My Jewish London*, particularly Chapter 1, Table 1 and Appendix A; and Black, *Jewish London: An Illustrated History*, 140–2, and Chapter 7.

39   Laura Vaughan (ed.), *Suburban Urbanities* (London: UCL Press, 2015).

40   Black, *Jewish London: An Illustrated History*; Gidley 'Diasporic memory and the call to identity: Yiddish migrants in early twentieth century East London'.

41   Boyarin and Boyarin, 'Diaspora: Generation and the ground of Jewish identity'; Charmé, 'Varieties of authenticity in contemporary Jewish identity'.

42   Morrison, *A Sense of Belonging*.

43   Vaughan, *Suburban Urbanities*, 1.

44   Benjamin, *Illuminations*, 249. This process of narrative switching is discussed in detail by Gabriela Spector-Mersel when exploring the use of multiple interpretive 'lenses' to analyse both the 'what' and the 'why' of a narrative, and also the identity

presented therein. Gabriela Spector-Mersel, 'Guest editor's introduction', *Narrative Works* 4, no. 1 (2014): 1–18.

45 Kochberg, *My Jewish London*, Appendix E.

46 Kochberg, *My Jewish London*, Appendix I.

47 Julis Kristeva, *Strangers to Ourselves* (Chichester: Columbia University Press, 1991), 32.

48 Charmé, 'Varieties of authenticity in contemporary Jewish identity'.

49 David M. Barnes and Ilan H. Meyer, 'Religious affiliation, internalized homophobia, and health in lesbians, gay men, and bisexuals', *American Journal of Orthopsychiatry* 82, no. 4 (2012): 505–15; Adrian Coyle and Deborah Rafalin, 'Jewish gay men's accounts of negotiating cultural, religious, and sexual identity: A qualitative study', *Journal of Psychology & Human Sexuality* 12, no. 4 (2000): 21–48.

50 Searle Kochberg, *Pride Seder* (2015), [Documentary] Dir. Searle Kochberg. UK: *Ritual Reconstructed*.

51 In recent years, the mainstream Progressive 'cathedral' synagogues have welcomed LGBT+ rabbis and 'out' members to their congregations. Following in the footsteps of the more radical lesbian and gay pioneering religious communities and their leaders from the 1990s, these mainstream central London congregations have integrated LGBT+ identities into mainstream Jewish religious practice to the extent that Eve of Pride services are now an annual occurrence.

52 The term 'Seder' is usually associated with the festival of Passover, marked every year in the spring, an iconic narrative core to Jewish identity and community narrative.

53 Terry Eagleton, *Why Marx Was Right* (London: Yale University Press, 2011), 130.

54 Hey, 'The politics of performative resignification', 452.

55 See www.rainbowjews.com (project legacy website 2012–14).

56 The Jewish Gay Group was founded in 1972.

57 Over time this group has evolved into what is now called the LGBT+ Jewish Group, meeting monthly at the Liberal Jewish Synagogue (St Johns Wood).

58 The late Barry Davis, actor, author, Yiddish translator and scholar, interviewed on film as part of the co-produced *Ritual Reconstructed* research, 6 March 2015.

59 Barry Davis, interviewed on film as part of the co-produced *Ritual Reconstructed* research, 6 March 2015.

60 Bee Scherer, 'Queerthinking religion: Queering religious paradigms', *The Scholar & Feminist Online* 14, no. 2 (2017): 1–2. Available at: http://sfonline.barnard.edu/queer-religion/queerthinking-religion-queering-religious-paradigms/2/ (accessed 5 March 2020).

61 Coyle and Rafalin, 'Jewish gay men's accounts of negotiating cultural, religious, and sexual identity: A qualitative study'; Scherer, 'Queerthinking religion: Queering religious paradigms'.

62 Levi-Strauss, *The Savage Mind*.

63 For more information, see https://www.chabad.org/library/article_cdo/aid/564247/jewish/What-is-Tashlich.htm.

64 Hey, 'The politics of performative resignification'.

65 Victor Turner, *The Anthropology of Performance* (New York: PAJ Publications, 1988), 25.

66 Catherine Bell, *Ritual: Perspectives and Dimensions* (Oxford: Oxford University Press, 2009), 74.

8

Brighton beach: Pleasures and politics of queer community, 1950–94

Louise Pawley

Introduction

The cover of a 1990 newsletter from Brighton Area Action against Section 28 featured two women running along the beach holding hands, one holding an ice cream; the iconic pier is just visible in the background. With its familiar, cartoon style and tag line 'wish you were here', activism here meets saucy souvenir postcard.[1] This single image combines queer visibility and politics with Brighton's reputation for camp seaside fun in a way that speaks to the central theme of this chapter. I show how, in the 1950s and 1960s, the beach became closely associated with relatively carefree queer pleasures and how, in the 1980s, these associations were shifted into activism and politics relating to the AIDS crisis and Section 28 – an addition to the Local Government Act 1988, which prohibited the 'promotion' of homosexuality in schools and other local authority-run sites including libraries and museums.[2] The oral history testimony, newsletters and ephemera I use demonstrate that the beach was a crucial site for Brighton's queer community organizing in both of these periods, and I argue that queer activism here often blurred the boundaries between politics and pleasure.

Much of the material I discuss comes from the Brighton Ourstory collection, now held at the Keep Archive Centre on the outskirts of Brighton. Ourstory was a community group created in 1989 with the purpose of documenting the town's gay and lesbian history. According to the group, even by the early 1990s, official bodies held no records of lesbian and gay life in the 1950s and 1960s, and it was as though gay men and lesbians 'ha[d] not existed, ha[d] made no contribution to the culture and economy of the town'.[3] Brighton Ourstory was 'committed to ensuring that our lesbian and gay lives are recorded, known, and valued'[4] at a moment of threatened erasure – by the stipulations of Section 28 and in the context of the AIDS crisis in Brighton. The material included in the Brighton Ourstory archive ranges from the 1940s to the present day, although the bulk of the collection relates to the later twentieth century. It uncovers Brighton's queer geography – revealing through flyers and event programmes which venues hosted lesbian and gay events, spots which were good for parties and areas that were seen as dangerous. Correspondences of political organizations and minutes

Figure 8 Brighton Area Action Against Section 28 newsletter, May 1990. Papers of Melita Dennett: OUR 123/1, East Sussex and Brighton and Hove Record Office at The Keep archive centre. Reproduced with permission of Melita Dennett.

from campaign meetings demonstrate changing political aims and vistas locally and nationally. Individual testimonies and personal photographs meanwhile reveal various dimensions of personal lives. Throughout, Brighton's beach is omnipresent: the site where the interplay between politics, pleasure and community is most apparent.

In what follows I first look at the selection of Ourstory oral histories published as *Daring Hearts* in 1992, with testimonies describing seafront bars and cafes, beach socializing, relaxing and cruising (especially in the nudist sections) in the 1950s and 1960s, and the way these opportunities drew queer visitors to the town (as it was then: city status was given to the twin towns of Brighton and Hove in 2000).[5] The second part focuses on newsletters, flyers and other activist ephemera relating to Section 28 protests and demonstrates how the beach and seafront was often used self-consciously as a space of visibility, protest and pleasure in the late 1980s and early 1990s.[6] This material anchors this chapter and is testament to the significance of such local history and archive projects and illuminates the importance of 'lesbian' and 'gay' as organizing categories of identity and collecting in the 1980s and 1990s. Although Brighton Ourstory later included the documentation of bisexual history in its aims, material across the collection largely relates to lesbians and gay men; other queer voices are almost completely absent. As a result the chapter is framed through those identity lenses. I nevertheless use the word 'queer' to encompass and signal a broader community in the town and as a reminder that 'gay' and 'lesbian' were not in widespread use until the 1970s.

Beach pleasures in the 1950s and 1960s

By the early nineteenth century, Brighton was gaining popularity as a seaside resort. The patronage of the cultural and fashionable Prince Regent, along with the supposed benefits of the sea air, made Brighton a popular watering hole for the elite during this period. By the end of the century, advances in the railway network and uneven increases in disposable income and holiday entitlements led to Brighton, along with other British seaside resorts, becoming more accessible and popular.[7] For those who were able to make the trip, the beach was a free, democratic, public, outdoor space and one where it was possible to let your hair down and express a sense of difference – albeit with some caution. This is partly why the beach became so crucial to queer expression and Brighton's identity as a 'gay mecca' (as one Ourstory interviewee had it). The beach was a place of escape from everyday life, played host to a number of venues frequented by queer individuals and provided a space for relaxation and sex (for queer men at least). Michael, who was born in Luton and 'escaped to Brighton in 1960', remembers that 'coming to Brighton was like arriving in Disneyland. All the wonderful Regency buildings and the seafront'.[8] For Birmingham-born Sandie, 'there was the sea and the sand… and it just seemed like everything, everything was there and we loved it'.[9] In these narratives, the beach and sea was part of what made Brighton special as a place to visit or settle. It was a place where visitors and locals could discard expectations. Sandie remembered, 'My ex-girlfriend['s] mum used to put her in frilly dresses and she used to go down the beach and bury them. So she was quite convinced that she was born butch.'[10] This was a place where Sandie's ex literally buried societal and familial convention.

While permissiveness and escapism were associated with many seaside towns, for queer people Brighton felt exceptional in part because of its long-standing Bohemian associations. Various well-known West End actors had second homes in Brighton, and the lively arts scene – fuelled by the arts school and, from 1967, the Brighton Festival – made it especially appealing during a time when male homosexual acts were criminal and lesbians widely derided.[11] One Ourstory contributor remembered, 'A friend of mine came down from Glasgow and he was quite amazed about Brighton. He thought it was a dream come true, he didn't think it could happen, he didn't think it was England.'[12] Ted, who 'found it very difficult in Southampton', where he felt 'very much an outcast', was 'a bit euphoric' on coming to Brighton, where he 'didn't have to conform' and there 'was no restrictions'.[13] For Siobhan, who lived in London, 'Brighton represented… an escapism from my own anger, from the struggle of my own life. I had a different feel about myself when I was down here... I preferred myself'.[14] Testimonies from both lesbian and gay men collected by Ourstory regularly emphasize this exceptionalism of Brighton, and note the freedom queer people felt compared to other parts of Britain.

The seafront and streets just beyond provided the space for many of the venues frequented by lesbians and gay locals and visitors alike. The Fortune of War and the Belvedere pubs, located in Brighton's seafront arches, were popular with butch lesbians who 'really looked like navvies, with bower boots, and suits, and chains' (as Eddie recalled in his testimony).[15] Beachfront cafés, notably the Wanderin and Lorelei, stayed open all night and were popular places for queer people to meet after pubs and clubs had closed. James remembered how George, the owner of the Wanderin, was also known as 'Fat Emma' and 'was quite outrageous with his picking up of soldiers and things'.[16] Sandie recalled that Lorelei 'would be crammed to the doors' on a Saturday night, and you would 'always see someone gay'.[17] These venues and others nearby meant that Brighton's beachfront was closely associated with queer nightlife in the post-war era.

Beyond the central beach and beachfront venues were other important social and sexual sites for queer locals and holidaymakers, especially the men. The Men's Beach in Hove just to the west of Brighton was 'notoriously gay'.[18] 'It was too fantastic', Grant recalled; 'Everybody knew about the Men's Beach. There was nothing in the rest of the country to compare'. Visitors 'just went down, if the weather was fine, [and] probably slept there all night'.[19] 'You just walked around and when you found somebody that hadn't got a friend, or wasn't talking, you sat yourself down, and started chatting away. And if you didn't click, well, you got up and you walked around again'.[20] Peter describes this cruisiness too: men would 'sunbathe in the nude, you see, troll around'; 'little caves and things, rocks where you could hide behind' were often used 'for a bit of trade', he said.[21] Peter may have conflating Hove beach with the nudist beach below Telscombe Cliffs, which fits his description better and, according to locals, attracted 'the wrong kind of naturists' and was a 'tramping ground for perverts and homosexuals'.[22] Peter's possible confusion is significant: considering the two beaches were closely connected for him, certainly both were cruisy and both were used almost exclusively by men. On the Men's Beach in Hove 'any women or children strayed on it they were promptly told to get off'.[23] It was perhaps partly for this reason that the South Downs countryside surrounding Brighton proved a more popular destination for many lesbians who visited the area in the post-war era.[24]

The Men's Beach and Telscombe beach were certainly not free from danger, however. One interviewee remembered that 'occasionally there'd be little sort of groups of police albeit sometimes plain clothes, even in the nude, strolling along Telscombe beach for example in the hope of catching gay men at sex'.[25] Peter mostly 'kept away' from the men's beach due to police patrols and worries about his 'professional reputation'.[26] Similar fears were felt throughout Brighton, despite the apparent tolerance and freedom. Vicky recounted apprehension when publicly dressing outside of expectations, remembering, 'If you went anywhere, you went by taxi. You didn't walk on the streets dressed like we used to dress, for instance. If you couldn't get in a car or get a taxi, then you didn't go'.[27] Various testimonies recount homophobia, stories of arrest and police raids on queer-friendly bars. Bill remembers using fake names because he was 'terrified by the law', while Dennis never wrote down names or addresses of Brighton friends so as not to incriminate them in the event of an arrest.[28] Women feared losing their jobs or damaging their reputation. This was particularly true for women who had children: 'it was always thought that the children would be taken away' if their lesbianism was revealed.[29]

Despite the dangers, Ourstory testimonies indicate that in post-war Brighton the seaside provided queer visitors and residents a degree of freedom which was rare in the rest of Britain during this period. Various pubs, bars and cafes provided a place for individuals to meet and socialize; outdoor spaces such as the Men's Beach and Telscombe beach were used for sex and relaxation by men especially. Testimonies recalling post-war Brighton in the 1980s were often tinged with more than a hint of nostalgia, and the pleasure evoked by the seaside in Brighton was not available to all. There were dangers there, as we've seen, and 'class-based, occupational and age-related cliques'.[30] Janine recalls the Brighton scene being 'selfish' in the post-war era. Middle-class people would buy a house here, make a small circle of queer friends and exist in relative isolation with little support given to 'gay causes', she said.[31] For those who were able to take advantage of it, though, Brighton beach provided a site of escape, pleasure and relative freedom.

Beach politics in the 1980s and 1990s

While the beach remained an important queer site in the 1970s, and many of the post-war bars and cafes on and near the seafront endured, queer counterculture in Brighton was often associated with places further back from the front. The gay liberation campaigns, which resulted in the first ever Pride event in Brighton, in 1973 were closely associated with the University of Sussex, founded at Falmer on the northern edge of the town in 1961 (hence 'Sussex' rather than 'Brighton' Gay Liberation Front). Preston Circus, a junction about a mile inland, gained attention as an important site for counterculture in Brighton with gay-friendly bookshops and venues where community groups met in the 1970s.[32] In addition, whilst the association with queer tourism and escapism continued, cheaper flights from the 1970s took many holiday-makers elsewhere.[33]

The focus of queer life switched back to the front in the 1980s, however, as it became central to rhetoric surrounding Brighton's queer community with the advent of AIDS.[34] In its 'AIDS Seaside Shocker', *The Sunday Mirror* reported in 1985 that four men had already died in Brighton, 'famous for its nudist beaches'.[35] Particularly for the popular press, during the AIDS crisis the pleasures of the seaside now became associated with danger and death. For activists, meanwhile, the beach became a focal point in their response to the crisis. In October 1988, campaigners held a vigil outside the Conservative Party conference at the Brighton Centre on the seafront. Rather than evoking notions of fun and pleasure, the seaside was chosen in this event for its alternate associations with calm and remembrance. The event was organized to challenge the homophobic policies and values of the Conservative government, and activists lined the beach from pier to pier to hold a sunset vigil. During the initial phase of the event, participants were invited to make their way down the beach to the edge of the sea at low tide to 'remember and wish for those of us who have been forgotten, those of us who have died, and those of us whose lives have been made a misery'.[36] The time given to quiet reflection and remembrance at the beginning of the vigil was particularly poignant in Brighton due to the intensity of the AIDS crisis here; the chain of protestors then formed on the beach between the two piers. One organizer said that the event should be seen 'not as a demonstration or a march against the Tories, but a demonstration for ourselves... we want to make a resonant statement of our loveliness and strength'.[37]

In ephemera relating to the 1988 beach vigil, imagery of waves and the shore were touched notions of power, strength and solidarity as well as remembrance. An event flyer asked participants to listen to what 'the wild waves are saying' and stated that 'With one voice, as one people, as a single wave inevitably crashing on the shore, we say to you that our time for freedom has arrived'.[38] The sea and setting provided an opportunity to emphasize new and particular strength and defiance of local community. The start of the event was an opportunity to reflect not only on local residents and issues but on the historic and global oppression of the worldwide queer community, reinforced by the act of looking out to sea. 'Today we join lesbians and gay men across America on their National Coming Out Day – "Lets stand up and be counted"', read the event information sheet.[39] *Capital Gay* meanwhile reported that 'protesters from Scotland, Wales and Yorkshire are expected to descend on the south coast resort to join the vigil'.[40] Although the event was framed by and closely related to its location, it was also thus part of a larger resistance movement that transcended place. This changing focus represents a move from Brighton being an isolated queer 'haven' and escape to being a gathering point and beacon for a wider national and international movement and community.

In the final part of this protest participants were invited to move back up the beach to form a second chain from pier to pier, now turning to face inward towards the Conservative Party with torches lit by a flame which 'passes person to person from one end to the other'. In this way, the information sheet went on, 'we celebrate our power... '.[41] The imagery of this final part of the vigil changed the tone of the demonstration from reflection to assertive action. Activists were staking their claim to the beach and to Brighton more widely. It is significant that the beach was the site of this change, not only because of its proximity to the building hosting the Conservative Party conference but also because it is the classic site of the last stand, the 'end of the line'. There was nowhere further to go and a fight with the Conservatives was inevitable. The information sheet declared that 'we are here, and our love is permanent and strong' – echoing the 'we're here, we're queer' slogan of the new queer movement, and emphasizing presence in the face of eradication.[42] The reflective and memorial tone of the vigil and its transformation to assertive protest perhaps gained some of its power precisely from turning seaside pleasure-seeking on its head. The protests that followed against Section 28, on the other hand, determinedly traded in that long-standing reputation for seaside fun and visibility.

Brighton Area Action against Section 28 held its first meeting in February 1988. By the end of the campaign, the group, and several other spin-off groups, had been a part of local and national marches, direct action, community-building initiatives (including Ourstory), a national and European tour and the first Pride event in the town.[43] As Melita Dennett, who was part of Brighton Area Action against Section 28, remembers, countering the government's directive, 'We did a bloody good job of promoting homosexuality'.[44] While the urgent need for personalized care at the beginning of the AIDS crisis left little energy for an explicitly political response, Section 28 sparked the community into more fervent political action in Brighton. After Section 28 became law in May 1988, significant effort was put into challenging the spirit of the legislation in Brighton, and the beach was key to that: while Section 28 sought to diminish gay and lesbian visibility, here was a place where it could be enhanced. The pleasure associated with the seaside also became a useful tool in championing fun and community in the face of legislation that isolated and shamed gay people. In one case, Brighton and Hove's lesbians were called to 'celebrate the end of patriarchy with a beach ball' as part of a 'beach rebellion' around 1990.[45] Here, the beach is seen once again as a site of pleasure, joy and resistance. Although organized by lesbians (for further information, potential participants were directed to Lesbian Line) this event was open to all women. Again, this is significant as all women, regardless of their sexual orientation, have been denied access to public spaces, either explicitly or through fear and unease. Here was a visible beach party affirming the right to use public spaces safely and to demand equality there.

The queer beaches of Brighton were historically peripheral – to the east and west – providing a shelter from a hostile heterosexual world.[46] However, for this beach party, organizers chose a central portion of the beach rather than a section shielded from 'the outside world'. While Section 28 encouraged invisibility and shame, lesbians were called on to have very evident fun. Participants of this beach party were 'Hove dykes in action creating women only beaches and planets', signalling again that the struggle went beyond the beaches of the twin towns of Brighton and Hove.[47] In this event, as with the earlier beach vigil, there were clear connections to a wider political movement. The Brighton Ourstory archive contains several documents reinforcing this, including correspondence with various national and international organizations, newsletters from American gay rights campaigns and an education pack relating to global lesbian and gay rights.[48] Brighton Area against Section 28 went on to a national, and later a European, tour in which Brightonians shared experiences with others.[49]

The flyer for the event indicated a range of activities. Some, such as 'networking for further actions', were explicitly political, but most were leisure activities: women were invited to come along to play sports, meditate, gossip and knit.[50] This range made the event more accessible and less intimidating than more traditional campaign meetings or marches. This is not to say the event was not radical, however. In his work on the London club night Duckie, Ben Walters demonstrates that 'queer fun' is a crucial part of the imagining and creating better worlds.[51] For Walters, queer fun has to be low stakes to aid an 'understanding of how fun supports relief from normative pressures, collective engagement, experimentation with new forms and processes and critical engagement with what counts as serious'.[52] In the case of the beach party then, the seemingly 'low-stake' activities described by the flyer had the potential to encourage

Figure 9 Flyer promoting Hove & Brighton 'Beach Rebellion', *c.* 1990. Papers of Melita Dennett: OUR 123/1, East Sussex and Brighton and Hove Record Office at The Keep archive centre. Reproduced with permission of Melita Dennett.

participants to explore their identity and community, and radically imagine a better world. It is significant that the beach party had the utopian aim of 'celebrat[ing] the end of patriarchy'.[53]

Queer fun was also at stake in a night of cabaret and resistance at the Zap Club in 1988.[54] The Zap Club was a nightclub at Kings Road Arches on the beach front. The club's location attracted a less mainstream clientele than many other clubs in the town and became famous in the late 1980s and the early 1990s as a venue which pulled together radical arts and performance with acid house. Zap Club nights 'Shame' and 'Wild Fruit' became, according to some, 'the prototype of gay clubbing in the 90s'.[55] The night advertised on this flyer was about music, dancing and cabaret but also about fighting oppressive legislation, again bringing politics and pleasure together on the beach. This interplay between pleasure and politics becomes even more apparent in the copy of the flyer held in the Ourstory collection: someone had used the reverse side to make notes at a campaign meeting against section 28, with various duties and jobs within the campaign allocated to those present.[56]

The re-initiation of Pride in 1991 Brighton underlined this connection of beach, pleasure and politics in the town. The parade often went along the seafront, the Zap Club playing host to afterparties throughout the 1990s. The importance of the seaside to Brighton Pride events is a legacy that continued beyond the Section 28 era, with 'Pride beside the Seaside' in 2009.[57] While more recent Pride events in the new city of Brighton and Hove have been criticized for commercialization and perceived depoliticization, in the 1990s, Pride politics and community were deliberately aligned with seaside fun; publicity and coverage regularly included the pier and beach. Pride and the other events I've described represented ways of 'doing' politics that challenged assumptions surrounding what 'serious' politics should look like. These were fun-filled events which combined the sauce and camp of the seaside with the spirit of early Gay Liberation Front protests.

Conclusion

This chapter has charted the importance of Brighton beach as a queer space of pleasure and politics. In the post-war era, the beach played a significant part in attracting people to visit and settle in the town. It developed a permissive and tolerant reputation and exercised an especially strong draw for queer people seeking an escape from social expectations and oppression in their hometowns across Britain. The beach was central, free and open to everybody and the seafront played host to a number of queer-friendly venues. The peripheries of the beach were also important sites, with Telscombe nudist beach and Hove Men's Beach providing gay men with a space for relaxation and the opportunity to pick up. Although testimonies suggest that fear of the police and the necessity for discretion existed in Brighton in the 1950s and 1960s, they also communicate a feeling of relative queer ease and pleasure – and on the seafront especially. Perhaps partly because of this reputation AIDS and Section 28 hit queer Brighton hard;[58] seaside permissiveness became associated with danger and death rather than tolerance and freedom in this period. The 1988 beach vigil used the beach as a site of reflection and remembrance, but also as a place to assert the community mobilized by AIDS. With Section 28, the beach became an important site to champion the queer visibility that the legislation threatened. Fun was taken seriously, and for many of the actions that took place in the town against Section 28, seaside pleasures were used as political tools. Pleasure and politics were conjoined in lesbian beach party, the Zap Club cabaret and Pride events.

In 2019, residents of Brighton were invited to 'queer the pier' as part of a Brighton Museum community exhibition. The project was a community-led collaboration between the Queer in Brighton heritage project, a group of local LGBTQI+ community curators and Brighton Museum and Art Gallery. The aim was to 'highlight the rich cultural history of the LGBTIQ+ community here in Brighton'.[59] The exhibition in the landmark, local authority-run Brighton and Hove Museum and Art Gallery (the former Royal stables), just a five-minute walk from the beach, showcases a vast array of queer history in a seaside form in a venue from which, under Section 28, would not have been possible.[60] The exhibition includes an automata machine to showcase the life of Vesta Tilley, a music hall singer and male impersonator; a 'gipsy fortune telling machine' which explores local Roma LGBTQ+ experiences; and arcade games exploring the lives of historic queer residents. The exhibition is presented as if along the pier, with typical seaside novelties and attractions, anchoring this queer history very specifically in Brighton and feeds into a sense of seaside nostalgia. The fact that the exhibition should be framed by the seaside seemed natural; to Anna, who helped to promote the project, 'Brighton's salty mix of hedonism, sea air plus a sense of Queer empathy was seemingly embedded within the community'.[61] It is 'both playful and powerful at the same time', said curator E-J Scott, signalling again the politics associated with queer fun and the significance of seaside and its history to both.[62]

Notes

1   Brighton Area Action Against Section 28, 'newsletter #16', Ourstory Archive, The Keep, Brighton. Papers of Melita Dennett: OUR 123/1 (1990).

2   Section 28 of the *Local Government Act 1988* stated that local authorities 'shall not intentionally promote homosexuality or publish material with the intention of promoting homosexuality' or 'promote the teaching in any maintained school of the acceptability of homosexuality as a pretended family relationship'. Before enactment, it was known as Clause 28, thereafter as Section 28. It is thus the latter I use here. Local Government Act 1988 (c.9, section 28): http://www.legislation.gov. uk/ukpga/1988/9/section/28/enacted (accessed 2 January 2020).

3   Brighton Ourstory, *Daring Hearts: Lesbian and Gay Lives in 50s and 60s Brighton* (Brighton: QueenSpark, 1992 E-book edition 2015), loc. 200.

4   Ibid., loc. 2744.

5   Ibid.

6   For example, see 'Papers of Brighton Area Action against Section 28', Ourstory Archive, The Keep, Brighton, Papers of Dani Ahrens: OUR 37/2, 1988–1992; 'Papers of Melita Dennett relating to Brighton Area Action against Section 28', Ourstory Archive, The Keep, Brighton, Papers of Melita Dennett: OUR 123/1, c.1987–c.1992.

7   Anya Chapman and Duncan Light, 'The "heritigisation" of the British seaside resort: The rise of the "old penny" arcade', *Journal of Heritage Tourism* 6, no. 3 (2011): 209–26.

8   Ourstory, *Daring Hearts,* loc. 1351.

9   Ibid., loc. 228.

10 Ibid., loc. 263.

11 Matt Cook, 'Local matters: Queer scenes in 1960s Manchester, Plymouth and Brighton' *Journal of British Studies* 59, no. 1 (2020): 35–7. Available at: https://eprints. bbk.ac.uk/id/eprint/30017/ (accessed 27 September 2021).

12 Ibid., loc. 260.

13 Ibid., loc. 249–53.

14 Ibid., loc. 247.

15 Ibid., loc. 1465.

16 Ibid., loc. 2329.
17 Ibid., loc. 1596.
18 Ibid., loc. 2223.
19 Ibid., loc. 2208–12.
20 Ibid., loc. 2215.
21 Ibid., loc. 2227.
22 Spokesperson for Telscombe Cliffs Ratepayers Association, quoted in Janet Cameron, *LGBT Brighton and Hove* (Amberley: Gloucestershire, 2009), 72.
23 Ourstory, *Daring Hearts*, loc. 2218.
24 Ibid., loc. 1309.
25 Ibid., loc. 2070.
26 Ibid., loc. 2224.
27 Ibid., loc. 806.
28 Ibid., loc. 818 & 836.
29 Ibid., loc. 885.
30 Cook, 'Local matters: Queer scenes in 1960s Manchester, Plymouth and Brighton', 38.
31 Ibid., loc. 2034–39.
32 Matt Cook and Alison Oram, *Queer Beyond London* (Manchester: Manchester University Press, 2022), 23.
33 Ourstory, *Daring Hearts,* loc. 1340–4.
34 Cook and Oram, *Queer Beyond London*, 29.
35 'AIDS Seaside Shocker', *Sunday Mirror*, 15 December 1985.
36 'Lesbian and gay vigil: Brighton 11 October Information Sheet', Ourstory Archive, The Keep, Brighton, Papers of Melita Dennett: OUR 123/1, 1988.
37 'Brighton ready for Tory conference protests', *Capital Gay,* 7 October 1988.
38 'Brighton beach vigil flyer', Ourstory Archive, The Keep, Brighton, Papers of Melita Dennett: OUR 123/1, 1988.
39 'Lesbian and gay vigil: Brighton 11 October information sheet'.
40 Ibid.
41 Ibid.
42 Ibid.
43 'Papers of Melita Dennett relating to Brighton area action against Section 28', Ourstory Archive, The Keep, Brighton, Papers of Melita Dennett: OUR 123/1, c.1987-c.1992.
44 Queer Looks Voices, 'Melita', 2018: http://queerlooks.brightonmuseums.org/brighton/melita/ (accessed 29 February 2020).
45 'Hove and Brighton Lesbian Beach Rebellion', Ourstory Archive, The Keep, Brighton, Papers of Melita Dennett: OUR 123/1, c.1900. The flier is – typically – undated.
46 Michael Levine, 'Gay ghetto', in *Social Perspectives in Lesbian and Gay Studies: A Reader*, ed. Peter Nardi and Beth Schneider (London: Routledge, 1979), 194–206; Stephen Quiley, 'Manchester's "village in the city": The gay vernacular in a post-industrial landscape of power', *Transgressions* 1, no. 1 (1995), 36–50; Kathe Browne and Leela Bakshi, 'We are here to party? Lesbian, gay, bisexual and trans leisurescapes beyond commercial gay scenes', *Leisure Studies* 30, no. 2 (2011), 179–96.
47 'Hove and Brighton Lesbian Beach Rebellion'.
48 'Papers relating to national and international lesbian and gay rights organisations', Ourstory Archive, The Keep, Brighton, Papers of Dani Ahrens: OUR 37/8, 1989–1995.

49 'Papers of Melita Dennett relating to national and international lesbian and gay rights organisations', Ourstory Archive, The Keep, Brighton, Papers of Melita Dennett: OUR 123/2, c.1987-c.1993.

50 'Hove and Brighton Lesbian Beach Rebellion'.

51 Ben Walters, 'Dr Duckie Homemade Mutant Hope Machines the PhD', 2020, based on Ben Walters, 'Queer fun, family and futures in Duckie's performance projects 2010–2016' (unpublished doctoral thesis, Queen Mary University of London, 2018), available at: https://duckie.co.uk/media/documents/PhD%20ebook%20Dr%20 Duckie.pdf (accessed 25 May 2020).

52 Ibid., 136–7.

53 'Hove and Brighton Lesbian Beach Rebellion'.

54 'Cabaret against Section 28', Ourstory Archive, The Keep, Brighton. Papers of Melita Dennett: OUR 123/1 c.1990.

55 *Gay Times*, October 1990.

56 'Cabaret against Section 28'.

57 *Pride beside the Seaside: Official Souvenir Guide 2009*.

58 Cook and Oram, *Queer Beyond London*, 30.

59 Cameron Tallant, 'Introducing queer the Pier', 2019: https://brightonmuseums.org. uk/discover/2019/05/09/introducing-queer-the-pier/ (accessed 2 June 2020).

60 'Queer the Pier' is on display in Brighton Museum & Art Gallery as of June 2020.

61 Anna Goodman, 'The word Is out: Promoting LGBTQI+ heritage', https:// brightonmuseums.org.uk/discover/2020/05/18/the-word-is-out-promoting-lgbtqi- heritage/ (accessed 6 June 2020).

62 E.-J. Scott in Vic Parsons, 'Introducing queer the Pier Meet E-J Scott, whose new exhibition queer the Pier delves into the history of the queerest city in the UK', *Pink News*: https://www.pinknews.co.uk/2020/02/20/queer-the-pier-ej-scott-brighton- lgbt-history-exhibition/ (accessed 4 June 2020).

9

Taking pride in Plymouth's past

Alan Butler

On Saturday 22nd August 2009, approximately 100 people gathered at the Plymouth City Centre, Piazza, to take their positions surrounding a fifty-metre rainbow flag. The flag had been laid there for just over an hour to serve as what the local newspaper had referred to as 'a symbol of Gay Pride'.[1]

Weekend shoppers and other passers-by looked on as marshals blew whistles and directed the milling crowd around the flag. At 11.30 am, the procession lifted and carried it towards the City Guildhall led by veteran human rights activist Peter Tatchell. This was his first visit to the city, made at the request of a group called 'Plymouth Pride Event', who had organized this rather understated, though significant, spectacle. Although local news coverage used the term 'parade' in referring to this event, the journey from the city centre's piazza to the Guildhall was a very short one – a little over 350 metres – and was interrupted by a tentative crossing of a main road in the middle of the short pilgrimage. The notion of a 'parade' has become synonymous with gay pride, and the act of carrying the flag across to the Guildhall was viewed in just such a way by many of the spectators and indeed many of the participants. It lasted only minutes before the procession moved out of public view and disappeared inside the building but was, at that time, the most public display of the existence of an LGBT+ community to have ever occurred in the city of Plymouth.

Subsequently, in 2011, the Plymouth City Museum and Art Gallery (now The Box) approached the local LGBT+ community to see if the local archive could be extended to include some more stories of hidden queer lives and spaces. With the support of the Heritage Lottery Fund (now the National Lottery Heritage Fund), work began on creating the Plymouth LGBT+ Archive, through the Pride in our Past project. The initial oral history interviews (over seventy of them) were conducted principally by myself, but also by members of the community and a paid research assistant. The archive also includes a collection of ephemera and would come to sit as a hybrid accession both in The Box collection and, also, as a community archive maintained by the Pride in Plymouth organization in their role as the city's LGBT+ local social enterprise. What was particularly significant in terms of visibility though was the opportunity for the queer community of Plymouth to plan and curate their own exhibition in the Plymouth City Museum and Art Gallery's Hurdle Gallery between 28 April and 30 June 2012.

When considering the limited duration and spatial containment of the 2009 parade, it became clear it had been a very appropriate representation of the lived experience of Plymouth's queer communities. Tatchell bemoaned the absence of the Royal Navy – in part because sailors had played a large part in the city's queer life – but then that part of the city's queer past had largely played out below the proverbial radar. Among those who recounted Plymouth's underground scene in the (now 100 plus) interviews gathered for the city's LGBT+ archive by the Pride in Our Past project (2011), many talked of the fun to be had but also of the desire not to 'make a fuss' or 'draw attention'. Sixteen years earlier, in the wake of a horrific homophobic murder in the city, journalist Jason Bennetto wrote in the national *Independent* newspaper of reticence among Plymouthians in discussing queer community. He felt this was strange as 'Plymouth is not particularly squeamish about sex – it has a notorious red-light district and a history of sex connected with its status as a garrison town for the Royal Navy, Royal Marines, and Army. Added to a population of about 270,000 it appears doubly strange that the gay community appears so timid'.[2] Yet, as I'll show in this chapter, timid may not really be the word to describe queer life here. Instead, pride was taken in remaining undercover, in spaces that were deemed appropriate, rather than more conventional displays like the 2009 event. In what follows I move through some of Plymouth's iconic spaces to show how the city has been a queerly vibrant if not a queerly visible place.

Cruising Union Street

Historically, Plymouth's identity as a city has been strongly linked to its role as a port. While all the armed forces have been based there at various stages in its history, its strongest link is with the Royal Navy and that culture has had a significant impact on Plymouth's social norms and values. After the city was virtually razed in the blitz of the Second World War, engineer J. Paton Watson and Professor Patrick Abercrombie sought to create 'a new Plymouth worthy of both its fame and its site between the hills and the water' but 'without sacrificing the amenities of Plymouth or blurring its traditional quality'.[3] Some of these traditions were associated with spaces where servicemen and travellers had revelled – and most obviously the Union Street area of the city. The street remained relatively intact after the blitz and so perhaps clung to a well-established reputation as a place for revelry and some of its seedier aspects. It 'had already achieved a degree of international notoriety long before the war on a par with Bugis Street in Singapore and Gut in Malta. Servicemen, particularly Bootnecks (Royal Marines) and Matelots, would attempt to drink their way from one end of the "Strip" to the other and back'.[4]

Union Street had been built in 1815 to unite the three towns which subsequently became the city of Plymouth: Plymouth, Stonehouse and Devonport, and with over twenty pubs along its route, it had a colourful reputation. Its primary attractions were referred to as 'The "Three P's" – Pubs, Prostitutes and the Paramount'[5] – the latter a small first floor dance club at the heart of Union Street drawing people from the city's various social groups and backgrounds. Oral histories show that the three P's along

Union Street opened up an array of queer opportunities – opportunities in which servicemen and especially Royal Navy sailors (locally referred to as 'matelots') were frequently implicated; they created a very particular queer dynamic and subculture in this post-war space.

In his interview in December 2011, Ted Whitehead, a 75-year-old man at the time, who had founded a gay group called 'Goodfellas' and produced their newsletter for a number of years, recalled being introduced to Plymouth's underground scene in 1954 having just left the army. He shared that groups of men,

> Would come from the Lockyer [a queer bar at the city centre end of Union Street] [and] walk down through, you could go into the Paramount dance hall or you could carry on down to the Castle pub or, if it was too late for that, you'd go down to the Mambo [an all-night coffee lounge]. We'd all meet up under the canopy of the Palace Theatre and pay the odd call to the loo up in Phoenix Street. Memories![6]

Matelots, he said, 'would spend their money on the girls and then the girls would say "Good night" and go home. Different with the prostitutes, but the ordinary girls who were just out for the evening, for a dance and so on, they were quite well behaved'.[7] As the matelots were paid each fortnight, these activities were usually restricted to the weekend closest to their pay day. Between these were the 'blank weeks' when they could not afford to go out drinking. Some gay men knew they should take to the town during these 'blank weeks' because many of the sailors would be happy to be entertained for the night in return for drinks. As Ted recounted, 'Of course the matelots would be at a loose end and would come into the Mambo [a gay-owned café] and you know, you'd probably buy them a coffee and get off with a matelot'.[8]

Figure 10 Ted and a friend in a Union Street bar. Donated from a private collection and reproduced with permission of the Plymouth LGBT+ Archive.

The matelots and Plymouth's gay men came to create a subculture which was organized around specific interactions in a specific moment of time and happened in a specific place. As Ted recalls, 'Oh, yeah, yeah. I never knew any trouble with them. You know, they were very "pro-gay".'[9]

The Paramount Dance Hall in the 1950s was something of the jewel in the crown for the Union Street area and was the place to go for young heterosexual couples wanting to dance – and many others besides. Ted, who would often go there alone, was aware of standing out from the crowd at the Paramount, recognizable to the matelots as different from other patrons:

> I sat there this particular night and a group of matelots came in and came over and sat beside me. And I was at the back of the dance hall. And there were five of them and they started coming on to me, chatting me up, and I was very wary, you know, five. You can cope with one. Or maybe two. They started to say you know, 'Come back with us' and I said, 'Where are you?' and they said 'We're off the frigate. You can come back on board with us'. And I said 'No' and they said 'No, we're all right', and they all started kissing each other to prove they were OK. This was in the full lit dance floor. Nobody took any notice if two men or two matelots got up and danced together. It was okay.[10]

The Paramount was at the centre of Union Street, balancing the sensibilities and desires of the matelots from the frigate at the western end with those of the gay men coming to the dance hall from the Lockyer Tavern to the east.

The Lockyer Tavern

The rebuilding and reinterpretation following the city's wartime decimation enabled a kind of queer reclamation of some places. This queer reclamation could endure for long periods, as with some bars and cafes, or for just fleeting moments when the darkness and seclusion gave space to explore and negotiate sexual opportunities. Long-standing spaces tended to be viewed as downmarket and so were more accessible to those on the fringes: gay men, lesbians, prostitutes and even the visiting sailors, all of whom formed their own rules of engagement in this underground scene. The matelots crossed perceived lines and boundaries, engaging with each of these groups on their own terms.

The Lockyer Tavern had a back bar with its own entrance and own toilet – well set up as a separate space that could accommodate Plymouth's queer clientele. Mavis Arnold, who worked as a barmaid in the back bar from 1967 to 1969, recalls, 'Where the toilets were situated, they [gay men] would never have gone through the [main] bar because the toilets were on either side. So, it was really "That's your part". She also explained, 'There was a complete red line, went down through the middle.'[11]

In his interview in 2012, Peter Buckley, a 67-year-old hairdresser, recalled of his first visit to the Lockyer in 1967: he 'walked in eating an apple which is very strange.

I don't know if Freud would make something about that'. Remembering the other patrons, Peter continued, 'There was a guy in there called Sophie and he was very camp and there were some very positive gay people in there. Very butch and very in your face and slightly aggressive. Which kind of was refreshing'.[12] While Peter had found it 'refreshing' that some gay people did not conform to his expectations of camp behaviour in this space, camp men like Sophie didn't quite fit his image and experience of queer life in Plymouth.

When considering perceived lines of engagement that affected behaviour and identity, Ted also recalled of the Lockyer that the 'straight people would come in for the evening. Young women, on a night out with the girls. They would come in because they felt safe. They knew they could sit and watch the queers or the gays'.[13] These women perhaps found these men amusing; they perhaps also felt safer going out here than in other parts of the city.

Queer Plymouthians expressed their sexual identities in multiple and seemingly contradictory ways across the spaces they inhabited. When Kevin Kelland, a sixty-year-old professional photographer, first visited the Lockyer Tavern, he recalls feeling that he was 'fighting being gay, or in those days being queer, very much',[14] but he quickly saw how easily he could become part of the subculture that existed within this space:

> I thought 'Ooh, this is the world'. You know, I felt fully accepted. It was like a duck to water. You would open the door and all the gay men would look around. And once I figured everything out. I remembered I would wear the more bizarre and, sort of, flamboyant things to attract men. Like a peacock. You were on show in there, yes, and you wanted to catch men's eye.[15]

Significantly, however, this watching gaze inspired in many gay men a sense of excitement in their hunt for potential sexual partners. Peter recalled, 'to be absolutely truthful I liked it like that because there was a sense that was something illegal about it, it kinda had a "frisson" to cruising that made it much more exciting'.[16]

The Lockyer Tavern came to be regarded as a safe space for Plymouth's gay scene until 1982, when it was demolished. The space was never forgotten by those who used and loved it, but, as some of my interviews show, people were fully aware that its physical attributes – separate entrances, exits and facilities – meant their presence was tolerated and their permission to use the space could be withdrawn at any point.

The Mambo

At the other end of Union Street was another queer space but with a different dynamic to the Lockyer. Ted recalled that 'the back of The Mambo had a garden with a loo in it and that was (laughs) a danger zone. The garden was pitch black and it would be matelots out there. Really, you didn't know what was happening out there half the time as you couldn't see a thing!'[17] The 'danger zone' to which Ted was referring, with his laugh and knowing smile, was the location for anonymous sex with a sailor.

The Mambo was a rather rundown venue, with egg boxes on the ceiling to provide soundproofing from neighbours, and it found its customer base through word of mouth. It was run primarily as a venue for gay men by a gay man called Reg, who, Ted recalled, 'wouldn't stand any nonsense from anybody. He would tell them [straight customers] where to go if they were causing trouble, if they were laughing at anybody'.[18] The Mambo principally served coffee and Reg would open up during the day and serve food. It would then close and in the evenings open again at 10 o'clock when he returned from one of the pubs himself, with friends in tow. Ted remembers, 'we would all go in and the girls would go in, the prostitutes, and they'd bring in their matelots and all the single matelots would come in and chat us up or we'd chat them up, whichever'.[19] One of the prostitutes, Rosie, would hide one of her arms and pretend it was missing to try and win some sympathy and sell more of her roses to an unsuspecting clientele. Unfortunately, she would often forget which one she had hidden on a previous occasion so would have switch from left to right. Either way, she had no problem with telling the gay men she shared the space with to '"F off" if you didn't give her some money for her flowers'.[20]

In terms of public visibility, the Mambo was at the other end of the spectrum from the Paramount or, to a lesser extent, the Lockyer Tavern. As the owner of the venue, Reg had the ability to decide when it opened and who was invited in to be the clientele of the space. Again, the matelots were welcomed as part of this scene and Reg's skill was to separate the inner sanctum of the Mambo from the world that remained outside its door. In this way, he created a space, within those walls, where permission did not need to be sought.

Mr. Harry's

By the early 1980s, The Lockyer Tavern, which had become something of a fading star, was gone and this gave way to new spaces such as Mr Harry's, In Other Words bookshop and The Swallow pub, which has endured as an LGBT+ drinking establishment to the present.

Unlike other venues, Mr Harry's was a ramshackle edifice on Plymouth Hoe, the space where Plymouth city centre touches the seafront. Peter, as many others, recalls it was 'a really seedy place... you know that sort of place, the water came through the ceiling, the toilets didn't work, all a bit run down'.[21] Yet, despite this, Mr Harry's was incredibly important and became a far more visible queer space in the city than had been seen before – and for both men and women. Jo Pine, a sixty-year-old physiotherapist, looked back on this period of time reminiscing that 'we had Harry's which was like – legendary! The place to go and we loved it. Harry's was a great place and we always felt very looked after there'.[22]

Mr Harry's was known as a queer space and attracted a wider clientele who saw themselves belonging there as club 'insiders', as opposed to some of the 'outsiders' visiting the Locker Tavern to spectate and jeer. Jo remembers, 'it was straight and gay. A lot of matelots back in those days with the girls. And the trouble would tend to start more or less between them and then it would spill over. But it was fun'.[23] The matelots, as we have seen, had long been a feature of Plymouth's queer culture and considered themselves as belonging in this space as much as they had in previous gay bars.

The club was visibly queer in part because the owner Harry Greenslade was himself openly gay. But while others loved this venue, Peter recalls the man, his business practices and the bar more negatively: 'People kept going on about how wonderful Harry was running a gay bar, but he wasn't a wonderful person at all. He exploited gay people... OK, but... he was himself, but he wasn't a nice character.'[24] He recalls Harry taking 'a knife out of his boot once and holding it to somebody's throat, a big knife. He was a funny person if you accepted the fact that he wasn't a good person'.[25]

Harry was not in any way camp. Instead, he combined his identity as a gay man with his role as a club owner who could maintain, and indeed defend, that business. His public profile, therefore, challenged some of the traditional stigma that had been previously attached to queer identity in the city. Mr Harry's bar resonated with the people of Plymouth on a number of levels: it was run down in a way that Plymouth as a city was often perceived to be while having a proprietor who was not afraid to use violence to maintain order. This sense of violence, or being able to withstand and deal with violence, chimed with the scenes being enacted on a weekly basis around the pubs on Union Street. The city's gay community was thus simultaneously like and unlike the wider Plymouth night-time scene.

Lynne Roberts, a 67-year-old factory worker, recalled the place with a similar sense of affection as Jo: 'It was very busy. It was amazing in those days. Harry's was amazing and I kept meeting people. It was packed, you couldn't move.'[26] However she also shared some of Peter's concerns about the club and its clientele: 'We used to say that we didn't like it when young girls used to come just to dabble... we would all say that they were dabbling and these bisexual women we always had a downer on them.'[27] She went on to say, 'We found that Harry's was very much a voyeuristic place where straight people used to go especially on "Hen Nights" and "Stag Nights" to see what gay people were up to and my friend Sandy was what was called "gay bashed" a few times.'[28] Even at Mr Harry's, queer spaces remained dangerous and also contested; different punters experienced them in different ways.

In Other Words

Another space, distanced from the gay clubs and pubs by being on a retail street at the other end of town, was the 'In Other Words' bookshop, seen as a safer space for LGBT+ people and as a meeting point for Plymouth's relatively few but determined radical activists. Opened in 1982, the bookshop was owned and run by Prudence de Villiers and her partner Gay Jones and had broken new ground for Plymouth by selling a wide range of literature including anti-war, environmental and gay and lesbian titles.

In a feature on its opening, *Evening Herald* reporter Jill Blight wrote that 'There is none of the hushed "library" in this warm and friendly emporium. The joint owners Prudence de Villiers, 34, and Gay Jones, 33, have cleverly created the right conditions for study and perusal where customers may have a cup of tea or coffee while browsing or just chatting'.[29] Blight defined the shop's 'alternative' nature as 'not conforming to stereotypes', and as Gay explained thirty years later, people used the shop to explore different ways of living – alternative medicine, alternative sources of energy and so on, not to mention 'alternative ways of living'.[30] Prudence had said at the time, 'We are not trying to threaten anyone. We're just making certain material available. There's no question of evangelising'.[31] The bookshop became an archive itself for those seeking access to ideas that were not always readily available in Plymouth. Gay reflects on Plymouth at the time of its opening as being very much 'a military city. And, as we know, for the military to be able to come out, was, oh, twenty-five years off. It was one of the last bastions of prejudice, basically. And about the last place where you could still be sacked for being gay. So that whole ethos made it very difficult'.[32]

As a result, the shop became a haven for many of Plymouth's queer citizens and also their likely allies during the 1980s and 1990s – Plymouthians who considered themselves to be activists, radicals or who generally held 'alternative' attitudes. In Other Words established itself as a non-threatening, indeed queer space in a very visible and public position on a high street where people of all sexualities could interact openly and explore more radical viewpoints and narratives. In an unrecorded conversation Gay did observe that there may have been a degree of cruising going on in the shop, though this was not something they actively encouraged. Often, in the oral history interviews, certain subtleties of the lives people lived were negotiated in the interview or saved to be shared until a time when the recorder was turned off.

Gay and Prudence were viewed as supportive activists, particularly by their younger LGBT+ customers. Gay recalls becoming something of a counsellor: 'We'd find ourselves talking to mostly younger people who were worried about their sexuality and wanted reassurance and wanted to be able to discuss it'.[33] She believes the most important aspect of the shop was the fact that it provided 'somewhere where they could come and have a safe haven and know that they're accepted and they could talk about things and they could buy books in which gay people were normal – you know, it was hugely important'.[34] This was especially significant during a decade in which prevailing discourses ensured that representations of homosexuality centred on HIV and AIDS. Gay reflects:

It wasn't a safe time. I mean the 80s were a particularly bad time to be gay because of HIV, AIDS and because a number of newspapers would have headlines about, you know, sending all gay people to camps and so on. You know there were outbursts like that and, you know, you could feel horribly insecure. And, no, it was very, very unpleasant. It was a very difficult time to be openly gay.[35]

During the debates about Section 28 in 1988, In Other Words became the most visible place in Plymouth where political opposition was expressed. The new law aimed to restrict the discussion and representation of gay lives in the work of local authorities and in schools. Gay and Prudence displayed newspaper coverage with slogans in their shop window which highlighted the oppressive nature of Section 28 while also displaying books that would shortly be regarded as inappropriate for use in schools.

Central Park

At this point in the chapter, I move on to discuss how other LGBT+ people in Plymouth also displayed their identity more visibly and how a horrific murder came to highlight homophobia and the dangers queer people faced. Jono Madeley was twenty-six when he moved to Plymouth, from London, in 1988 to work in education. He described how he had been struck by the great differences, in terms of both representation and attitudes, between the two cities. He recalls initially being fascinated by its location 'close to the sea, fantastic moorland around me, it was absolutely fantastic. I loved the idea of living in Plymouth'.[36] However, he found examples of LGBT+ lives in short supply which did not match his experiences of living in the capital. He felt that London had 'found a political voice, HIV and AIDS – that whole notion – had kind of galvanised the community together'.[37] Despite the best efforts of spaces such as In Other Words, this had simply not occurred in the same way in Plymouth.

Jono shared that he found it difficult to describe what the Plymouth queer community looked like because its focus had always been on the people who accessed the discreet gay scene: 'there was never a sense of people who, you know, may not use those facilities, who also identified themselves as being lesbian, gay, bi-sexual, trans-gender. And where was *their* voice?'[38] The problem was further compounded by 'a sense of, that as long as you keep it underground and as long as you don't put your head above the parapet and make too much noise, then we'll be OK'.[39] Jono, at the time, also attributed this to Plymouth's historical links with the armed forces. He perceived the city as 'still very much dominated by the military, you know the Dockyard was kind of at its peak, the Navy was growing, and we had the army down here. So it felt as though attitudes and behaviours were very much geared towards what the military might expect'.[40] As Matt Cook has suggested, 'in Plymouth, the ban on homosexuals in the military and the surrounding culture of discretion acted as a brake'.[41]

Paul Cooke, a youth worker who had grown up in the city, and was a teenager at this time, agreed that representations of homosexuality in the 1980s were either missing or else seemed very stereotypical. He recalled that, you would 'put on the telly and there's no representation. Or the only representation is a camp gay man... and there's nothing wrong with being a camp gay man at all but that's how society viewed me and that's how they viewed gay people'.[42] Paul met a man called Kieran in the early 1990s when volunteering for a gay men's health project which the older man was managing. He recounted, 'I started doing voluntary work with him and I think Kieran was probably... a cantankerous old bastard... but he was an amazing man because he was angry, he was HIV positive but he was really challenging Plymouth.'[43] As Paul recalls, 'he was challenging both people... not gay and gay... because he would wear leather waistcoats, Levi jeans, Doc Martens, pink triangles. He was very out; when he met you he would give you a kiss and at the time that was pretty out there'.[44] Queer theorist Michael Warner suggests, 'queers exist by virtue of the world they elaborate together, and gay or queer identity is always fundamentally inflected by the nature of that world'.[45] Kieran's public demonstration of queer identity, in a world and a place that had seen little of this type of performance, drew upon many of the recognized subcultural symbols employed in gay culture to create some visibility of queer lives in a city that still found that rather uncomfortable.

Discourses of shame and stigma continued to endure within the city, particularly around the practice of men cruising public spaces looking for sexual encounters with other men. Jono recalls how his work with the Youth Service brought him into contact with local police in this regard:

> There had been quite a crusade amongst the police nationally in kind of tackling people having sex in public places and the consequence of that had been highlighted by a couple of cases across the country where men who were having sex with men. They'd been caught having sex in a public place with another man and had actually committed suicide.[46]

Paul, when recalling his own initiation into the Plymouth gay scene, discussed public cruising:

> there was Club 91 and Harry's club, and obviously the Swallow, and there was cruising on the Hoe and Central Park. I have to say, before the murder, I went to Central Park a lot. I think that's a great advantage in being gay. You can get sex on tap. It may not be good sex, but it is sex. There's a negative and positive for cruising.[47]

The murder to which Paul refers came to light when, after midnight on Tuesday 7th November 1995, two severely injured men were found lying 200 yards apart in the city's Central Park area, some distance from Union Street. One of the men, Terry Sweet, aged sixty-four, died shortly after the police arrived. Sweet lived alone and was well known within Plymouth's gay community. His attackers had slashed his genitalia and face and hit him around the head. The other man, Bernard Hawken, survived the attack, but had similar life-altering injuries.

Reflecting on the incident two years later, *The Guardian* painted a picture of the three assailants entering the park 'on a hunting expedition. Armed with knives, their fists and boots, the men were hunting queers'.[48] Members of the gay community were horrified to find such hatred in the city directed against them. It shook an implied assumption that their quiet existence was tolerated, if not accepted, up until this point. Reflecting on this time, one man, outside of an interview, told me, 'We didn't realise until then that they hated us'.

After the three men's conviction, their friends and followers daubed the space with graffiti. On the path, close to where Sweet was found, someone spray-painted the outline of a body and wrote: 'Please step over spilt AIDS!'[49] while the killers reportedly received fan mail while in jail. Interviewees recalling this time shared how the police response was swift and considerate of their situation while also acknowledging how it caused the queer community, which had always prided itself on staying under the radar, to step up and take action to aid in the capture of these men. An underground scene that had always prided itself on going mostly unnoticed was effectively outed by this attack and that unexpected level of queer visibility led to the formation of groups and representation in the city.

The Museum

By the late 2000s, the two most visible and recorded moments in Plymouth's queer history were this terrible attack and the 2009 'parade that was not a parade' described at the beginning of this chapter. These were the legacies handed to the city's queer community in the creation and curation of a ground-breaking exhibition that shared their stories with Plymouth's wider community in 2012.

In this exhibition, at the Plymouth City Museum and Art Gallery, the city's LGBT+ inhabitants were provided with a new space to explore and represent their histories. This, however, would be a far more public space than had ever been cultivated before. It was temporary, as queer spaces often tend to be, but a nine-week-long exhibition was welcomed and, for a community that had always prided itself on avoiding public gaze, it was a significant sea change. Many of the people who contributed went on a real journey through the twelve-month planning process in terms of the extent to which they were prepared to go public with their stories. People went from being coaxed into being interviewed to standing proudly next to an exhibit about their lives on the opening night of the exhibition.

In the process of curation, it quickly became apparent that the best way to truly acknowledge the lives and culture that had taken pride in passing and so gone mostly unnoticed was to use this newly queered space to recreate in differing ways the places that I have talked about in this chapter. Large displays about the Lockyer Tavern and other drinking establishments were included around the gallery, while the more intimate spaces of the various oral history interviews were recreated with sound bites and listening stations.

The 'In Other Words' bookshop was recreated in one corner of the gallery to evoke its sense of a safe place in time but also to offer visitors an opportunity to stop and peruse materials that charted the spirit of activism that had brought us to this open celebration of queer Plymouth. The museum's Hurdle Gallery is positioned at the rear of the museum so this provoked recollections of being in the back bar once again, but for the most part the response from the majority of contributors was that this exhibition was not something they expected to see shared so publicly in their lifetime. Through the exploration and acknowledgement of how pride had been interpreted, felt and lived in this city, the LGBT+ community came to see how they fitted into Plymouth's wider heritage and how that might look going forward.

Plymouth's links to the sea and the armed forces have had a major impact on its citizens, including on the lives of its queer inhabitants. It became apparent that this needed to be reflected in the exhibition. On Union Street and beyond, customs and codes of behaviour were created as much in response to the Plymouth lived experience as to individuals' sexuality and gender roles. What was felt to be specific to Plymouth was the involvement of the matelots in both the public and underground recreational spaces. Their engagement with the underground scene made it a space where, rather than experiencing the more conventional sense of pride, which we might attach to rainbow flag waving and activism, the Plymouth queers took pride in passing, for the majority of their time, and then revelling in such moments where buying a sailor a drink or taking him home for the night was something to feel proud about.

The 'out and flag-waving' kind of LGBT+ pride did not fit with how the queer communities of the city felt at the time of the somewhat tentative 2009 parade. Local people's perceptions have since been reconsidered and reshaped through an active engagement in telling, sharing and preserving the stories of their queer heritage. The impact of creating this heritage was demonstrated within just three years. After the formation of the Plymouth LGBT Archive and the exhibition, Plymouth held its first outdoor Pride event in 2012, and, over the years since, large-scale Pride marches have become an annual feature. This more conventional and open sense of pride, however, is still framed and grounded against a particular and local – perhaps more authentic – sense of what pride has meant and might mean to the queer communities of Plymouth today and in the future.

Notes

1   J. O'Mara, 'Pride event is a part of city life', *The Herald*, 19 August 2009, p.13. Print.
2   Jason Bennetto, 'Stigma creates fear of reporting attacks'. *The Independent*, 9 November 1995.
3   James Paton Watson and Patrick Abercrombie, *A Plan for Plymouth*, 2nd edition (Plymouth: Underhill Ltd., 1943), Preface V.
4   Chris Robinson, *Plymouth in the Forties & Fifties* (Plymouth: Pen & Ink Publishing, 2011), 165.
5   Ibid., 165.
6   *Interview with Edward Whitehead*, 5 December 2011. Plymouth and West Devon Record Office Accession number [hereafter PWDRO] 3901/24.
7   *Interview with Edward Whitehead*, 5 December 2011. PWDRO 3901/24.
8   Ibid.
9   Ibid.
10 Ibid.
11 *Interview with Mavis Arnold*, 10 March 2012. PWDRO 3901–28.
12 *Interview with Peter Buckley*, 30 January 2012. PWDRO 3901/41.
13 *Interview with Edward Whitehead*, 5 December 2011. PWDRO 3901/24.
14 *Interview with Kevin Kelland*, 5 December 2011. PWDRO 3901/27.
15 Ibid.
16 *Interview with Peter Buckley*, 30 January 2012. PWDRO 3901/41.
17 *Interview with Edward Whitehead*, 5 December 2011. PWDRO 3901/24.
18 Ibid.
19 Ibid.
20 Ibid.
21 *Interview with Peter Buckley*, 30 January 2012. PWDRO 3901/41.
22 *Interview with Joanna Pine*, 16 December 2011. PWDRO 3901/25.
23 Ibid.
24 *Interview with Peter Buckley*, 30 January 2012. PWDRO 3901/41.
25 Ibid.
26 *Interview with Lynne Roberts*, 24 February 2012. PWDRO 3901/44.
27 Ibid.
28 Ibid.

29 J. Blight, 'Kooking the books'. *Evening Herald*. 11 June 1988. Print.
30 Ibid.
31 Ibid.
32 *Interview with Gay Jones*, 20 November 2011, PWDRO 3901/33.
33 Ibid.
34 Ibid.
35 Ibid.
36 *Interview with Jono Madeley,* 17 November 2011, PWDRO 3901/26.
37 Ibid.
38 Ibid.
39 Ibid.
40 Ibid.
41 Matt Cook, 'Local matters: Queer scenes in 1960s Manchester, Plymouth and Brighton', *Journal of British Studies* 59, no. 1 (2020), 35–7. Available at: https://eprints.bbk.ac.uk/id/eprint/30017/ (accessed 27 September 2021).
42 *Interview with Paul Cooke,* 1 March 2012. PWDRO 3901/43.
43 Ibid.
44 Ibid.
45 Michael Warner, *Publics and Counterpublics* (New York: Zone Books, 2002), 57.
46 *Interview with Jono Madeley,* 17 November 2011. PWDRO 3901/26.
47 *Interview with Paul Cooke,* 1 March 2012. PWDRO 3901/43.
48 Kevin Toolis, 'Licence to Hate', *The Guardian Weekend*, 30 August 1997. Print.
49 Ibid.

10

A 'queer collection': The Anglo colony in Florence, 1840s–1950s

Rachel Hope Cleves

Aldous Huxley would not deny that Florence had its charms. Brunelleschi's dome, the Michelangelo tombs and the terraced hillsides overlooking the city all impressed him with their beauty. But as for the cultured British and American expatriates who admired the city's charms so passionately that they had relocated there permanently, Huxley thought them a 'queer collection; a sort of decayed provincial intelligentsia', and during his first visit to the city in 1921 he did his best to steer clear.[1] He was not much fonder of the tourists who constantly streamed through the city, ticking off the sights listed in their red leather Baedeker's guides. 'Patriotic English and Americans should not walk too much in the streets of Florence.... No one visiting Florence can look at his fellow tourists and still be proud of his birth', Huxley wrote in a 1923 travel piece for *Vanity Fair*.[2] Obviously, despite his earlier reservations, he had returned to the city for a subsequent visit. Indeed, he would return to Florence many times over the years. Despite his pose of disapproval, Huxley was drawn to the city.

A great deal has been written about the history of queer migrations to the big city during the twentieth century. London, Paris and New York have each spawned robust historiographies tracing the development of sexual subcultures, political movements and domestic formations in the safe anonymity of their densely populated streets.[3] A more recent wave of scholarship has argued that sustained focus on big cities has overlooked the significance of queer life in provincial cities and rural communities.[4] This chapter seeks to build on that intervention by looking closely at a provincial city that drew queer British and American migrants from across national boundaries. What might the history of queer Anglosphere localities look like through a transnational lens? Did expatriate life in the city trespass sharp boundaries of national and sexual identity? Or did the provincial nature of Florence allow the queer Britons who relocated there in significant number to fashion for themselves a little queer England outside of England?

That Florence was a provincial city, despite its many notable sights, cannot be disputed. Because of the city's relatively small size, which remained below half a million until after the Second World War, the city's Anglo colony had a dominating effect on Florentine life. As early as the mid-nineteenth century, the Goncourt brothers called Florence a '*ville toute anglaise*', or, an all English city.[5] Increasing numbers of

Americans travelled to the city in the second half of the nineteenth century, reaching nearly 2,000 a year by 1858.[6] But British culture continued to dominate within the Florentine Anglosphere, both because of sheer numbers – 35,000 Britons were living in Tuscany, mostly in Florence, by 1900 – and perhaps also because the sort of Americans who wished to immerse themselves in Europe valued the (supposed) deeply rooted and historical quality of English culture over the (supposed) brash newness of American culture. To many well-to-do Americans in the nineteenth century, English culture represented class, a standard to be aspired to, while to many wealthy Britons, American culture was gauche and a subject for scorn. The Anglo colony in Florence retained a distinctly British flavour.

As Huxley unkindly put it, during a later 1925 visit to the city, Florence was a 'third-rate provincial town, colonized by English sodomites and middle-aged Lesbians'.[7] This provinciality, I argue, made Florence's Anglo-American queer community distinctive from the sexual subcultures that characterized a 'genuine metropolis' such as Paris, London or Rome, to which Huxley unfavourably compared the city. Most significantly, the insular quality of what was known by residents and visitors as the Anglo 'colony' led to the mixing together of people with non-normative sexualities that are often treated separately within queer historiography. Unlike 'gay New York' or the 'lesbian Left Bank', queer Florence encompassed individuals with a wide range of illicit sexual predilections. The city's 'queer collection' included not only the 'sodomites' and lesbians whom Huxley noted but also spinsters, adulterers, pederasts, voyeurs and various personages of sui generis erotic inclinations, all of whom might be considered queer for the ways in which they transgressed the normative sexual order, and who mixed together in more promiscuous constellations than those typical of larger cities. Historian Laura Doan problematizes this usage of the term 'queer' for giving too much credence to the normative, which is 'already intrinsically riddled with inconsistency'. David Halperin's definition of queer as 'whatever is at odds with the normal' lacks differentiation, according to Doan.[8] The example of Huxley's 'queer collection' restores that differentiation by revealing a social world not constructed along a binary of transgressive/normative but arranged according to complex geometries of erotic inclinations, class, affinity, gender, kinship, age, shared history and other intersecting characteristics. A person need not be a 'sodomite' or lesbian to be part of Huxley's queer collection. Just choosing to live in the Anglo colony in Florence, by Huxley's definition, might be enough.

Origins

While some in the Anglo colony were drawn to Florence because of its collections of Renaissance art, or because of its supposedly healthful climate, others were attracted from the outset by the city's reputation for sexual tolerance. That reputation dated back centuries and related principally to the city's association with sex between males. In fact Middle High German had a verb, *florenzen*, which meant 'to sodomize'.[9] Renaissance Europe's rediscovery of classical sources about 'Greek Love', or eroticized relations between males, began in Florence when the Byzantine philosopher Gemistus Pletho gave a series of lectures on Plato and Platonism while visiting the Italian city in 1438. After Pletho, the art, literature and philosophy of the Greek world became a primary vocabulary for early modern Europeans to express same-sex desire.[10] Pletho's time in Florence, for its part, became a subject within queer literature. E. M. Forster, for example, wrote about Pletho at least three times: in an early essay; in a failed historical novel; and in his 1908 novel *A Room With a View*, in which Mr Eager, a member of 'the English colony at Florence', describes another member of the colony who 'is working at Gemistus Pletho'.[11]

Pletho's lectures may have found a receptive audience because they were delivered at a moment when Florence had a particularly flourishing culture of male same-sex sexuality. In 1432, the city had even established a special judiciary magistracy called the 'Office of the Night' just to handle the policing of such relations. Working from the records produced by the Office, historian Michael Rocke calculated that between 1459 and 1502, at least one of every two youths in Florence was formally implicated in a sodomy charge before the age of thirty.[12] Other scholars have quarrelled with Rocke's use of statistics; however, his conclusion that same-sex relations constituted a common part of male experience in Florence in the fifteenth century remains persuasive.[13] The Office of the Night records reveal a paederastic sexual culture that was structured by age, with relations taking place almost entirely between adults over the age of eighteen who took the 'active' role, and youth between the ages of twelve and twenty who took the 'passive' role. While the special magistracy's very existence indicates the illegality of this apparently ubiquitous sexual culture, the Office of the Night typically meted out fairly mild discipline for consensual, non-violent same-sex relations. Contemporary popular songs and literary sources also treated Florence's acceptance of male same-sex relations as a source of humour, rather than condemnation. This toleration enraged the Dominican friar Girolamo Savonarola, who targeted pederasts with particular savagery when he waged his infamous campaign to cleanse Florence of sin at the end of the fifteenth century.[14]

Despite Savonarola's campaign, Florence's same-sex sexual culture persisted throughout the early modern era. English tourists discovered Florence as a queer locality in the seventeenth century when wealthy young gentlemen visited the city during the Grand Tour. By the eighteenth century, Florence hosted a lively colony of queer British and German expatriates who took part in intimate social relationships with each other and with Italian men. The British diplomat Sir Horace Mann, a friend of the queer belletrist Horace Walpole, and 'a well-established sodomite', was a central figure in this international set.[15] Mann hosted gatherings at his Palazzo Manetti, where friends like the artist Thomas Patch, the poet Thomas Gray and Antonio Cocchi, Mann's Italian doctor, socialized with visitors to the city. The writer Hester Thrale referred to Mann and his friends as 'Finger-Twirlers', which she said was 'a decent word for Sodomite'.[16] Thomas Patch gaily acknowledged the questionable sexual dynamics at play in Mann's gatherings in his 1761 painting *The Golden Asses*, showing an all-male drinking party at Mann's house, the title of which made reference to Apuleius's notorious work of classical pornography, *The Golden Ass*.[17] In a more serious vein, an essay written by Cocchi titled *Del Matrimonio* illustrated the development within Mann's circle of a new transnational homoerotic subculture, comprised not of libertines and street boys, as in the fifteenth century, but of urbane sophisticated men in love who cultivated egalitarian, emotionally supportive same-sex relationships.[18]

In the early nineteenth century, after the end of the Napoleonic Wars, Florence's Anglo colony expanded in size. Stendhal complained in 1817 that the city was filled with English tourists.[19] As the colony grew, it expanded to include increasing numbers of women, and the city's association with queer sexuality stretched to include relations between women as well as between men. Victorian England's most famous female poet, Elizabeth Barrett Browning, moved to Florence with her husband Robert Browning in 1846, and the couple began to host a literary salon at their home, Casa Guidi, which became a central gathering point for the city's growing Anglo colony. The American sculptor Harriet Hosmer, who had erotic relationships with women and often dressed in trousers and other male attire, stayed with the Brownings when she visited Florence from Rome. Browning found Hosmer's mannish looks attractively original.[20] Browning also counted among her acquaintances the art collector Ellen Heaton and the writer Fanny Haworth, two women who, in her words, were living in a 'matrimonial alliance' in which the independently wealthy Heaton took the role of 'monsieur le Mari', and Fanny Haworth supplied the feminine charm.[21]

Another friend of Elizabeth Browning, the minor novelist and poet Isabella Jane Blagden, frequently incorporated lesbian themes into her works. Blagden's apartment in the Villa Brichieri was the site of a distinctive and regular salon frequented both by resident and visiting women writers and artists. Blagden shared her home with a series of female friends, finding that in Florence it was possible for two women to live together with propriety. In her 1861 novel *Agnes Tremorne*, Blagden expounded on why it was better for women to live together than to live with husbands: 'In the personal intimacy which exists in such a relation, there is an entire comprehension and knowledge of each other. This is seldom attained, even in the holiest and truest of marriages. It requires a sixth sense, which few possess, for a man to penetrate every fold of a woman's character.'[22] Blagden's metaphor for intimacy – *to penetrate every fold* – hinted at the erotic potential of unions between women, which she certainly understood if not from personal experience, then from her frequent visits to the overtly lesbian household led by Charlotte Cushman in Rome.

Rival Florentine *salonnière* Theodosia Garrow Trollope, the daughter-in-law of Fanny Trollope, also maintained close female intimacies alongside her marriage. She was particularly close to the writer Margherita Mignaty, originally from Corfu. George Eliot, who met Mignaty in Florence, described the writer as royal in appearance, with 'large, very black eyes' that were 'aflame' with sentiment.[23] Mignaty's and Trollope's correspondence to each other was passionate, and filled with declarations of longing. Trollope 'tested the elasticity of Victorian sexual relationships, as well as the boundaries between public and private, in her intense and eroticized female friendships', according to Alison Chapman's study of the networks of British and American female writers who flocked to the city in the mid-nineteenth century.[24]

By the 1870s, 30,000 of Florence's 200,000 residents were British or American.[25] There were shops where customers could buy all sorts of English imports from marmalade to mackintoshes, frequented by expatriate customers, some from families who had made their homes in Florence for generations. Most of the long-term residents were people of means. In the twentieth century, Aldous Huxley would refer to these households as 'the Villadom'.[26] Expatriates with more limited wallets could still live comfortably in apartments and pensions in the city proper, thanks to a favourable exchange rate. Rich or not, all members of the colony could feed their appetites for tea and seedcakes in the city's English shops. But if the Britons and Americans who flocked to Florence in the mid-nineteenth century longed for commodities from Britain, they most decisively chose not to import the stringent moral codes that structured social life there. *Firenze la Bella* was a place to escape such narrow confines.

Queer Florence

Perhaps the first account to describe the Anglo Florentine colony as 'queer' came from the pen of Henry James, an American expatriate writer whose own queerness has long transfixed scholars and critics. James first visited Florence in the winter of 1886–7. Arriving on 8th December, he rented a furnished room in a villa that had been leased by his friend, the writer Constance Fenimore Woolson, on the south-eastern outskirts of town, at the top of Bellosguardo hill. James remained in Florence for ten weeks before moving on to Venice. Writing later to his friend Grace Norton, James complained that he found Florence beautiful but he thought the people there to be tiresome. 'I did see a great many people', he told Norton, 'they were members of the queer, promiscuous polyglot (most polyglot in the world) Florentine society'.[27] He was so fond of this formulation that he used it again in a letter to Sarah Butler Wister, a good friend whose long intimate friendship with Jennie Musgrave may have been one of James' inspirations for his lesbian novel, *The Bostonians* (1886). James wrote to Wister on the same day that he wrote to Norton, and recounted his encounters with the 'queer, promiscuous polyglot society' in Florence. James dismissed the colony as a 'vain agitation of insignificant particles', before going on to namedrop several of its luminaries with whom he had passed his time, including Vernon Lee, Janet Ross and Princess Troubetzkoi.[28] His inclusion of Lee on this list suggests that James intended the word 'queer' not simply in its traditional sense, as a synonym for odd or eccentric, but also in its emerging sexual sense, to connote deviance from sexual norms.[29] Like Huxley, three decades later, James felt both repelled by and drawn to Florence's queer society, mirroring his likely sentiments about his own sexuality.

James considered the most impressive member of Florence's queer society to be the British writer Vernon Lee, also known by her birth name Violet Paget. She had been born in France to British parents, and her family drifted from town to town in France, Switzerland, Germany and Italy as she grew up, finally settling in Florence in 1873, when she was seventeen. She soon began publishing under the intentionally gender ambiguous nom-de-plume Vernon Lee, which became far more than a pen name.[30] Vernon Lee captured the writer's masculinity, reflected as well in her choice to dress *a la garçonne* in high starched collars, cropped hair and bowler hats. Throughout her life, Lee engaged in a series of intense romantic relationships with other women, and she is commonly treated as a lesbian within the historiography, although this label has been disputed.[31] No one disputes Lee's brilliance of mind or conversation, which made her such an attractive and central figure in Florence's Anglo colony for half a century, until her death in 1935. Lee frequently hosted gatherings at the Casa Paget, in the hills between Florence and Fiesole.

'How many men and women, of how many types, characters, and nationalities!' visited there, recalled the English poet Mary Robinson, who lived with Lee for a period. The intimacy between the women made Robinson's friend John Addington Symonds so jealous that this early supporter of homosexual rights wrote to his friend the sexologist Havelock Ellis, who replied that the women's relationship 'might serve as a possible case-history for the section on Lesbianism in *Sexual Inversion*.'[32] A large number of the visitors to Casa Paget were queer women who regarded Lee with reverence. One observer noted that when the Florence train stopped by the Casa Paget, 'it was boarded by several manly-looking women. One of them seemed to be the central figure. Her face in spite of its snout-like ugliness was fascinatingly witty and intelligent. Somebody told me that her name was Violet Paget and that she wrote books as "Vernon Lee"'.[33]

Lee's conversational brilliance attracted many queer men as well. Their numbers were growing in the late 1880s, owing at least in part to the passage of the 1885 Labouchère Amendment in Britain, which criminalized acts of 'gross indecency' between men, lowering the threshold for prosecution of homosex from the earlier, more stringent and more harshly punitive, sodomy statute. Sex between males had been decriminalized in southern Italy in the early nineteenth century. After Unification, Italy passed the 1889 Zanardelli Code, decriminalizing sex between males nationally, creating a legal environment that appealed to British men who faced troubles at home.[34] Even before Labouchère, Italy appealed to British refugees like Lord Henry Somerset, the Conservative politician, who fled to Florence in 1879 following the exposure of his relationship with a teenage boy.[35] Many queer male migrants to the city found their way to the Casa Paget.

Lee's charms were far from universal, however. Not everyone appreciated her habit of dominating conversations, nor her sharp judgements. A strong enmity developed between Lee and another pillar of the Anglo colony, Bernard Berenson, a Lithuanian-born Jewish American art historian who had moved to Florence in 1892 and converted to Catholicism. Berenson and Lee visited art galleries together in Italy and London, but soon their personalities clashed, with Berenson complaining that Lee talked 'like a steam engine' and that her talk was full of *spropositi*, or nonsense, and Lee complaining that Berenson was 'a dreadful poseur, always flitting about'.[36] Dislike later evolved into professional rivalry, with Lee criticizing Berenson's artistic discernment and Berenson in turn disparaging Lee's scholarship, suggesting that she and her romantic friend Kit Anstruther-Thomson had plagiarized ideas from his books *Venetian Painters of the Renaissance* (1894) and *Florentine Painters of the Renaissance* (1896). Lee felt that Berenson's attacks were personal, driven by rancour, rather than professional critique.[37] Lee's biographer suggests that Berenson's hostility to Lee originated in his antipathy towards her sexuality.[38]

Berenson may have disdained lesbianism, but his own sexual habits contributed to his step-granddaughter Barbara Strachey's observation that Florence's 'large expatriate community abounded in "Sapphists," eccentrics and those whose marital arrangements were irregular'.[39] In other words, Strachey grouped together Berenson, along with his wife Mary Berenson (Strachey's grandmother), and the couple's sometimes friend, Vernon Lee, as all members of Florence's broader queer collection. Strachey had good cause to make this remark. Bernard Berenson was notoriously unfaithful to his wife, Mary Berenson, an art historian in her own right, whom many credit with having written substantial portions of her husband's books. His lovers included Bella da Costa Greene, librarian to J. P. Morgan, and Nicky Mariano, his long-time live-in secretary at I Tatti, the villa where he lived from 1901 until his death in 1959.

Mary Berenson's extra-marital affairs made her as fitting for inclusion within the grouping 'sapphists, eccentrics, and those whose marital arrangements were irregular', as her husband – perhaps even more so, since Mary Berenson could be argued to have flirted with all three categories. Mary commenced her relationship with Bernard while still married to her first husband, an Irish barrister named Benjamin Costelloe. When Mary relocated to Florence in 1895 to join Berenson, she initially hired an aspiring art historian named Maud Cruttwell to be her housekeeper and secretary at her villa, a few doors down from Berenson's. Cruttwell, who was a former secretary of Vernon Lee, dressed like her mentor in men's collars and ties, accessorized with thick tweed jackets. She also smoked cigars. According to one reference text, Cruttwell 'among other things, endorsed and perhaps encouraged Mary Berenson's increasing physical size (Mrs. Berenson was quite fat in later years)'.[40] The suggestion of an erotic feeder-type relationship between the two women coincides with an equally surprising suggestion in the sources that despite her lesbianism, and general disdain for men, Cruttwell entertained a passion for Bernard Berenson, who for his part 'could not bear to see her', and considered her to be both ugly and intellectually inferior. Cruttwell, however, outgrew her passion for Berenson by 1907 when she came under the influence of Gertrude and Leo Stein, who were spending the summer in Florence. By that time, Mary wrote that Cruttwell 'was a maniac *à rebours* loathing men and adoring women'.[41] Mary, for her part, fell in love with Geoffrey Scott, a young architectural historian whom she had introduced into the household as a companion to her children, and who later married their neighbour Sybil Cutting, with whom Bernard Berenson was having an affair, leading Mary to attempt suicide.[42] Irregular marital relationships indeed!

After the Great War

Florence's queer reputation flourished in the early twentieth century, reaching perhaps its apogee during the interwar era, when the value of the lira declined, permitting more British and American migrants of ordinary means to move to the city. Florentine society after the First World War was 'expansive without being expensive', as the dilettante author and art collector Harold Acton put it. Acton was born in Florence, to a wealthy Anglo-American family, and he grew up in La Pietra, a villa on the city's northern outskirts. In his 1948 memoir, Acton recalled that during his adolescence in the 1910s, 'One was continually hearing that certain men in Florence were queer, not that it made much difference to their popularity: on the contrary! the queerer the dearer'. When he was young, Acton wrote, he wondered what the word 'queer' meant. 'Wherein did this queerness reside?' He remembered one young man he saw at a cafe.

> In trying to solve this problem I stared at the young man until he flushed with embarrassment. 'But I can't see anything queer about him,' I exclaimed, and was told to mind my own business, which led to further cogitation. Thinking him over, I came to the conclusion that he was prettier than a man was supposed to be and that might have something to do with it.[43]

It's impossible to take Acton's story at face value. His memoir is less than forthcoming about his own homosexuality, despite being full of portraits of Florence's famous queer literati, many of whom he counted as friends. Acton had grown up very much embedded in James' queer, polyglot, promiscuous Florence. His father, Arthur Acton, was an art dealer and collector of a decidedly questionable sexual reputation. Bernard Berenson referred to him as a 'bounder'.[44] There were rumours that Arthur Acton had shared a sexual relationship with his American friend Guy Mitchell when the two were students at the Ecole des Beaux Arts together in Paris before Acton entered into a marriage of convenience with Mitchell's sister Hortense.[45] Arthur Acton first moved to Florence in 1894 and, according to one story, began renting and living in Villa La Pietra by 1897. In the early twentieth century the Actons made La Pietra into a social capital of the Anglo colony, but according to some accounts it was not a happy family home. Hortense spent much of her time away from Florence, in Paris or London. Their sons Harold and William went to school in England.[46] Arthur used his spare time to take naked photographs of young girls and to pursue affairs with Florentine women, including his personal secretary Ersilia, with whom he had a daughter, Liana, an event that would lead to a dramatic inheritance battle that has continued for over thirty years.[47]

While Acton passed without comment over his father's questionable character, his memoirs acknowledged the fascination of 'Florentine gossip'. As Acton learned growing up, 'every other member of the foreign colony had a purple past. Though the purple had faded, there was a piquancy in knowing that the suave Lord X had had to flee from the London police because he was "a Greek born out of due time" and that the motherly Mrs. Y had been the power behind a throne'.[48] By Lord X, Acton probably had in mind the self-exiled Conservative politician Lord Henry Somerset, still living in Florence until 1932; and by Mrs Y, Acton was making reference to Alice Keppel, who had made a profession of serving as a mistress to wealthy men, ending with a long season as the mistress of King Edward VII. With the King's money, Alice Keppel bought the Villa dell'Ombrellina in Florence, to which she retired in the company of her husband George Keppel. Acton, by grouping together Henry Somerset and Alice Keppel, drew the same connection between Florence's queer men and its irregular wives that had earlier been drawn by Henry James. George Keppel, for his part, was a voyeur who liked to watch young people swim in his hillside pool. Kinta Beevor, who was the grand-niece of Florentine hostess Janet Ross, recalled that when she was a young woman in the 1930s, Keppel would drive around the city in his red Lancia sports car trying to pick up girls and invite them to the villa for a swim.[49]

Acton had friendships with many of the men and women in the colony whom he described as having 'purple pasts'. His memoir includes comic portraits of well-known figures in Florence, like Reggie Turner, Oscar Wilde's devoted defender. Turner, a minor novelist, had fled to Florence after Wilde's conviction, and he spent the rest of his life in the Italian city. Acton described him as

> small, quietly dressed, with a sallow complexion, thick purplish lips and perpetually blinking eyes. Not prepossessing at a first glimpse, but his features were intensely mobile and this highly expressive mobility counteracted his ugliness and made you forget it. His wit had the lightest butterfly touch and fluttered its wings from what he left unsaid as well as from what he said.[50]

Acton's butterfly metaphor and allusion to things 'left unsaid' implied Turner's homosexuality, without naming it. Although he was frank about his sexuality with friends, Acton remained publicly closeted until the end of his life, refusing to speak to author Selina Hastings, for example, after she outed him in her 1986 biography of Nancy Mitford.[51] But Acton's reticence was unusual for his milieu. Turner and many of his Florentine friends were very public about their sexualities.

Other prominent figures in interwar Florence included Ronald Firbank, a writer of such queer affect that Harold Acton called him 'airy faery Ronald'; Maurice Magnus, an American eccentric who was Isadora Duncan's former manager and who wrote a salacious memoir about buggery in the French foreign legion; and Giuseppe 'Pino' Orioli, an antiquarian bookseller and publisher who arranged for D. H. Lawrence's *Lady Chatterley's Lover* to be printed in Italy, to evade censorship in Britain (Figure 11).[52] Orioli, who lived in London before the First World War, had been the lover of Irving Davis, a bookseller and member of the Bloomsbury crowd. A notorious scamp with a taste for male adolescents, Orioli liked to sing the praises of Florentine youth who had their 'gabardine trousers specially tailored to show off their genitals'.[53] Orioli delighted in ribald humour and outré behaviour, making no secret of his erotic leanings.

The same could be said of Orioli's dearest friend in interwar Florence, the writer Norman Douglas. Born in Austria to a Scottish industrialist family that operated a mill along an Alpine waterway, Douglas was a notorious pederast, who could often be found in the city's *trattorie* in the company of Italian boys.[54] Reggie Turner used to joke, 'On occasions when other men visit a jeweller's shop, Norman buys a toy train.'[55] Not all of queer Florence was so forgiving. Osbert Sitwell, the British novelist and aesthete who spent much of his time living at the Castello di Montegufoni, south of Florence, complained of the blatancy of Douglas' behaviour. One time he had taken Douglas to dinner and the writer brought along a child in a sailor suit, 'sitting throughout the meal with him on his knee', much to Sitwell's displeasure.[56] But for every critic, Douglas drew twice as many admirers. His presence on the piazza was one of Florence's main draws, attracting visitors like Aldous Huxley, who came to see Douglas despite his

Figure 11 D. H. Lawrence reading *Lady Chatterley's Lover* to Norman Douglas, Pino Orioli and Reggie Turner in Orioli's Florence living room in 1928 by Collingwood Gee (1933). From the collection of Deirdre Sholto Douglas and reproduced with her permission.

reservations about the city.[57] Taboos against intergenerational sex had not yet reached the fever pitch of today, leaving more space for humoured indulgence. Many people agreed that Douglas was a 'wicked' man, but they enjoyed his company nonetheless. D. H. Lawrence's wife Frieda Lawrence called him 'the only wicked man I have known, in a medieval sense, but, oh, so witty'.[58] The city's pederasts did not stand apart from the broad agglomeration that comprised queer Florence. The centrality of pederasts to Florence's 'queer' reputation in the early twentieth century points to the limitations of academic historians' use of the term as both a shorthand for the LGBTIA2S umbrella of identities and a means of demarking 'whatever is at odds with the normal'. First, few self-identified queer people today would welcome the inclusion of pederasts (or paedophiles) within the umbrella term. Second, the relative acceptance of pederasts within Florentine circles in the early 1900s suggests that adult-child sex was less 'at odds with the normal' than we might expect.

In fact, during the early twentieth century, Florence was as well known for pederasts as for any other sexual type. Douglas used to jokingly call the men who gathered in the city to chase after its boys, 'the Paederastic Congress'.[59] The city's pederasts included men from many nations. In his memoirs, Pino Orioli recalled that when he first moved to Florence in 1910, he would frequently encounter in the city's *caffès* a group of about ten men, 'most of them Germans, and all of them queer', who sat together, 'saying charming things about Donatello or Dante or Michelangelo or Bruno or Benvenuto. If you took a table near enough to overhear what they were saying, you soon realized that they were not comparing the merits of those famous Italians of bygone days, but those of the best-looking modern youngsters about town who bore the same names'.[60] Paederastic humour was an open element of the risqué repartee to be heard among the queer circles that gathered at the city's venues.

Many authors who visited Florence during the interwar years tried to capture this conversational milieu in their novels. D. H. Lawrence lampooned Douglas, Turner and Magnus in *Aaron's Rod* (1922), about the peripatetic adventures of an earnest English union official who leaves his family behind in the Midlands for adventures among the Bohemians of London and Florence. In Florence, the city's notorious characters engage in wicked conversations filled with sexual innuendo. Lawrence's outlook on Florentine society was rather censorious. For all his modern reputation as a libertine, many of Lawrence's contemporaries saw him as an uptight puritan.[61] As much as he felt drawn to Italy's sexual permissiveness, he also felt deeply uncomfortable about its toleration for same-sex sexuality. Italy, he wrote to his childhood friend May Holbrook, 'is a queer country'.[62] According to Douglas, the sight of the Florentine boys in their tight trousers made Lawrence feel squeamish.[63] He dismissed Lawrence's novel as 'Aaron's Rot'.[64] Nonetheless, the book captured recognizable aspects of queer Florence.

In one scene, a character asks,

> Why is it, do you think, that English people abroad go *so* very QUEER – so ultra-English – INCREDIBLE! – and at the same time so perfectly impossible? But impossible! Pathological, I assure you. – And as for their sexual behaviour – oh, dear, don't mention it. I assure you it doesn't bear mention. – And all quite flagrant, quite unabashed – under the cover of this fanatical Englishness.[65]

Lawrence's observation that Florence's sexual self-exiles fashioned themselves as 'ultra-English' in their absence from home suggests how significant national identity remained to many of these putative cosmopolitans. The most wealthy English residents often had little intercourse with Italians 'except through their cooks and gardeners'.[66] Many lived in the country for decades without ever learning the language, socializing only with other Anglo-Florentines. Other expatriates, like Norman Douglas, had plenty of intercourse (of the wrong sort) with Italians and spoke the language fluently, but nonetheless maintained a strong sense of Britishness. Douglas dressed in tweeds and insisted on his identity as a Scot, despite having been born and raised in Austria, and never having lived in Scotland for more than a few weeks at a time. The appeal of Florence was that it allowed queer Britons to live their sexual lives unhampered without sacrificing their national identities.

Lawrence's friend Richard Aldington, another writer who frequented Florence in the interwar years, described the city's *caffè* society in similarly acerbic terms. Aldington mixed, for a time, on friendly terms with Orioli and Douglas, but a series of perceived personal slights led to a rupture in Aldington's relationship with Douglas. In 1937, Aldington published a novel, *Seven against Reeves*, which painted his former Florentine friends in scabrous terms. Transplanting the action from Florence to Venice (presumably for the sake of deniability), Aldington depicted a dinner table conversation between 'Mr. Philboy' (Douglas) and 'Erasto Paederini' (Orioli), pseudonyms that plainly revealed the men's sexual inclinations towards boys and youth.[67] After Douglas died and could no longer sue for libel, Aldington wrote a tell-all biography of Douglas that included details of the writer's paederastic sexual affairs.[68] Douglas, for his part, disavowed sexual morality, and thus expressed no moral objections when Aldington abandoned his long-term lover Brigit Patmore to run away with her son's new wife, Netta. But Douglas did enjoy gossiping about the tawdry affair and poking fun of Aldington. 'Thank God I don't get messed up with other people's wives', he wrote to his friend Bryher.[69]

In contrast to Lawrence and Aldington, the writer Ronald Firbank depicted Florence with a much lighter touch in his 1920 play, *The Princess Zoubaroff*. Firbank was notoriously shy, but his characters idled away their days in chit-chat. *Zoubaroff* included characters based on Oscar Wilde ('Lord Orkish') and his lover, Lord Alfred 'Bosie' Douglas ('Reggie Quintus'), who visited the city after Wilde's release from prison. In one scene, Lord Orkish comments to Lady Rocktower, 'I don't know at all what the Arno is coming to. I was leaning on my window-sill and there were some youths who appeared to be bathing without false modesty of *any* kind'. When Lady Rocktower says, 'How dreadful', Lord Orkish responds, 'I'm sure if I looked it was quite involuntary'. Indeed, says Lady Rocktower, 'I'm sure you couldn't help yourself from standing and looking'. The Arno River's notoriety, as a swimming spot for Florentine youth that gathered a daily crowd of enthusiastic male spectators, dated back centuries.[70]

Like Henry James and Harold Acton, Firbank's understanding of queer Florence encompassed the city's women as well as its men. One of the characters in the play is 'Blanche Negress', an author known for her book 'Lesbia, or Would He Understand'. Another character quizzes Blanche about her romantic inclinations:

> Blanche: Men amuse me sometimes. But I have never really loved one.
> Eric: You have never loved *any* man?
> Blanche: Never!
> Lady Rocktower: It's a pleasure to meet now and again a woman of really
>   advanced morals.
> Blanche: I can safely say I prefer the society of other women to that of men.[71]

At the play's end Firbank's female characters reject their marriages to live together in a convent. Their husbands celebrate this outcome, which sets them free to pursue their own same-sex affairs. In humorous fashion, Firbank captured a queer community in Florence that extended to pederasts, men who loved men, lesbians and women who rejected marriage for homosocial conviviality.

Blanche Negress and Lady Rocktower may have had no direct correlates within Florence's Anglo colony, but they represented the many British and American women who fashioned independent sexual lives in interwar Florence. The most glamorous may have been Alice and George Keppel's daughter Violet Trefusis, who had love affairs with Vita Sackville-West and Winnaretta Singer.[72] Radclyffe Hall first visited Florence in 1921 with her partner Una Troubridge, who had relatives among the Anglo colony's old families and spoke fluent Italian. The women returned frequently to the city that Hall referred to as 'our beloved Florence'.[73] Vernon Lee continued to hold court at Villa Paget until her death in 1935, attracting new admirers all the while. The painter Romaine Brooks, who frequented Florence during the 1920s and 1930s, moved to the city with her long-time lover Natalie Barney in 1940.[74] But by then, the decision to retreat to Florence had taken on very different meaning than it had a decade earlier. No longer was the city a refuge from Victorian persecution. The city's queer expatriate scene had come to a crashing halt, brought down by the Second World War.

Fascism and its aftermath

Florence's climate of sexual toleration resisted the rise of Italian Fascism until the late 1930s. Unlike Nazi Germany, the dictatorship of Benito Mussolini did not criminalize same-sex relations. Italian Fascists did seek to repress the public visibility of same-sex relations, however, to promote their ideal of the virile new man. Gangs of black shirts attacked gatherings of queer men. The government used a strategy of censorship, imprisonment and isolation to suppress homosexuality, or as it was mostly referred to at the time, pederasty. For a while, the colony continued on blithely undisturbed. As the novelist Lettice Cooper described the prewar scene, 'life went on… in the English and American society round Florence as if Mussolini hardly existed'.[75] Some, like Bernard Berenson, passively opposed the Fascists, while doing their best to stay out of trouble. Others, like the biographer Iris Origo – born in London to an American father and an Anglo-Irish mother – passively supported the Fascists.[76] Several expatriates were even enthusiastic supporters of Mussolini, including Una Troubridge and Radclyffe Hall.[77] Other expatriates despised the Fascists but remained in Florence because they had nowhere else to go, like Norman Douglas, who had previously been arrested and driven from Britain and Austria.

Eventually, however, queer, promiscuous, polyglot Florence had to give way to the new Italian reality. The persecution of the Anglo colony stepped up after 1935, when Italy invaded Ethiopia, prompting protest from the British government.[78] Anti-British posters and graffiti appeared around the city.[79] Many long-time Anglo residents fled the city, including people who had been born there and been resident for their entire lives. Some moved to England or the United States. Others, who were *personae non gratae* in their countries of origin, like Norman Douglas, abandoned Italy for Switzerland or Portugal, seeking neutral ground.

The rush to return began as soon as Allied troops hit the ground in Italy. Many members of the interwar community had passed away. Orioli died in exile in Portugal in 1942. Some could not return, like Norman Douglas, whose Florentine apartment had been occupied by a politically connected family after he fled the city in 1937. But other prominent figures returned and tried to resume their old lives, like Harold Acton, who fashioned Villa La Pietra into a centre of post-war Florentine queer society. The American writer David Plante began to visit La Pietra in the 1960s. 'For many young homosexual men', Plante recalled 'La Pietra was an entrée into a world they had fantasized about', a world of privilege, high culture and exclusivity.[80] Entrée to Acton's home allowed a new generation to imagine themselves as the inheritors of a lofty queer historical lineage.

Despite political and religious efforts to repress nonmarital sex during the post-war era, 1950s Italy had a flourishing queer sexual scene characterized both by the sort of youthful street hustlers that had attracted men like Norman Douglas before the war and by an emerging homosexual subculture of same-sex attracted men. New waves of Anglo travellers gleefully participated in this scene.[81] Enough of the spirit of the old colony was resuscitated after the war that Henry James' original remarks about the city's queer nature struck the writer Sinclair Lewis as still entirely apt. Lewis set his final novel, *World so Wide* (1951), in post-war Florence. The novel's main character is an American everyman, Hayden Chart, who following a car accident that kills his wife, decides to leave Newlife, Colorado, for a sojourn abroad, and ends up settling in Florence. The name of Chart's hometown connects him to one of James' earliest innocents abroad, his character Christopher Newman, from *The American* (1877). Lewis makes his debt to James clear. 'Mr. Henry James was breathless over the spectacle of Americans living abroad and how very queer they are', Chart thinks, 'But just how queer they are, Mr. James never knew.'[82] Well, perhaps he knew, but he was reluctant to say. Lewis had the advantage to be writing at a moment when codes of censorship were beginning to crumble. Chart's friend from home, Roxanne Eldritch, who comes to see him in Florence, rejects the city's queer colony and upbraids Chart in plain-spoken Americanisms: 'You got to get out of Florence – I mean, the Limey-Yankee Florence. It's such a hick village!… And then that ratty bunch of American pansies that sit at the same bar, every afternoon, out on the sidewalk, exhibiting their beauties to any visiting firemen fairies that may happen to hit the town.'[83] Eldritch's speech shakes Chart out of his Florentine torpor. The novel resolves with Eldritch rescuing Chart from Florence by marrying him, and carrying him away to new, monogamous, heterosexual adventures.

Eldritch's rant demonstrates that, at least in Lewis's view, Florence's sui generis admixture of provinciality and sexual diversity survived into the 1950s. The war hadn't destroyed the city's character. But, ultimately, the loosening of Victorian sexual mores that permitted Sinclair to describe Florence in language that James wouldn't dare undermined the Anglosphere's need for a city of its nature. The loosening of both legal and social restrictions on sexual behaviour made it unnecessary for gay men and lesbian women to find refuge abroad. Possibilities for queer life expanded at home. No longer did Britons need to construct a queer England outside England. And with that expansion of domestic possibilities came hardening boundaries between sexual identity communities.

In her pathbreaking 1984 article 'Thinking Sex', Gayle Rubin proposed a model of the 'charmed circle' of sexuality, in which some types of sexual activity (married, heterosexual, monogamous) fell within the circumscribed boundaries of the 'good', and other forms of sexuality (queer, promiscuous, commercial, intergenerational, etc.) fell outside the circle into the illicit.[84] During the heyday of Florence's Anglo-American colony, from the 1840s through to the 1950s, the charmed circle was so narrowly drawn that all sorts of people were grouped together outside its boundaries.

In Florence, this led to the construction of a queer society inclusive of all sorts of sexual nonconformists. But the broadening of the charmed circle, especially during the 1990s, meant that sexual groups who claimed their place within the 'good', such as promiscuous women, gay men and lesbians, increasingly did not share in common a status as excluded deviants. Certainly, they did not claim a shared positionality with those groups that remained outside the circle, like pederasts, who were now called paedophiles and had become more hated than ever before.[85] Unlike gay men and lesbians, paedophiles in the late twentieth century felt increased need to travel outside the borders of Britain and the United States to pursue sexual encounters, concentrating in new locations including southeast Asia. The 'queer collection' atomized into its separate components.

For a century or so, from the mid-nineteenth century to the mid-twentieth century, Florence's provincial Anglo-American colony divided more along personal antipathies and gradations of wealth than it did by discrete sexualities. There was the villadom versus the city, or, in other words, the wealthy elites who lived perched on the hillsides around Florence versus the bohemians and poor students who lived in small flats in the city proper. Norman Douglas avoided the villadom, forcing friends like Harold Acton to come down to the city and join him for meals. Within the villadom, there were animosities and divides. Janet Ross, who hosted Sunday salons at her Poggio Gherardo, a villa described by Boccaccio in the *Decameron*, hated Vernon Lee. At one time, Ross was friends with Ouida (Louise de la Ramée), a popular novelist. Later, Ross and Ouida were said to have fallen out over their rivalry for a man, the Marchese della Stufa. Ouida exacted her retribution by satirizing Ross in her novel *Friendship*. Ross retaliated by horse-whipping Ouida in the streets of Florence, and keeping a copy of the novel in her bathroom to use for toilet paper.[86] Other stories attribute the divide between the women to a disagreement stemming from a dog bite.[87] Whatever the origin, the battle between Ross and Ouida divided villadom more sharply than did differences of sexual expression.

Finally, tales of the fractures within villadom point to an obvious conclusion about Florence's queer collection: it was founded on privilege. Florence attracted Britons and Americans in part because exchange rates often made Italy inexpensive to expatriates. As Georgina Grahame observed in *In a Tuscan Garden*, her 1902 guide to life in Florence, 'It is astonishing how many Englishwomen of small means there are living here in respectability and comfort in their own small *étage*, who, if in London, would be in comfortless suburban lodgings'.[88] Many of the writers who were drawn to the city, like D. H. Lawrence and Norman Douglas, were constantly scrambling for the funds to stay afloat. Even they, however, had the privilege of wealthy friends and patrons. Douglas could count on the Harold Actons and Osbert Sitwells of the world to take him out to dinners at his favourite *trattorie*, where he ordered the best dishes and left his hosts with the bill. Florence's queer collection shared in common their possession of sufficient capital – economic, social or both – to support their divergent lifestyles. Florence was a provincial city in terms of both its numbers and its limitations. Yet, it long played an outsized role as a queer locality within the transnational Anglosphere.

Notes

1   Aldous Huxley to Leonard Huxley, 31 May 1921, Grover Smith (ed.), *Letters of Aldous Huxley* (New York: Harper & Row, 1970), 197; Aldous Huxley, 'The tyranny of the guide book', *Daily Mail*, 31 August 1923.

2   'From a tourist's notebook', *Vanity Fair*, 20 August 1923.

3   A brief list of examples includes George Chauncey, *Gay New York: Gender, Urban Culture, and the Making of the Gay World, 1890–1940* (New York City: Basic Books, 1995); Matt Houlbrook, *Queer London: Perils and Pleasures in the Sexual Metropolis, 1918–1957* (Chicago: The University of Chicago Press, 2005); Andrea Weiss, *Paris Was a Woman: Portraits from the Left Bank* (Berkeley: Counterpoint, 2013).

4   See for example John Howard, *Men Like That: A Southern Queer History* (Chicago: University of Chicago Press, 2001); Valerie J. Korinek, *Prairie Fairies: A History of Queer Communities and People in Western Canada, 1930–1985* (Toronto: University of Toronto Press, 2018).

5   de Goncourt Edmond and de Goncourt Jules, *L'Italie d'hier: Notes de voyages 1855–1856* (Paris: G. Charpentier et E. Fasquelle, 1894), 73.

6   Catherine Trundle, *Americans in Tuscany: Charity, Compassion, and Belonging* (New York: Berghahn, 2014), 26–8, 185 fn5. See also Levenstein on the expansion of the American colony in Paris after the Civil War; Harvey Levenstein, *Seductive Journey: American Tourists in France from Jefferson to the Jazz Age* (Chicago: University of Chicago Press, 1998), 104–6.

7   Aldous Huxley to Julian Huxley, 21 April 1925, Smith, *Letters of Aldous Huxley*, 246.

8   Laura Doan, *Disturbing Practices: History, Sexuality, and Women's Experiences of Modern War* (Chicago: University of Chicago Press, 2013), 169.

9   Giovanni Dall'Orto, 'Florence', in *Encyclopedia of Homosexuality*, ed. Wayne R. Dynes, Warren Johansson and William A. Percy (New York: Garland, 1990).

10   Alastair J. L. Blanshard, 'Chapter 34: The early modern erotic imagination', in *A Companion to Greek and Roman Sexualities*, ed. Thomas K. Hubbard (Hoboken: John Wiley & Sons, 2014), 578.

11   Lionel Trilling, *E. M. Forster* (New York: New Directions, 1943), 36; E. M. Forster, *A Room with a View* (New York: Vintage Book, 1961), 57.

12   Michael Rocke, *Forbidden Friendships: Homosexuality and Male Culture in Renaissance Florence* (New York: Oxford University Press, 1996), 115.

13   See, for example, Samuel K. Cohn, Jr., 'Forbidden friendships: Homosexuality and male culture in Renaissance Florence. By Michael Rocke', *Speculum* 74, no. 2 (1999): 481–83.

14   Rocke, *Forbidden Friendships*, 5–14, 87–92.

15   Clorinda Donato, 'Where "reason and the sense of Venus are innate in men": Male friendship, secret societies, academies, and antiquarians in eighteenth-century Florence', *Italian Studies* 65, no. 3 (2010): 334.

16   George E. Haggerty, 'Queering horace walpole', *Studies in English Literature, 1500–1900* 46, no. 3 (2006): 552.

17   Apuleius, *The Golden Ass, or Metamorphoses*, trans. E. J. Kenny (New York: Penguin Books, 1998). Haggarty states that the title of the painting comes from a poem by the Florentine writer Niccolò Machiavelli, which is, in fact, a reworking of the classical original.

18   Donato, 'Where "reason and the sense of venus are innate in men"'.

19   Harold Acton, *Memoirs of an Aesthete*, 1970 ed. (London: Methuen & Co., 1948), 9.

20   Martha Vicinus, *Intimate Friends: Women Who Loved Women, 1778–1928* (Chicago: University of Chicago Press, 2006), 36.

21   William S. Peterson, "'My spiritual face": A newly discovered portrait of Mrs. Browning', *Browning Institute Studies*, 5 (1977): 8.

22   Blagden is quoted in Alison Chapman, *Networking the Nation: British and American Women's Poetry and Italy, 1840–1870* (New York: Oxford University Press, 2015), 28.

23   Francesca Bugliani, '*Romola* in England and Italy (1868–1924)', in *The Reception of George Eliot in Europe*, ed. Elinor Schaffer and Catherine Brown (London: Bloomsbury, 2016), 205.

24   Chapman, *Networking the Nation*, 55.

25   David Leavitt, *Florence, a Delicate Case* (London: Bloomsbury, 2002).

26   Kinta Beevor, *A Tuscan Childhood* (New York: Viking, 1993), 104.

27   Henry James to Grace Norton, 27 February 1887; Leon Edel (ed.), *Henry James Letters*, Vol. III: 1883–1895 (Cambridge, MA: Belknap Press, 1980), 165. James described many people he met in Florence as 'queer' in other letters, including Henry James to Mr and Mrs William James, 23 December 1886; Henry James to John Hay, Christmas Eve, 1886; and Henry James to Frances Anne Kemble, 20 May 1887; ibid., 151, 53, 83.

28   Henry James to Sarah Butler Wister, 27 February 1887; ibid., 169.

29   James also uses the term 'queer' in this sense in Henry James, *The Bostonians* (New York: Random House, 2003), 76–84.

30   Sally Newman, 'The archival traces of desire: Vernon Lee's failed sexuality and the interpretation of letters in lesbian history', *Journal of the History of Sexuality* 14, no. 1/2 (2005): 51fn1.

31   Vineta Colby, *Vernon Lee: A Literary Biography* (Charlottesville: University of Virginia Press, 2003); Newman, 'The archival traces of desire', 53–4.

32   Colby, *Vernon Lee*, 49–51.

33   Ibid., 175.

34   Chiara Beccalossi, 'The "Italian Vice": Male homosexuality and British tourism in southern Italy', in *Italian Sexualities Uncovered, 1789–1914*, ed. John H. Arnold, Joanna Bourke and Sean Brady (London: Palgrave, 2015).

35   Leavitt, *Florence, a Delicate Case*, 82.

36   Colby, *Vernon Lee*, 159.

37   Mandy Gagel, '1897, a discussion of plagiarism: Letters between Vernon Lee, Bernard Berenson, and Mary Costelloe', *Literary Imagination* 12, no. 2 (2010): 154–79.

38   Colby, *Vernon Lee*, 161.

39   Barbara Strachey, *Remarkable Relations: The Story of the Pearsall Smith Family* (London: Victor Gollancz, 1980), 124.

40   'Cruttwell, Maud', in *Dictionary of Art Historians*: http://arthistorians.info/cruttwellm.

41   Tiffany L. Johnston, 'Maud Crutwell and the Berensons: "A preliminary canter to an independent career"', *Interdisciplinary Studies in the Long Nineteenth Century* 28 (2019). The phrase 'à rebours', meaning *against nature* or *against the grain*, referenced Joris-Karl Huysman's 1884 novel by that title, a favourite within queer aesthetic circles.

42   Richard Maxwell Dunn, *Geoffrey Scott and the Berenson Circle: Literary and Aesthetic Life in the Early 20th Century* (Lewiston, NY: Edwin Mellen Press, 1998).

43   Acton, *Memoirs of an Aesthete*, 9, 40.

44   A. Richard Turner, *La Pietra: Florence, a Family and a Villa* (Florence: Edizioni Olivares, 2002), 54.

45 Rumors of Acton's and Mitchell's same-sex relationship are from R. Terry Schnadelbach, *Hidden Lives/Secret Gardens: The Florentine Villas Gamberaia, La Pietra and I Tatti* (LAUD Press and iUniverse, 2009). This text is self-published and perhaps unreliable, which seems to be the case for all information about Arthur Acton. Nonetheless, Schnadelbach's claims are cited in Felicia Caponigri, 'Who owns Villa La Pietra? The story of a family, their home, and an American university under Italian law', *Notre Dame Journal of International & Comparative Law* 5, no. 1 (2015): 211. Sorting out the facts from the fiction in Arthur Acton's personal history, and the history of the Villa La Pietra, is beyond the scope of this chapter or the powers of this author.

46 Turner, *La Pietra*, 22.

47 On Acton's photography, see Leavitt, *Florence, a Delicate Case*. On the ongoing property dispute, see Victor Porcelli, 'Italian princess sues NYU for billion-dollar art collection', *Washington Square News*, 24 August 2019: https://nyunews.com/news/2019/08/25/nyu-florence-acton-inheritance/.

48 Acton, *Memoirs of an Aesthete*, 102.

49 Beevor, *A Tuscan Childhood*, 149.

50 Acton, *Memoirs of an Aesthete*, 64–5.

51 David Plante, 'A last fantasy in Florence', *The New Yorker*, 10 July 1995, 46.

52 For Firbank, see Acton, *Memoirs of an Aesthete*, 105. For Magnus, D. H. Lawrence (ed.) *Memoirs of the Foreign Legion by M. M.* (London: Martin Secker, 1924). For G. Orioli Orioli, *Adventures of a Bookseller* (New York: Robert M. McBridge & Co., 1938), 232–4.

53 Ian Littlewood, *Sultry Climates: Travel & Sex* (Cambridge, MA: Da Capo Press, 2001), 131.

54 For more on the friendship of Orioli and Douglas, see my book; Rachel Hope Cleves, *Unspeakable: A Life beyond Sexual Morality* (Chicago: University of Chicago, 2020).

55 Constantine FitzGibbon, 'Norman Douglas: Memoir of an unwritten biography', *Encounter*, September 1974, 37.

56 John Pearson, *Façades: Edith, Osbert & Sacheverell Sitwell* (London: Macmillan, 1978), 259.

57 Smith, *Letters of Aldous Huxley*, 223–4.

58 E. W. Tedlock (ed.), *Frieda Lawrence: The Memoirs and Correspondence* (New York: Alfred A. Knopf, 1964), 345.

59 Michael Allan (ed.), *Straining Friendship to Breaking Point: Letters from John Mavrogordato to Norman Douglas and a Selection of Letters from Douglas to Mavrogordato*, Vol. 7, Norman Douglas Selected Correspondence (Graz/Feldkirch: W. Neugebauer Verlag GMBH, 2014), 128.

60 Orioli, *Adventures of a Bookseller*, 118.

61 Norman Douglas, *Looking Back: An Autobiographical Excursion* (New York: Harcourt, Brace and Company, 1933), 287.

62 George J. Zytaruk and James T. Boulton (eds), *The Letters of D. H. Lawrence*, Vol. II: June 1913–October 1916 (Cambridge: Cambridge University Press, 1981), 149.

63 Norman Douglas, *Late Harvest* (London: Lindsay Drummond, 1946), 53–4.

64 Norman Douglas to Hellé Flecker, 5 July and 29 August, 1922. Berg Collection. New York Public Library.

65 D. H. Lawrence, *Aaron's Rod* (New York: Penguin Books, 1922), 251; *Memoirs of the Foreign Legion*.

66   Isabelle Richet, 'The "Irresponsibility of the outsider"? American expatriates and Italian fascism', *Transatlantica [Online]*, no. 1 (2014): 7.

67   Richard Aldington, *Seven against Reeves: A Comedy-Farce* (London: William Heinemann, 1937).

68   Richard Aldington, *Pinorman: Personal Recollections of Norman Douglas, Pino Orioli and Charles Prentice* (London: William Heinemann, 1954).

69   Norman Douglas to Bryher, 16 March 1937, box 21, folder 338. Norman Douglas Collection. Beinecke Library.

70   Steven Moore, *Ronald Firbank Complete Plays* (London: G. Richards Ltd., 1994), 76.

71   Ibid., 77.

72   Philippe Jullian and John Phillips, *Violet Trefusis: Life and Letters* (London: Hamish Hamilton, 1976), 27–8, 93–5.

73   Richard Ormrod, 'Gabriele D'annunzio and Radclyffe Hall', *The Modern Language Review* 84, no. 4 (1989): 842.

74   Romaine Brooks, 'A war interlude or on the hills of Florence during the war', in *Romaine Brooks Papers* (Washington, DC: Archives of American Art, 1940s).

75   Lettice Cooper, *Fenny* (London: Virago, 1987), 146.

76   Richet, 'The "Irresponsibility of the Outsider"'.

77   Gregory Woods, *Homintern: How Gay Culture Liberated the Modern World* (New Haven, CT: Yale University Press, 2016).

78   Lorenzo Benadusi, *The Enemy of the New Man: Homosexuality in Fascist Italy* (Madison: University of Wisconsin Press, 2012).

79   Acton, *Memoirs of an Aesthete*, 382–3.

80   Plante, 'A last fantasy in Florence'.

81   Alessio Ponzio, '"What they had between their legs was a form of cash." Homosexuality, male prostitution and intergenerational sex in 1950s Italy', *Historical Reflections/Réflexions Historiques* 46, no. 1 (2020): 62–78.

82   Sinclair Lewis, *World so Wide* (New York: Random House, 1951), 96.

83   Ibid., 229.

84   Gayle Rubin, 'Thinking sex: Notes for a radical theory of the politics of sexuality', in *Culture, Society and Sexuality: A Reader*, ed. Richard Parker and Peter Aggleton (New York: Routledge, 1984).

85   Steven Angelides, 'The emergence of the Paedophile in the late twentieth century', *Australian Historical Studies* 36, no. 126 (2005): 272–95.

86   Beevor, *A Tuscan Childhood*, 104.

87   Caroline Moorehead, *Iris Origo: Marchesa of Val D'orcia* (London: John Murray, 2000), 28.

88   Georgina S. Grahame, *In a Tuscan Garden* (London: J. Lane, 1902), 204.

Selected bibliography

Ackroyd, Peter. *Queer City: Gay London from the Romans to the Present Day*. London: Chatto and Windus, 2017.

Aldrich, Robert. *Colonialism and Homosexuality*. London: Routledge, 2003.

Avery, Simon and Katherine M. Graham, eds. *Sex, Time and Place: Queer Histories of London, c.1850 to the Present*, 115–31. London: Bloomsbury Academic, 2016.

Beachy, Robert. *Gay Berlin: Birthplace of a Modern Identity*. London: Penguin Random House, 2015.

Bengry, Justin. 'Courting the Pink Pound: *Men Only* and the Queer Consumer, 1935–1939'. *History Workshop Journal* 68 (2009): 122–48.

Bonner-Thompson, Carl. '"The Meat-market": Production and Regulation of Masculinities on the Grindr Grid in Newcastle upon Tyne, UK'. *Gender, Place and Culture* 24, no. 11 (2017): 1611–25.

Boyd, Nan Alamilla. *Wide-Open Town: A History of Queer San Francisco to 1965*. Berkeley: University of California Press, 2003.

Brady, Sean. 'Why Examine Men, Masculinities and Religion in Northern Ireland?'. In *Men, Masculinities and Religious Change in Twentieth-Century Britain*, edited by Lucy Delap and Sue Morgan, 218–51. Basingstoke: Palgrave Macmillan, 2013.

Bressey, Caroline. 'Cultural Archaeology and Historical Geographies of the Black Presence in Rural England'. *Journal of Rural Studies* 25, no. 4 (2009): 386–95.

Brickel, Chris. *Mates and Lovers: A History of Gay New Zealand*. Auckland: Godwit, 2008.

Brighton Ourstory Project. *Daring Hearts: Lesbian and Gay Lives in 50s and 60s Brighton*. Brighton: QueenSpark Books, 1992, 2015.

Brooks, Ross. 'Beyond Brideshead: The Male Homoerotics of 1930s Oxford'. *Journal of British Studies* 59 (2020): 821–56.

Brown-Saracino, Japonica. *How Places Make Us: Novel LBQ Identities in Four Small Cities*. Chicago: The University of Chicago Press, 2017.

Browne, Kath and Leela Bakshi. *Ordinary in Brighton: LGBT Activisms and the City*. London: Routledge, 2016.

Buckle, Sebastian. *The Way Out: A History of Homosexuality in Modern Britain*. London: I.B. Taurus, 2015.

Cant, Bob. *Invented Identities? Lesbians and Gays Talk about Migration*. London: Cassell, 1997.

Cant, Bob. *Footsteps & Witnesses: Lesbian and Gay Lifestories from Scotland*. Edinburgh: Word Power Books, 2008.

Carroll, Sam and Maeve Devine, eds. *Brighton Trans*formed*. Brighton: QueenSpark, 2014.

Casey, Mark. 'De-dyking Queer Space(s): Heterosexual Female Visibility in Gay and Lesbian Spaces'. *Sexualities* 7, no. 4 (2004): 446–61.

Chauncey, George. *Gay New York: Gender, Urban Culture, and the Making of the Gay Male World, 1890–1940*. New York: Basic Books, 2019.

Cleves, Rachel Hope. *Unspeakable: A Life beyond Sexual Morality*. Chicago: University of Chicago Press, 2020.

Cook, Matt. *London and the Culture of Homosexuality, 1885–1914*. Cambridge: Cambridge University Press, 2003.

Cook, Matt. *A Gay History of Britain: Love and Sex between Men since the Middle Ages*. Oxford: Greenwood, 2007.

Cook, Matt and Jennifer Evans, eds. *Queer Cities, Queer Cultures: Europe since 1945*. London: Bloomsbury, 2013.

Cook, Matt. 'Local Turns: Queer Histories and Brighton's Queer Communities'. *History Compass* 17, no. 1 (2019).

Cook, Matt. 'Local Matters: Queer Scenes in 1960s Manchester, Plymouth and Brighton'. *Journal of British Studies* 59, no. 1 (2020): 32–56.

Cook, Matt and Alison Oram, *Queer Beyon London*. Manchester: Manchester University Press, 2022.

Donato, Clorinda. 'Where "Reason and the Sense of Venus Are Innate in Men": Male Friendship, Secret Societies, Academies, and Antiquarians in Eighteenth-Century Florence'. *Italian Studies* 65, no. 3 (2010): 329–44.

Dowling, Linda. *Hellenism and Homosexuality in Victorian Oxford*. London: Cornell, 1994.

Duggan, Marian. *Queering Conflict: Examining Lesbian and Gay Experiences of Homophobia in Northern Ireland*. London: Routledge, 2012.

Ellis, Nadia. *Territories of the Soul: Queered Belonging in the Black Diaspora*. Durham: Duke University Press, 2015.

Galford, Ellen, Ken Wilson and Remember When Project. *Rainbow City: Stories from Lesbian, Gay, Bisexual and Transgender Edinburgh*. Edinburgh: Word Power Books, 2006.

Flynn, Paul. *Good as You*. London: Ebury Press, 2017.

Higgins, Patrick. *Heterosexual Dictatorship: Male Homosexuality in Postwar Britain*. London: Fourth Estate, 1996.

Higgs, David, ed. *Queer Sites: Gay Urban Histories since 1600*. London: Routledge, 1999.

Homfray, Mike. *Provincial Queens: The Gay and Lesbian Community in the North-West of England*. Oxford: Peter Lang, 2007.

Houlbrook, Matt. *Queer London: Perils and Pleasures in the Sexual Metropolis, 1918–1957*. Chicago: University of Chicago Press, 2005.

Howard, John. *Men Like That: A Southern Queer History*. Chicago: University of Chicago Press, 1999.

Howes, Robert. *Gay West: Civil Society, Community and LGBT History in Bristol and Bath 1970 to 2010*. Bristol: SilverWood, 2011.

Jastrzebska, Maria and Anthony Luvera, eds. *Queer in Brighton*. Brighton: New Writing South, 2015.

Jennings, Rebecca. *A Lesbian History of Britain since 1600: Love and Sex between Women since 1500*. Oxford: Greenwood, 2007.

Jennings, Rebecca. *Unnamed Desires: A Sydney Lesbian History*. Clayton: Monash University Publishing, 2015.

Jennings, Rebecca. *Tomboys and Bachelor Girls: A Lesbian History of Postwar Britain, 1945–1971*. Manchester: Manchester University Press, 2017.

Johnson, E. Patrick. *Sweet Tea: Black Gay Men of the South*. Chapel Hill, NC: UNC Press, 2008.

Kennedy, Elizabeth and Madeline Davies. *Boots of Leather, Slippers of Gold: The History of a Lesbian Community*. New York: Routledge, 1993.

Knowles, James. '"Hypothetical Hills": Rethinking Northern Gay Identities in the Fiction of Paul Magrs'. In *Territories of Desire in Queer Culture – Refiguring Contemporary Boundaries*, edited by David Alderson and Linda Anderson, 130–50. Manchester: Manchester University Press, 2000.

Korinek, Valerie J. *Prairie Fairies: A History of Queer Communities and People in Western Canada, 1930–1985*. Toronto, Buffalo and London: University of Toronto Press, 2018.

Leavitt, David. *Florence, a Delicate Case*. London: Bloomsbury, 2002.

Leeworthy, Daryl. *A Little Gay History of Wales*. Cardiff: University of Wales Press, 2019.

Leeworthy, Daryl. 'Rainbow Crossings. Gay Irish Migrants and LGBT Politics in 1980s' London'. *Studi Irlandesi: A Journal of Irish Studies* 10 (2020): 79–99.

Lewis, Mark. 'A Sociological Pub Crawl around Gay Newcastle'. In *The Margins of the City: Gay Men's Urban Lives*, edited by Stephen Whittle, 85–100. Aldershot: Ashgate Press, 1994.

Lin, Jeremy Atherton. *Gay Bar: Why We Went Out*. London: Granta, 2021.

Meek, Jeff. *Queer Voices in Post-War Scotland: Male Homosexuality, Religion and Society*. Basingstoke: Palgrave Macmillan, 2015.

Nayak, Anoop. 'Last of the "Real Geordies"? White Masculinities and the Subcultural Response to Deindustrialisation'. *Environment and Planning D: Society and Space* 21 (2003): 7–25.

Nayak, Anoop. 'Displaced Masculinities: Chavs, Youth and Class in the Post-industrial City'. *Sociology* 40, no. 5 (2006): 813–31.

Oram, Alison and Annmarie Turnbull. *The Lesbian History Sourcebook: Love and Sex between Women in Britain from 1780–1970*. London: Routledge, 2001.

Oram, Alison. *Her Husband Was A Woman!: Women's Gender-Crossing in Modern British Popular Culture*. London: Routledge, 2007.

Oram, Alison. 'Making Place and Community: Contrasting Lesbian and Gay, Feminist and Queer Oral History Projects in Brighton and Leeds'. *Oral History Review* (forthcoming 2022).

Pollen, Annebella. 'Utopian Bodies and Anti-fashion Futures: The Dress Theories and Practices of English Interwar Nudists'. *Utopian Studies* 28, no. 3 (2017): 451–81.

Romain, Gemma and Caroline Bressey. 'Claude McKay: Queering Spaces of Black Radicalism in Interwar London'. In *Sex, Time and Place: Queer Histories of London, c.1850 to the Present*, edited by Simon Avery and Katherine M. Graham, 115–31. London: Bloomsbury Academic, 2016.

Romain, Gemma. *Race, Sexuality and Identity in Britain and Jamaica: The Biography of Patrick Nelson*. London: Bloomsbury Academic, 2017.

Roseneil, Sasha. *Common Women, Uncommon Practices: The Queer Feminisms of Greenham*. London: Cassell, 2000.

Smith, Helen. *Masculinity, Class and Same-Sex Desire in Industrial England, 1895–1957*. London: Palgrave Macmillan, 2015.

Stein, Marc. *City of Sisterly and Brotherly Love: Lesbian and Gay Philadelphia, 1945–1972*. Philadelphia: Temple University Press, 2004.

Taylor, Yvette and Emily Falconer. '"Seedy Bars and Grotty Pints": Close Encounters in Queer Leisure Spaces'. *Social & Cultural Geography* 16, no. 1 (2015): 43–57.

Weeks, Jeffrey. *Between Worlds: A Queer Boy from the Valleys*. Cardigan: Parthian, 2021.

Weston, Kath. 'Get Thee to a Big City: Sexual Imaginary and the Great Gay Migration'. *GLQ: A Journal of Lesbian and Gay Studies* 2, no. 3 (1995): 253–77.
Wotherspoon, Garry. *Gay Sydney: A History*. Sydney: New South, 2016.

For further commentary, links and information on queer localities in Britain see especially:
Pride of Place: https://historicengland.org.uk/research/inclusive-heritage/lgbtq-heritage-project/
Queer Beyond London: http://queerbeyondlondon.com

Index

Printed in the USA
CPSIA information can be obtained
at www.ICGtesting.com
LVHW011320220424
778092LV00001B/73